The Impact of Extreme Weather on School Education

This book introduces an emerging area of research exploring the influence of extreme weather events on school systems.

Chapters explore a range of extreme weather events such as snowstorms, bushfires, extreme winds, heavy rainfall and prolonged heat waves, and their potentially widespread impacts. It also covers key challenges faced by schools, including how to protect students, levels of teacher preparation to counter extreme weather conditions and how students' learning is impacted by extreme weather patterns.

Drawing on a broad range of research in this field, this book will appeal to environmental and educational researchers, as well as those currently studying or practising in education.

Brendon Hyndman is Associate Dean (Research) of the Faculty of Arts and Education at Charles Sturt University, where he also holds an Associate Professor of Education position within the School of Education. Hyndman's research career and approaches have largely revolved around his teaching philosophy of promoting participant-centred and autonomous approaches to education. His widely disseminated PhD research was based upon exploring both student-centred (and student-informed) strategies to provide improved activity choices within outdoor-school-recreation settings. Hyndman is a national board member for Play Australia and Australian representative on the Global Recess Alliance.

Jennifer Vanos is Associate Professor in the School of Sustainability at Arizona State University. She focuses on extreme heat, thermal comfort and air pollution in her research, and examines health impacts on vulnerable populations, such as children and athletes. She is currently running numerous field projects in Arizona and collaborates with schools, government and non-profits in community-based research. Vanos is an active member of the Urban Climate Research Center at ASU and a scientific advisor for the Korey Stringer Institute and National Program for Playground Safety.

The Impact of Extreme Weather on School Education
Protecting School Communities

Edited by Brendon Hyndman
and Jennifer Vanos

LONDON AND NEW YORK

First published 2024
by Routledge
4 Park Square, Milton Park, Abingdon, Oxon OX14 4RN

and by Routledge
605 Third Avenue, New York, NY 10158

Routledge is an imprint of the Taylor & Francis Group, an informa business

© 2024 selection and editorial matter, Brendon Hyndman and Jennifer Vanos; individual chapters, the contributors

The right of Brendon Hyndman and Jennifer Vanos to be identified as the authors of the editorial material, and of the authors for their individual chapters, has been asserted in accordance with sections 77 and 78 of the Copyright, Designs and Patents Act 1988.

All rights reserved. No part of this book may be reprinted or reproduced or utilised in any form or by any electronic, mechanical, or other means, now known or hereafter invented, including photocopying and recording, or in any information storage or retrieval system, without permission in writing from the publishers.

Trademark notice: Product or corporate names may be trademarks or registered trademarks, and are used only for identification and explanation without intent to infringe.

British Library Cataloguing-in-Publication Data
A catalogue record for this book is available from the British Library

ISBN: 978-0-367-61086-9 (hbk)
ISBN: 978-0-367-61088-3 (pbk)
ISBN: 978-1-003-10316-5 (ebk)

DOI: 10.4324/9781003103165

Typeset in Times New Roman
by Apex CoVantage, LLC

Contents

List of Figures	*viii*
List of Tables	*x*
List of Contributors	*xi*
Foreword	*xii*
Preface	*xiii*

1 The Impact of Extreme Weather on School Communities   1
BRENDON HYNDMAN AND JENNIFER VANOS

Introduction 1
*Extreme Weather Impacts to School Children in a
    Changing Climate 3*
*The Importance of Protecting and Preparing School
    Communities From Weather Extremes 4*
*From Mitigating Impacts to Adaption to Weather Extremes
    for Protecting School Children 6*
Summary and Looking Forward 11

**2 The Impact of Indoor and Outdoor Heat Extremes
on Schoolchildren**   18
BRENDON HYNDMAN, ADORA SHORTRIDGE
AND JENNIFER VANOS

Introduction 18
Heat and Health Considerations 19
Developmental Risks on Schoolchildren 22
Schoolchildren's Thermal Comfort 25
*Indoor and Outdoor Heat Impacts Across International
    School Contexts 26*
Summary 31

3 The Impact of Air Quality on Schoolchildren — 38
GIOVANNI DI VIRGILIO, MELISSA HART, ANGELA MAHARAJ AND DONNA GREEN

Outdoor Air-Pollution Impacts on Schoolchildren 38
Indoor Air-Pollution Impacts 40
Current Policy and Mitigation Actions 41
The Need for Real-Time, Distributed Air Quality and Meteorology Data Networks 42
Real-Time, Distributed Air-Quality Monitoring Networks 43
Case Study I: Black Summer 46
Case Study II: Indoor Monitoring in Australia 50
Key Challenges and Opportunities 51

4 The Influences of Extreme Cold and Storms on Schoolchildren — 60
BRENDON HYNDMAN AND BRENTON BUTTON

Storms and Unplanned School Closures 62
Are Schoolchildren Losing Out From School Closures on Their Development? 66
Disrupting Play Behaviours and the School Day 67
What Are the Solutions to Be Able to Mitigate Extreme Cold Weather and Storm Events on School Activities? 71

5 Public Perceptions of Weather-Protection Strategies for Schools — 78
BRENDON HYNDMAN

What Research Has Considered Weather-Protection Policy for Schools? 79
What Should Be Considered in a Weather-Protection Policy? 80
Data Collection and Analyses 81
Social–Ecological Model 82
Social–Ecological Perceptual Insights 82
Individual Levels of Influence 83
Interpersonal (Social) Levels of Influence 84
Physical-Environment Levels of Influence 84
Policy/Organisational Levels of Influence 86
Situating the Findings 87

6 **Building and School-Playground Design to Protect From Weather Extremes** 94
JENNIFER VANOS AND SEBASTIAN PFAUTSCH

Weather Extremes and Schools 94
Weather "Smart" School Programs 95
Bioclimatic Design at Schools: A Global Lens 98
Case Study: Novel Surfacing Considerations for Playgrounds to Reduce Heat Exposure 108
Beyond Design: Responsiveness to Climate Extremes by School Communities 111
Conclusions 112

7 **Future Protection From Extreme Weather Influences in School Communities** 119
BRENDON HYNDMAN AND JENNIFER VANOS

Index *134*

Figures

1.1	Climate extremes, children's health, and impacts to learning	2
1.2	Example of the formation of a tornado	4
1.3	Example of a storm cell	4
2.1	A conceptual diagram linking climate drivers and urban-induced heating to multiscale effects, outdoor and indoor heat, heat-exposure pathways, thermal discomfort, physical activity and impacts on health and learning	20
2.2	An example of a group of schoolchildren huddled into a small, shaded area	21
2.3	An organisation tool for schools to determine their level of heat readiness based on 30 recommendations	31
3.1	The geography of Sydney and the locations of the Schools Weather and Air Quality sensors sited at primary schools in Sydney and the University of New South Wales (UNSW)	44
3.2	Schools Weather and Air Quality (SWAQ) Vaisala AQT420 air-quality sensor and WXT536 meteorology sensor located at a Sydney primary school in 2019, complete with SWAQ logo	45
3.3	(a–f) Diurnal variation in normalised $PM_{2.5}$, temperature and relative humidity at five Sydney schools during Black Summer	48
3.4	(top) Time series of 20-min-interval temperature (°C), wind speed (m/s), relative humidity (%), air pressure (hPa), and $PM_{2.5}$ (µg/m³) at SWAQ-Luddenham on 26 November 2019; (bottom) variation in meteorological and CO (ppm) observations at SWAQ-Luddenham during 26 November 2019	49
4.1	An example of a pupil actively travelling to school during snow conditions	68
4.2	An example of surfacing that can result in lost traction for recreational activities	69

4.3	Schoolchildren continuing to play outside, despite a flooded play area	70
4.4	A child wearing weather-equipped boots continues to play in a flooded play space	71
6.1	Example of wind roses for Rome, Italy in the cold season (left) and warm season (right)	98
6.2	Retention area and bioswale for floodwaters in South Phoenix at Paideia Academies School	99
6.3	Examples of warning signs used in playgrounds	102
6.4	Infrared images of playground equipment captured during a heat wave in January 2019 in western Sydney, Australia	103
6.5	Infrared images of common surface materials used in and around playgrounds across Sydney, Australia	104
6.6	Infrared images showing high surface temperatures in school outdoor areas. High surface temperatures usually lead to high emission of sensible heat, which accelerates heat stress in children	105
6.7	Infrared images of extreme surface temperatures observed during heat waves in playgrounds across Sydney, Australia	107
6.8	Infrared images documenting the surface-cooling effect of shade in playgrounds	109
6.9	(A–D) Differences in surface temperature of common playground materials according to material type and colour	110

Tables

2.1 Studies addressing heat protection and thermal comfort in schools (or as a model for schools) across diverse international contexts 28

6.1 Burn thresholds of skin according to ISO13732 (2006) for selected materials commonly found in outdoor play spaces 108

Contributors

Brenton Button, Faculty of Education, University of Winnipeg, Winnipeg, Canada

Giovanni Di Virgilio, Climate Research, Climate & Atmospheric Science Branch, NSW Department of Planning and Environment, NSW, Australia and Climate Change Research Centre, University of New South Wales, NSW, Australia

Donna Green, Climate Change Research Centre, University of New South Wales, NSW, Australia

Melissa Hart, Australian Research Council Centre of Excellence for Climate Extremes, University of New South Wales, NSW, Australia

Brendon Hyndman, School of Education, Faculty of Arts and Education, Charles Sturt University, NSW, Australia

Angela Maharaj, Climate Change Research Centre, University of New South Wales, NSW, Australia

Sebastian Pfautsch, School of Social Sciences, Western Sydney University, NSW, Australia

Adora Shortridge, School of Sustainability, Arizona State University, Arizona, United States

Jennifer Vanos, School of Sustainability, Global Institute of Sustainability, Arizona State University, Arizona, United States

Foreword

Across the globe, our communities have been facing the challenges and consequences of extreme weather events. These changing extremes are impacting on the health and well-being of our children and young people. The evidence presented in this book emphasises the link between educational attainment and opportunities and weather extremes. We must never underestimate the critical role schools play in equipping their communities to cope with these changing extremes.

Every day, schools are making decisions that will impact how well our children are prepared for the future. The capacity of children to engage in play and other physical activity at school is one such decision. Physical activity and play are essential for optimum health and development of our children. With children of school age spending up to seven hours a day in school, the school setting is an essential contributor for children's participation in physical activity and exposure to the multiple benefits of play. Ensuring a school has weather-protective strategies to maintain the recommended levels of physical activity and access to unstructured play is a critical decision with long-term impact.

It would be easy to feel overwhelmed when faced with the enormity of the evolving challenges our world now confronts. However, this book equips schools with evidence-based information, guidance and inspiration that will support them to take positive action. I hope this book will support schools to elicit a meaningful response to the evolving range of sustainable challenges, which not only focuses on ensuring the health and well-being of their school-age children, but supports children to access quality, accessible educational opportunities that will equip them to be agents of change to meet the challenges ahead.

Robyn Monro Miller AM
President, International Play Association
September 2022

Preface

The idea for writing the book *The Impact of Extreme Weather on School Education: Protecting School Communities* emerged from the widespread reports of extreme weather influences being regarded as the most significant global health threat of the 21st century. The fact that health directly intersects with a child's ability to learn – the underpinning purpose of education – is a concerning aspect of some of the global extreme weather trends. School students are our future, our next generation, to take society forward. Teachers also require a supportive environment to best facilitate learning and development of their students. Yet despite the current and proposed health challenges and vulnerability of school systems, there has been a scarcity of empirical insights for school communities to draw upon. It is also rare to see climate scholars from other disciplines working in collaboration with educational researchers that specifically investigate schooling systems.

The significance of the threat of extreme weather is reinforced by the wide-ranging environmental, health, societal and economic impacts. An increase in extreme and at times unpredictable weather events continues to occur, which can disrupt students' attendance at school. Examples of extreme weather impacts include extreme and prolonged heat waves, snowstorms, extreme winds, bushfires and heavy rainfall. The book was designed to provide key international insight into the direct impacts of these varying weather extremes (heat, snow, wind, rainfall) and indirect effects (e.g., air pollution) on international school systems. The book showcases how weather extremes influence teachers and students, and the strategies schools are undertaking, and could undertake, to counter the impacts of extreme weather.

Across the world, the number of children and adolescents meeting recommended physical-activity participation levels for optimal health has plummeted to alarmingly low levels. The school setting is recognised as one of the most important settings to develop students' activity levels given that students spend sizeable portions of their daily schedules within school communities. Further, school ages represent a critical period to establish positive physical-activity habits that can track into adulthood. The need to consider weather-protective strategies to help enhance or maintain schoolchildren's physical-activity levels indoors or outdoors is also vital. Not meeting the preventative physical-activity guidelines has been estimated to account for up to 3% of total healthcare costs in developed countries and 2 million deaths worldwide. Extreme weather impacts both physical activity and class-based learning, with thousands of school recess periods (often outdoors) affected globally – a substantial amount of time.

This book is primarily targeted at schools, school leaders, communities, graduate students, lecturers, researchers, policymakers, play organisations, parents and playgrounds designers. It has been written in a style that is accessible to readers entering this unique field from a variety of different disciplinary backgrounds. It should also be recognised that the term researcher is not just confined to those in academic institutions; this book is designed for all who are curious and want to gain insights into protecting school communities from extreme weather events.

Extreme weather conditions have a considerable impact in schools globally in the majority of jurisdictions. Amongst the effects of such extreme weather, students across the globe are expected to learn critical skills and habits to prepare themselves for adulthood and future careers. School safety is a major focus in many school curricula/syllabi, and the impact of extreme weather on learning, play and physical activities are only just being uncovered. Moreover, there are other considerations within schools, including teachers' preparation level, to counter extreme weather conditions for student protection and lessen the impact on students' learning. To date, many of the crucial questions outlined in this book have gone unanswered, and there is a paucity of research investigating extreme weather-related influences in schools with such pedagogical and classroom foci. This book uniquely articulates an emerging area of research that is becoming increasingly relevant in the world of education that is exposed to the dramatic impacts of extreme weather events.

The content of this book encompasses best practices to protect international school communities from extreme weather, how schools and education systems are countering severe weather, how students rely on adults for protective strategies, what training teachers are receiving for weather protection in schools, the influences of extreme heat on learning and health, research into public perceptions of weather-protective strategies, the impacts of snowfall, rainfall, air quality and building design on schools and schoolchildren and the impacts of school closures. This is the first book of its kind to provide a guide and introduction specifically focused on exploring and protecting extreme weather influences on school systems. This book will be of great interest to students and scholars of education, exercise science, environmental science, climate science, meteorology and health. The book will also be of interest to upper-level undergraduates and professionals working at the policy interface in the education and environmental arenas. Research programs across the world can use this book to provide insight into how schools and education systems can counter extreme weather effects to support both students and teachers in lessening the impacts to teaching and learning.

Lastly, we would like to thank the anonymous reviewers for their constructive comments on the book, and our relevant faculties for the ongoing support in the production of this important book. The many researchers across disciplines, their projects, study participants, including students, teachers, parents, principals and wider school communities that have dedicated time to engage in these topics of research, are thanked. The willingness and interest to engage in the projects we detail throughout the book have ensured that insights are able to be provided into these crucial settings. Your efforts are all appreciated. The book is dedicated to future generations of schoolchildren and their communities to ensure that detrimental weather impacts upon learning and development are mitigated over the decades to come.

Brendon Hyndman is associated with the School of Education, Faculty of Arts and Education, Charles Sturt University, Albury-Wodonga, NSW, Australia.

Jennifer Vanos is associated with the School of Sustainability, College of Global Futures, Arizona State University, Tempe, AZ, United States.

1 The Impact of Extreme Weather on School Communities

Brendon Hyndman and Jennifer Vanos

Introduction

The impact of extreme weather on school education continues to gain widespread international attention, especially with globalised data indicating that certain extreme weather events are becoming more intense, longer lasting and more frequent (IPCC, 2021a). For instance, the number of natural disasters from extreme weather events have approximately doubled compared to the 1980s (CRED, 2015; IPCC, 2021a). The increased occurrences of certain harmful and extreme weather events are potentially one of the greatest international health threats of the 21st century (Costello et al., 2009).

Disasters associated with extreme weather events have been previously estimated to negatively impact almost 200 million schoolchildren across the world each year (Save the Children, 2007). Schoolchildren are emphasised as a vulnerable group to extreme weather events due to not yet reaching their physical, mental and social maturity (Weissbecker et al., 2008; Peek & Stough, 2010). Schoolchildren and teachers may attend school for at least 30 hours each week, or around one-third of their time awake (Glander, 2016). The United Nations Children's Fund (UNICEF) anticipate that, in comparison to the 1990s, an additional 108.5 million children will be negatively impacted in 2023 by extreme weather events (Burgess, 2013). Despite such impacts upon school-aged children, Cox and colleagues (2017) detail that children are often not included during investigations to help support weather-protective initiatives (Cox et al., 2017).

Prior to the global pandemic, extreme weather caused over 90% of school closures in the United States (Wong et al., 2014). The diversity of extreme weather events can make it difficult to develop context-specific protection across the many climatic regions (Hyndman & Zundans-Fraser, 2021). Scholars are concerned with the elevated levels of predicted risk to schoolchildren's well-being from polluted water, physical injuries, drowning and dehydration (Rother et al., 2020). School communities across other parts of the world are concerned with rapidly changing impacts of extreme weather upon schoolchildren's learning, health and other developmental impediments due to schools

DOI: 10.4324/9781003103165-1

being unprepared to fully prevent the negative impacts of extremes upon schoolchildren (Miller & Hui, 2022). These adverse impacts include different severe storms and extremes (e.g., bushfires, cyclones/hurricanes, tornadoes, flooding, gale force winds, storm tides) causing school closures and preventing attendance in school classrooms, and extremely high (heat waves) or low (cold waves, blizzard) outdoor temperatures (Figure 1.1). These extremes can prevent schoolchildren development through outdoor activity engagements, respiratory concerns from bushfires causing air-quality declines or schools simply not being designed appropriately with necessary infrastructure or policies to be able to adapt to such weather extremes (Sheffield et al., 2017). Census data from

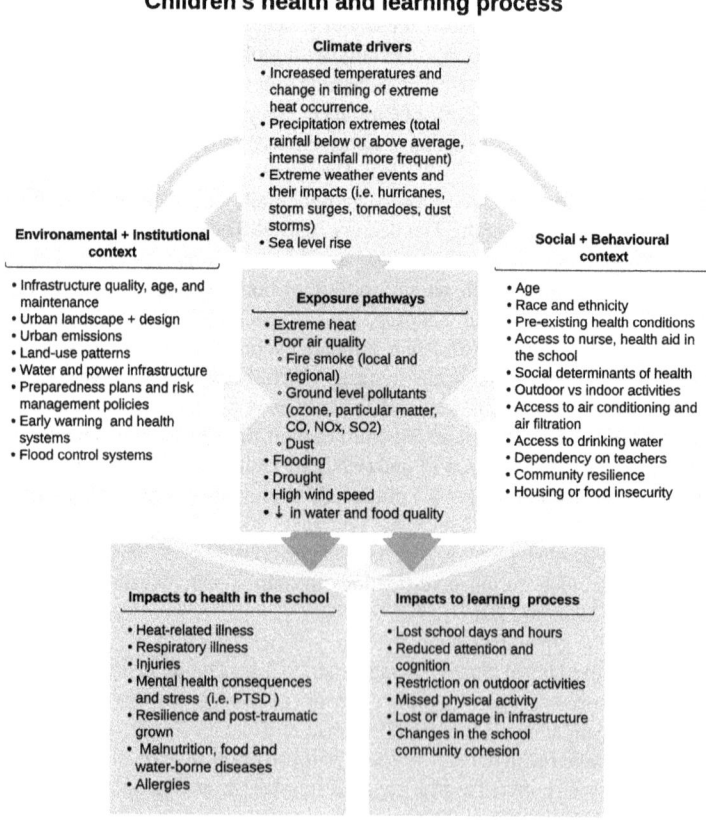

Figure 1.1 Climate extremes, children's health, and impacts to learning

Source: Original image by Gisel Guzman Echavarria, Arizona State University

across 29 countries shows that above-average temperatures, rainfall (in some countries) and drought negatively impact schoolchildren's educational attainment (Randell & Gray, 2019). Extreme weather disruptions also present various levels of intensity at varying timescales. Some disruptions, such as hurricanes, heat waves or winter storms provide more forewarning than flash flooding or a tornado, which can occur more unexpectedly. Ensuring that schools are well adept to find and heed guidance at various temporal scales from their local weather service is vital in the face of all extremes.

Extreme Weather Impacts to School Children in a Changing Climate

Weather is defined as the atmospheric conditions at any specific time, which regularly varies over both space and time. Weather and climate data generally include recordings of precipitation, temperature, wind speeds, humidity, pressure and cloud cover (Barry & Chorley, 2009). Extreme weather includes any hazardous meteorological event that has the potential to cause infrastructure damage, social disturbance and harm towards human life (NOAA, 2013). Extreme weather is part of the inherent variability within the global climate system. Extreme events vary by location, and thus preparedness efforts by schools should also differ based on the localised typical extreme weather and by time of year.

Various indicators of climate change that have been connected to anthropogenic (human-caused) impacts include: 1) increasing extremes of temperature and 2) precipitation changes (or drought) (IPCC, 2021a). Subsequent novel impacts to a given location or school site may arise on small-to-large scales due to these anthropogenic changes. Importantly, areas that often deal with extreme weather events throughout the year (e.g., flooding, hurricanes, heat waves) are now, on average, experiencing even greater intensities and/or more frequencies of the extreme weather events (i.e., different times of the year) based on insights from the Intergovernmental Panel on Climate Change (IPCC, 2021a). For example, across Africa, there have been concerns among the different regions relating to rising temperatures (in tropical West Africa), drought conditions (southern Africa), increased cyclones (southeastern Africa) and excess rainfall (East Africa) (Rother et al., 2020). Concerning evidence has reinforced that the economic, social and environmental factors that contribute to global morbidity and mortality will be accelerated in this new era of climatic extremes (Watts et al., 2018).

However, some types of extreme weather or weather variables are not directly linked (or "attributed") to climate change. For example, ultraviolet (UV) radiation, in general, is not directly linked to or impacted by climate change (Matthews-Trigg et al., 2019). Further, there is "limited evidence" from the IPCC (2021b) of a link between climate change and small-scale phenomena – such as tornadoes (Figure 1.2), convective storms (Figure 1.3),

Figure 1.2 Example of the formation of a tornado
Source: Image © M. Wright

Figure 1.3 Example of a storm cell
Source: Image © M. Wright

microbursts and lightning – both in observed trends and in projections. Nevertheless, these extremes cause loss of life, illness and economic and social damages. Thus all extremes, whether exacerbated by climate change or not, are important and potentially harmful that can, and do, affect schools and the users of school spaces.

The Importance of Protecting and Preparing School Communities From Weather Extremes

Schools play a major role as a point of access in supporting the population when there are disruptions from extreme weather (Bach et al., 2013; Rifai, 2012). School communities have a significant influence on the development of our next generation. In Western countries, such as the United States, the United Kingdom, Canada and Australia, there are approximately 200,000 schools combined (National Center for Education Statistics, 2017; Australian Bureau of Statistics, 2021; Council of Ministers for Education Canada, 2022; British Educational Suppliers Association, 2021). In the United States alone, it is reported that there are over 50 million schoolchildren with 3.1 million teachers (Glander, 2016). The types of extreme weather can vary considerably across large continents, which can include desert regions, mountainous regions, low-lying valley regions with rivers and subtropical or tropical regions (Rother et al., 2020). Although the scope of this book is to improve protection for schools and to optimise learning and development activities in-session, it should be acknowledged that school staff are also impacted, and any protective strategies that are implemented in more vulnerable groups (e.g., children) are also useful for the adult population. What is certain is that the intensity of extreme weather events can be unpredictable. From slight discomforts in the classroom that can impact cognitive functioning or attention within class (e.g., heat) to full-scale mortality (e.g., from severe storms).

For example, on the most extreme end of the scale, a mudslide in the Philippines killed 200 schoolchildren in 2006 (ISDR, 2007). Further, Rai et al. (2021) provide specific United States instances of reduced air quality from wildfire smoke directly leading to the death of multiple children, and extreme heat resulting in the fatal organ failure of a 16-year-old boy during football practice from a heat stroke. In the aftermath of Hurricane Katrina in New Orleans in the United States, almost 400,000 children were displaced from their schools (Save The Children, 2015). Although earthquakes are not a weather extreme (and thus are not covered within this book), preparedness efforts for earthquakes can be similar to that of weather extremes. In 2005, a Pakistan earthquake also resulted in the deaths of over 16,000 schoolchildren (ISDR, 2007).

Despite the wide scale of impacts that can impact the health and development of our schoolchildren from both extreme weather events (and natural disasters), Anderson (2005) previously outlined that children are largely excluded from important school policy decisions and research agendas. More recently, Hyndman (2016, 2017a) reinforced this finding, and that many decisions that impact the individual, social, physical-environment and policy within school spaces often do not consult the primary users that engage with such spaces: the schoolchildren. The Global Statement for Meaningful Adolescent and Youth Engagement (WHO, 2021, p. 1) states, "Meaningful adolescent and youth engagement recognises and changes the power structures that prevent young people from being considered experts regarding their own needs and priorities, while also building their leadership capacities." Scholars suggest that there are two factors that can better shape schoolchildren's responses to extreme weather events: 1) gaining knowledge and awareness, and 2) utilising such knowledge to inform schoolchildren's perception of risk (Mermer et al., 2018; Gellman, 2020).

From Mitigating Impacts to Adaption to Weather Extremes for Protecting School Children

The increasing occurrence of the "extremes" of weather are putting strain on our already stressed schooling systems, and subsequently our society's vulnerable population of children. Although the physiological harm from extreme weather has been well established, the social disruption and disturbance upon school communities often have not received the same level of research attention (Hyndman & Zundans-Fraser, 2021). Our next generation is now experiencing more prolonged droughts (causing more hazardous bushfire conditions) and more flooding and heat/cold waves that adversely impact schoolchildren's ability to continue their educational development (Iyer, 2020; Rother et al., 2020). The longer the interruption from extreme weather events, the more young people can developmentally fall behind other groups of schoolchildren that have not been exposed to such adverse weather circumstances or those in schools that have had comprehensive infrastructure, preparation and preventive measures in place (Miller & Hui, 2022). Forced displacement or migration from school districts is common from extreme weather events, and these circumstances can put schoolchildren's sense of routine, safety and security at risk (Schulze et al., 2020). Kousky (2016) and Lai et al. (2016) point to how the destruction of school structures and teacher/student relocations negatively impact upon scheduled classroom engagement and disrupt schoolchildren's mastering of educational skills and components (Kousky, 2016; Lai et al., 2016). Extreme weather events can also worsen existing challenges within schools due to aspects such as mould growth, overcrowding of learning spaces due to displacements and potential exposures to toxicities after flooding (Sheffield & Landrigan, 2011).

There is also the consideration that parental support can be impaired if adults are negatively impacted by climatic extremes with their own emotional, social and physical functioning providing challenges to families and employment (Clayton et al., 2017). In some Arctic indigenous communities, extreme weather changes can have detrimental impacts upon schoolchildren's mental health and lead to suicide due to losses of land, identity, culture and lifestyles (Hersher, 2016). The risks from displacement and migration away from normal school routines can also lead to depression, post-traumatic stress, negative emotional reactions and negative behavioural changes (Shepard et al., 2018). It is suggested that the shorter the duration of the impact from extreme weather events, the more favourable the outcome for schoolchildren's mental health outcomes (e.g., one-off events compared to recurrent) (Garcia & Sheehan, 2016). For instance, a short-lived flooding event would have a less adverse impact upon a child's mental health versus a longer-term severe drought. Therefore, the closely intertwined intersection between both health and education (Midford et al., 2020) needs to be carefully considered.

A major yet natural cause of global weather extremes are the El Niño/La Niña phenomena that are caused by the Pacific Ocean having reduced (El Niño) or elevated (La Niña) pressure due to elevated temperatures and a convergence of air masses that occur in the Pacific, causing increases in drought or intense precipitation in specific regions (Barry & Chorley, 2009). Cyclonic events are also a major cause of prolonged school closures due to the obvious high-risk nature of the extreme storm events, as well as the common flooding that results in cyclonic aftermaths (Barry & Chorley, 2009). Typhoons and hurricanes (both known as tropical cyclones) are intense low-pressure weather systems that emerge from warm, tropical waters in which there are high evaporation rates and excess moisture over the world's oceans. High-velocity winds are then generated due to the smoothness of ocean surfaces near coastal areas (Barry & Chorley, 2009). Although most of the impacts upon school systems from extreme storms are due to closure during tropical cyclones (Miller & Hui, 2022) from wind damage to the school or excess flooding, there has been some evidence of the negative impacts of lightning strikes from storms on schoolchildren (detailed in Chapter 4). The chapter also uniquely details the occurrence and impacts of tornadoes within vulnerable communities of the United States.

As with many school procedures, it is reported that there often is no streamlined, consolidated communications process or channel for alerting schools to unpredictable weather extremes (Hammer & Schmidlin, 2002; Schumacher et al., 2010; Hyndman, 2017b; Hyndman & Zundans-Fraser, 2021). It is outlined that common approaches to extreme weather warnings for schools include media dissemination of the possibility of hazardous weather two to three days prior, followed by a local emergency manager on standby to confirm with school leaders via phone/email if a warning has occurred in the area of the school community (alongside local media alerts). Each scenario would be unique to school scheduling to take action according to field trips, sporting events and the timing of the day, yet schools in high-risk areas would require the development of safety plans for quick implementation in such an event to fast-track decision-making processes for the safety of schoolchildren. School decision making is clearly a complex process, and most of the international research literature has focused on school decision making toward "school closures" from the events of cyclones, tornadoes and snowstorms (Hyndman, 2017c; Day, 2007). Decision-making processes are even more complex if severe weather develops rapidly, with the precise impact areas difficult to ascertain (Schumacher et al., 2010). More research is needed into how and why school leaders decide to implement school closures (Call & Coleman, 2014), and whether benchmark thresholds for implementing weather protection measures should be more consistent (Jacobs et al., 2019). Although determining whether to close a school or not according to extreme weather often enters policy debates (Hyndman & Zundans-Fraser, 2021), this book endeavours to delve deeper to provide holistic insights into the school system to also determine the multidimensional impacts of weather extremes at a microscale within schools, e.g., school structures, classrooms. Ergler (2020) describes that thinking about everyday weather experiences or seasons is very rare, despite weather and seasons playing such an essential role in our lives. There are research gaps in considering more micro-level supportive health and educative protection considerations when school communities are not being forced to close.

Research identifies direct links between schoolchildren not attending school and receiving less favourable results on both reading and maths assessments, even prior to kindergarten-age levels (Gottfried, 2014; Ehrlich et al., 2018). Lower academic scores have been linked to the absenteeism for male school children, minority groups and those from lower socioeconomic areas (Morrissey et al., 2014; Gottfried & Gee, 2017). There are also reported concerns on academic achievement relating to districts in which there have been forced, prolonged snow closures in Canada (Hyndman, 2017c). Higher annual temperatures have been suggested to reduce educational performances, especially in students from minority backgrounds (Park et al., 2021) or poorer countries (Randell & Gray, 2019). Extreme heat and related heat stress in particular is well known for negatively impacting cognitive functioning (Taylor et al., 2016). Worryingly, environmental stressors such as extreme-heat wave events exacerbate air-pollution levels due to stagnation of air, and thus have been indicated to lead to asthma problems and even impact the cognitive development of a baby prior to being born (Burke et al., 2018). Yet scholars have called for more research to determine the impact of weather events upon schoolchildren's educational and academic progress and outcomes (Peek & Stough, 2010; Hyndman, 2017b).

Hyndman (2017a) additionally points to under-researched influences within outdoor spaces in schools, in which schoolchildren are exposed to many influential weather patterns that do not force school closures. An Australian study that utilised nationally representative data over a ten-year period determined that as temperatures become more extreme (e.g., by getting hotter or cooler), schoolchildren spent much more time indoors, increasing engagement in screen-based entertainment and reducing physical-activity pursuits. It was summarised that extreme weather conditions have the potential to be detrimental to schoolchildren's long-term achievements, educational attainments and overall development. Interestingly, the winter cold extremes were determined to be more detrimental to schoolchildren's engagement in activity levels (Nguyen et al., 2019). Although more research is required, there are trends toward a demand for a greater collation of educational evidence and transparency of such emerging issues in order for more research to be financially supported (Anderson, 2010).

Research of high school students in Denmark revealed that the majority of children in Scandinavian countries have the perception that reformed approaches (e.g., avenues for discussion, debate, development of critical thinking) need to be put in place immediately at both local levels and by the government (Harker-Schuch & Bugge-Henriksen, 2013). Furthermore, there is consensus that by increasing awareness and knowledge of the issues associated with extreme weather, further prioritisation will be provided by state and national governments, alongside educational leaders. Internationally, large data sets continue to identify that schoolchildren and young people are seriously concerned about the increased occurrence of extreme weather events on their own futures (Tranter & Skrbis, 2014; United Nations International Children's Emergency Fund (UNICEF), 2014), their families, their investment hopes (Sanson & Burke, 2020), reaching their full potential (Clayton et al., 2017) and even that the planet could become unlivable prematurely (Albert et al., 2010) or negatively impact their future offspring (Sanson & Burke, 2020; Silburn, 2020).

Coverage within the curriculum of teaching related to extreme weather is also necessary to ensure that schoolchildren are correctly informed to help protect and counter modern challenges of extreme weather (Shepardson et al., 2009; Hyndman & Zundans-Fraser, 2021) and can be an ideal cross-disciplinary subject area. This need is further reinforced in the New Zealand context by Eames (2017), who argues that there is an absence of adequate focus and coverage of extreme weather influences across all curricula areas, despite the interdisciplinary study possibilities. Others note that a broader range of schoolteachers need to develop informed behaviours, attitudes and knowledge to model the prioritisation of preparedness and protection from extreme weather events (Monroe et al., 2013; Hyndman, 2017b). It is anticipated that if teachers are to prioritise considerations, policy and procedures relating to extreme weather impacts in the classroom, schoolchildren will then do the same. Similarly, Thaman's (2010) research reinforced the importance of beliefs and value systems underpinning the implementation of international education initiatives such as "Education for Sustainable Development" (ESD) at the regional and local-community level to ensure teaching and learning is more meaningful to the Pacific population. The ESD is a series of pedagogies, practices and processes to ensure educational contexts are more prepared for sustainable development complexities that are both current and emerging. Education is a major influencer in the international response to extreme environmental challenges, such as the increases in weather extremes (UNESCO, 2017), and clearly requires more widespread attention.

It is clear that we are at an important time for enacting societal adaption to increasing impacts of extremes. Adaptation is the phase of adjusting to change and its related effects to avoid harm (Pachauri et al., 2014), and in this case, extreme weather effects have changed the way school communities need to operate. The Intergovernmental Panel on Climate Change (IPCC) (Pauchari et al., 2014, p. 118) also states that "human intervention may facilitate adjustment to expected climate and its effects." The lack of broader intervention and the inconsistencies in weather protection across many educational contexts

(Hyndman, 2017b) also indicate that there is ample scope to better adapt to the changing weather patterns to reduce the vulnerabilities and build resilience and response systems within school-community populations. Hence, adaptation is indeed possible through careful collaboration and coordination between governments, societal stakeholders and individuals in order to make protective improvements (Adger et al., 2005).

Moreover, the United Nations Framework Convention on Climate Change (UNFCCC) pushes for urgent attention by governments to enhance adaptive efforts toward coping with weather extremes (Adger et al., 2005). Adger and colleagues (2005) emphasise that large-scale implementation of new strategies is important to ensure adaptation takes place. Hyndman (2017b) encouraged a similar approach in relation to the proposal of a national, consolidated heat protection policy for Australian schools. To ensure that all factors are addressed in adapting to enhanced weather extremes, Hyndman and Zundans-Fraser (2021) propose a multidimensional and angled framework considering all levels of influence. Similarly, Schipper (2007) previously argued for adaptive foci to further emphasise underlying factors of influence that can be often overlooked.

Adaptation and mitigation (Pachauri et al., 2014) are major global strategies to coping with increased weather extremes. This book emphasises the importance of school systems to appropriately adapt to current and future extremes to reduce educational vulnerabilities to school communities. Additionally, the UNFCCC urges jurisdictions globally to ensure improved development, promotion, implementation and increase of educational awareness of the effects of changing weather extremes (UNESCO, 2012). Successful educational programs therefore need to be better informed of the knowledge, strategies and actions required to adapt to such changes to global weather extremes (Anderson, 2010). To date, it is acknowledged that there have been very few investigations into how educational leaders can support children to cope with the vicarious, gradual and indirect nature of various weather extremes.

Schoolchildren are described as having strong capabilities to drive adaptive changes if they are informed with the necessary resources and are sufficiently socially supported by the community, teachers, friends, peers and parents (Haisma et al., 2018). Studies show that schoolchildren can inspire both parents and adults in general in advancing their concerns related to improving prevention toward weather extremes (Lawson et al., 2019). Rai et al. (2021, p. 8) describe how schoolchildren have had the least contribution to societal responses to extreme weather events, "yet they are among the most affected by the devastation it wreaks, both now and in the future." Therefore, there are a number of gaps in improving the protection of school communities from extreme weather events. This book advances awareness and presents a range of critical considerations to help school communities be informed, to develop and to plan improvements in protective and mitigating considerations.

Summary and Looking Forward

Extreme weather influences have been widely regarded as the most significant global-health threat of the 21st century and into the 22nd century. The significance of the threat of extreme weather is reinforced by the wide-ranging environmental, health, societal and economic impacts. An increase in the variability of extreme and unpredictable weather events continues to occur, which disrupts students' attendance at school. Examples of extreme weather impacts include more intense and prolonged heat waves, snowstorms, extreme winds, bushfires/wildfires and heavy rainfall. Yet amongst such extreme weather influences, students globally are expected to learn key skills and habits to prepare themselves for adulthood and future careers.

Moreover, further considerations exist within schools, including the level of preparation of teachers to respond to extreme weather conditions and to protect students, as well as how students' learning is impacted by extreme weather patterns. To date, many of these questions have gone unanswered and there is a paucity of research investigating extreme weather-related influences in schools with such extreme pedagogical and classroom foci. As outlined here in Chapter 1, the importance of this book is reinforced as a vital resource for widespread educational communities, researchers and for pre/in-service teachers, and that articulates an emerging area of research that is increasingly relevant in educational settings, which are exposed to the dramatic impacts of extreme weather events.

In Chapter 2, Hyndman, Vanos and Shortridge detail the holistic impacts of both indoor and outdoor heat extremes on schoolchildren, including how children are physiologically impacted by extreme heat exposure; how extreme heat can be detrimental to schoolchildren's outdoor physical activity, and development; and how a range of thermal comfort considerations can ensure that the balance of heat (e.g., regulating internal body temperature), sweat rates and skin temperatures fall within normal parameters. Moreover, sample exemplars are provided across international research that has investigated the heat impacts within various school contexts and what can and should be considered in heat protection guidelines for school communities, teacher training and potential learning impacts, both indoors and outdoors.

Chapter 3 details air-quality impacts upon schoolchildren, current policies at schools related to air quality and specific actions to reach a stage that optimally protects our school communities from air pollution. The University of New South Wales' Schools Weather and Air Quality (SWAQ) team details the physiological impacts of impaired air quality on schoolchildren, the types of air pollutants affecting schools and the impact of wildfire/bushfire smoke that is associated with extreme heat (and drought) conditions outlined in Chapters 1 and 2. The chapter provides detailed case studies of extreme weather associated with poor air quality (wildfire examples) and unique insights into indoor classroom air quality.

In Chapter 4, Hyndman and Button detail the physiological influences of extreme cold on schoolchildren, encompassing school-community impacts from extreme rain/snowfall, cyclones and tornadoes. The processes and impacts of school closures from extreme storms are outlined across various international communities, and considerations are raised in how to best maintain schoolchildren's important outdoor play behaviours at school. Beyond simply closing schools, the authors discuss ways that school communities might mitigate the impacts of cold-weather events from disrupting physically active pursuits that can be sidelined during the cooler months (Nguyen et al., 2019).

With the many discussions of what should be included in policy decision making for schools across the earlier chapters, Hyndman uniquely showcases what the public perceives as important in relation to weather protection in schools via Chapter 5's insights. Hyndman builds upon the suggestions from multiple scholars to recognise that drawing upon the collective beliefs of a population can play a vital role in having a positive impact upon policy outcomes and discourses. A multidimensional and holistic framework is used to showcase the varying public considerations towards weather protection policy for schools, which details both public support for consolidated school weather policies and also criticisms for the decision makers in schools relating to what is prioritised for funding.

In Chapter 6, Pfautsch and Vanos provide comprehensive insights into how the planning and design of built outdoor spaces can be better protected to modify "microclimates" within schoolyards and in schools. The evidence presented compels readers to think more deeply about how the design of outdoor school spaces can facilitate or restrict play behaviours (e.g., through weather-imposed injury), and create safer or more dangerous conditions related to extreme weather, with a large emphasis on heat, sun and precipitation. The authors detail novel insights and imaging to showcase environmental temperature exposures, shade considerations, climatic zones in schools and various temperature ranges. Design materials, insulation strategies, surface structures, shading and natural greening into school spaces are also highlighted throughout that chapter.

Finally, Chapter 7 showcases, in great depth, the protective considerations from across the international literature, including protective frameworks and consolidated suggestions from international scholars for educational communities and researchers to take forward to lessen the impacts of future extreme weather events.

In summary, the contents of this exciting book encompass how to protect international school communities from extreme weather influences, how schools and education systems are countering extreme weather, how schoolchildren can rely on adults (including staff and teachers) for protective strategies from the direct and indirect impacts of extremes, training that teachers are receiving for weather protection in schools, the influences of extreme heat, research into public perceptions of weather protective strategies, the influences of snowfall, rainfall and air quality on schools, the role of building design in said impacts and the effects of school closures on schoolchildren.

References

Adger, W. N., Arnell, N. W., & Tompkins, E. L. (2005). Adapting to climate change: Perspectives across scales. *Global Environmental Change, 15*(2), 75–76.

Albert, M., Hurrelmann, K., Quenzel, G., & Jugend, G. (2010). *Eine pragmatische generation behauptet sich (A pragmatic generation asserts itself)*. Fischer Taschenbuch Verlag.

Anderson, A. (2010). *Combating climate change through quality education*. Brookings Global Economy and Development.

Anderson, K. (2005). *Predicting the weather: Victorians and the science of meteorology*. University of Chicago Press.

Australian Bureau of Statistics. (2021). *Schools*. Retrieved from www.abs.gov.au/statistics/people/education/schools/latest-release

Bach, C., Gupta, A. K., Nair, S. S., & Birkmann, J. (2013). Critical infrastructures and disaster risk reduction. *National Institute of Disaster Management and Deutsche Gesellschaft für internationale Zusammenarbeit GmbH (GIZ), New Delhi*, p. 72.

Barry, R. G., & Chorley, R. J. (2009). *Atmosphere, weather and climate*. Routledge.

British Educational Suppliers Association. (2021). *Key UK education statistics*. Retrieved from www.besa.org.uk/key-uk-education-statistics/

Burgess, J. (2013). *Climate change: Children's challenge*. United Nations Children's Fund United Kingdom. Retrieved from www.unicef.org.uk/publications/climate-change-report-jon-snow-2013/

Burke, S. E., Sanson, A. V., & Van Hoorn, J. (2018). The psychological effects of climate change on children. *Current Psychiatry Reports, 20*(5), 1–8.

Call, D. A., & Coleman, J. S. (2014). The decision process behind inclement-weather school closings: A case-study in Maryland, USA. *Meteorological Applications, 21*(3), 474–480.

Centre for Research on the Epidemiology of Disasters (CRED). (2015). *The human cost of natural disasters: A global perspective*. Retrieved from www.preventionweb.net/files/42895_cerdthehumancostofdisastersglobalpe.pdf

Clayton, S., Manning, C., Krygsman, K., & Speiser, M. (2017). *Mental health and our changing climate: Impacts, implications, and guidance*. American Psychological Association and Eco-America. Retrieved from: http://ecoamerica.org/wp-content/uploads/2017/03/ea-apa-psych-report-web.pdf

Costello, A., Abbas, M., Allen, A., Ball, S., Bell, S., Bellamy, R., . . . & Patterson, C. (2009). Managing the health effects of climate change: Lancet and University College London Institute for Global Health Commission. *The Lancet, 373*(9676), 1693–1733.

Council of Ministers for Education Canada. (2022). *Education in Canada: An overview*. Retrieved from https://cmec.ca/299/Education-in-Canada-An-Overview/index.html

Cox, R. S., Scannell, L., Heykoop, C., Tobin-Gurley, J., & Peek, L. (2017). Understanding youth disaster recovery: The vital role of people, places, and activities. *International Journal of Disaster Risk Reduction, 22*, 249–256.

Day, R. E. (2007). *Cancellations tough to call, even for the best school chiefs-silberman retains credibility by not trying to snow anyone*. Retrieved from https://encompass.eku.edu/cgi/viewcontent.cgi?referer=&httpsredir=1&article=1038&context=ci_fsresearch

Eames, C. (2017). Climate change education in New Zealand. *Curriculum Perspectives*, *37*(1), 99–102.

Ehrlich, S. B., Gwynne, J. A., & Allensworth, E. M. (2018). Pre-kindergarten attendance matters: Early chronic absence patterns and relationships to learning outcomes. *Early Childhood Research Quarterly*, *44*, 136–151.

Ergler, C. R. (2020). *The power of place in play: A Bourdieusian analysis of Auckland children's seasonal play practices* (Vol. 17). Transcript Verlag.

Garcia, D. M., & Sheehan, M. C. (2016). Extreme weather-driven disasters and children's health. *International Journal of Health Services*, *46*(1), 79–105.

Gellman, M. D. (2020). Behavioral medicine. In *Encyclopedia of behavioral medicine* (pp. 223–226). Springer International Publishing.

Glander, M. (2016). Selected statistics from the Public Elementary and Secondary Education Universe: School Year 2014–2015. US Department of Education. *National Center for Education Statistics*. Retrieved from https://eric.ed.gov/?id=ED569170

Gottfried, M. A. (2014). Chronic absenteeism and its effects on students' academic and socioemotional outcomes. *Journal of Education for Students Placed at Risk (JESPAR)*, *19*(2), 53–75.

Gottfried, M. A., & Gee, K. A. (2017). Identifying the determinants of chronic absenteeism: A bioecological systems approach. *Teachers College Record*, *119*(7), 1–34.

Haisma, H., Yousefzadeh, S., & Boele Van Hensbroek, P. (2018). Towards a capability approach to child growth: A theoretical framework. *Maternal & Child Nutrition*, *14*(2), e12534.

Hammer, B., & Schmidlin, T. W. (2002). Response to warnings during the 3 May 1999 Oklahoma City tornado: Reasons and relative injury rates. *Weather and Forecasting*, *17*(3), 577–581.

Harker-Schuch, I., & Bugge-Henriksen, C. (2013). Opinions and knowledge about climate change science in high school students. *Ambio*, *42*(6), 755–766.

Hersher, R. (2016). The arctic suicides: It's not the dark that kills you. *National Public Radio: All Things Considered*. Retrieved from https://www.npr.org/sections/goatsandsoda/2016/04/21/474847921/the-arctic-suicides-its-not-the-dark-that-kills-you

Hyndman, B. (Ed.). (2017a). *Contemporary school playground strategies for healthy students*. Springer.

Hyndman, B. (2017b). Heat-smart schools during physical education (PE) activities: Developing a policy to protect students from extreme heat. *Learning Communities Journal: International Journal of Learning in Social Contexts (Special Edition)*, *21*, 56–72.

Hyndman, B. (2017c). Does bad weather affect student performance in school? *The Conversation*. Retrieved from https://theconversation.com/does-bad-weather-affect-student-performance-in-school-75461

Hyndman, B., Benson, A., & Telford, A. (2016). Active play: Exploring the influences on children's school playground activities. *American Journal of Play*, *8*(3), 325–344.

Hyndman, B., & Zundans-Fraser, L. (2021). Determining public perceptions of a proposed national heat protection policy for Australian schools. *Health Promotion Journal of Australia*, *32*(1), 75–83.

IPCC. (2021a). Climate change 2021: The physical science basis. In V. Masson-Delmotte, P. Zhai, A. Pirani, S. L. Connors, C. Péan, S. Berger, N. Caud, Y. Chen, L. Goldfarb, M. I. Gomis, M. Huang, K. Leitzell, E. Lonnoy, J. B. R. Matthews, T. K. Maycock, T. Waterfield, O. Yelekçi, R. Yu, & B. Zhou (Eds.), *Contribution of working group I to the sixth assessment report of the intergovernmental panel on climate change* (pp. 2061–2086). Cambridge University Press. https://doi.org/10.1017/9781009157896.015

IPCC. (2021b). Summary for policymakers. In V. Masson-Delmotte, P. Zhai, A. Pirani, S. L. Connors, C. Péan, S. Berger, N. Caud, Y. Chen, L. Goldfarb, M. I. Gomis, M. Huang, K. Leitzell, E. Lonnoy, J. B. R. Matthews, T. K. Maycock, T. Waterfield, O. Yelekçi, R. Yu, & B. Zhou (Eds.), *Climate change 2021: The physical science basis. Contribution of working group I to the sixth assessment report of the intergovernmental panel on climate change* (pp. 3–32). Cambridge University Press. https://doi.org/10.1017/9781009157896.001

ISDR. (2007). *Hyogo framework*. United Nations.

Iyer, R. N. (2020). *Natural disaster shocks: Does household response impact children's educational achievement*. Georgetown University.

Jacobs, L. E., Hansen, A. Y., Nightingale, C. J., & Lehnard, R. (2019). What is "too cold?" Recess and physical education weather policies in Maine elementary schools. *Maine Policy Review, 28*(1), 49–58.

Kousky, C. (2016). Impacts of natural disasters on children. *The Future of Children*, 73–92.

Lai, B. S., Esnard, A. M., Lowe, S. R., & Peek, L. (2016). Schools and disasters: Safety and mental health assessment and interventions for children. *Current Psychiatry Reports, 18*, 1–9.

Lawson, D. F., Stevenson, K. T., Peterson, M. N., Carrier, S. J., L Strnad, R., & Seekamp, E. (2019). Children can foster climate change concern among their parents. *Nature Climate Change, 9*(6), 458–462.

Matthews-Trigg, N. T., Vanos, J., & Ebi, K. L. (2019). Climate change and cancer. In *Cancer and society: A multidisciplinary assessment and strategies for action* (pp. 11–25). Springer, Cham. https://doi.org/10.1007/978-3-030-05855-5_2

Mermer, G., Donmez, R. O., & Daghan, S. (2018). The evaluation of the education for earthquake preparation addressed to middle school students. *JPMA. The Journal of the Pakistan Medical Association, 68*(12), 1809–1815.

Midford, R., Nutton, G., Hyndman, B., & Silburn, S. (Eds.). (2020). *Health and education interdependence: Thriving from birth to adulthood*. Springer.

Miller, R. K., & Hui, I. (2022). Impact of short school closures (1–5 days) on overall academic performance of schools in California. *Scientific Reports, 12*(1), 1–13.

Monroe, M. C., Oxarart, A., & Plate, R. R. (2013). A role for environmental education in climate change for secondary science educators. *Applied Environmental Education & Communication, 12*(1), 4–18.

Morrissey, T. W., Hutchison, L., & Winsler, A. (2014). Family income, school attendance, and academic achievement in elementary school. *Developmental Psychology, 50*(3), 741.

National Center for Education Statistics. (2017). *Educational institutions*. Retrieved from https://nces.ed.gov/FastFacts/display.asp?id=84

National Oceanographic and Atmospheric Administration (NOAA) and US Department of Commerce. (2013). *Storm Prediction Center*. Retrieved from www.spc.noaa.gov/faq/

Nguyen, H. T., Le, H. T., & Connelly, L. B. (2019). *Weather and children's time allocation*. Retrieved from https://mpra.ub.uni-muenchen.de/94442/

Pachauri, R. K., Allen, M. R., Barros, V. R., Broome, J., Cramer, W., Christ, R., . . . & van Ypserle, J. P. (2014). *Climate change 2014: Synthesis report. Contribution of working groups I, II and III to the fifth assessment report of the intergovernmental panel on climate change*. IPCC. https://www.ipcc.ch/site/assets/uploads/2018/05/SYR_AR5_FINAL_full_wcover.pdf

Park, R. J., Behrer, A. P., & Goodman, J. (2021). Learning is inhibited by heat exposure, both internationally and within the United States. *Nature Human Behaviour, 5*(1), 19–27.

Peek, L., & Stough, L. M. (2010). Children with disabilities in the context of disaster: A social vulnerability perspective. *Child Development, 81*(4), 1260–1270.

Rai, P., Sutter, J. I., Wheeler, J. G., Byron, R. G., & Byron, L. G. (2021). Pediatric climate change advocacy: A call to action for health care providers. *Journal of Applied Research on Children: Informing Policy for Children at Risk, 12*(1), https://doi.org/10.58464/2155-5834.146

Randell, H., & Gray, C. (2019). Climate change and educational attainment in the global tropics. *Proceedings of the National Academy of Sciences, 116*(18), 8840–8845.

Rifai, H. S. (2012). Hurricane impacts on critical infrastructure. In *After Ike: Severe storm prediction, impact, and recovery on the Texas Gulf Coast* (pp. 122–137). Texas A&M University Press.

Rother, H. A., Etzel, R. A., Shelton, M., Paulson, J. A., Hayward, R. A., & Theron, L. C. (2020). Impact of extreme weather events on Sub-Saharan African child and adolescent mental health: A protocol for a systematic review. *Atmosphere, 11*(5), 493.

Sanson, A. V., & Burke, S. E. (2020). Climate change and children: An issue of intergenerational justice. In *Children and peace* (pp. 343–362). Springer.

Save the Children. (2007). *Definition of child protection*. Retrieved from https://resourcecentre.savethechildren.net/document/save-childrens-definition-child-protection/

Save The Children. (2015). *2015 National report card on protecting children in disasters*. Retrieved from https://rems.ed.gov/docs/disasterreport_2015.pdf

Schipper, E. L. F. (2007). Climate change adaptation and development: Exploring the linkages. *Tyndall Centre for Climate Change Research Working Paper, 107*, 13.

Schulze, S. S., Fischer, E. C., Hamideh, S., & Mahmoud, H. (2020). Wildfire impacts on schools and hospitals following the 2018 California Camp Fire. *Natural Hazards, 104*(1), 901–925.

Schumacher, R. S., Lindsey, D. T., Schumacher, A. B., Braun, J., Miller, S. D., & Demuth, J. L. (2010). Multidisciplinary analysis of an unusual tornado: Meteorology, climatology, and the communication and interpretation of warnings. *Weather and Forecasting, 25*(5), 1412–1429.

Sheffield, P. E., & Landrigan, P. J. (2011). Global climate change and children's health: Threats and strategies for prevention. *Environmental Health Perspectives, 119*(3), 291–298.

Sheffield, P. E., Uijttewaal, S. A., Stewart, J., & Galvez, M. P. (2017). Climate change and schools: Environmental hazards and resiliency. *International Journal of Environmental Research and Public Health, 14*(11), 1397.

Shepard, S., Boudet, H., Zanocco, C. M., Cramer, L. A., & Tilt, B. (2018). Community climate change beliefs, awareness, and actions in the wake of the September 2013 flooding in Boulder County, Colorado. *Journal of Environmental Studies and Sciences, 8*(3), 312–325.

Shepardson, D. P., Niyogi, D., Choi, S., & Charusombat, U. (2009). Seventh grade students' conceptions of global warming and climate change. *Environmental Education Research, 15*(5), 549–570.

Silburn, S. (2020). The role of epigenetics in shaping the foundations of children's learning. In *Health and education interdependence* (pp. 321–330). Springer.

Taylor, L., Watkins, S. L., Marshall, H., Dascombe, B. J., & Foster, J. (2016). The impact of different environmental conditions on cognitive function: A focused review. *Frontiers in Physiology, 6*, 372.

Thaman, K. H. (2010). Teacher capacities for working towards peace and sustainable development. *International Journal of Sustainability in Higher Education, 11*(4), 353–364.

Tranter, B., & Skrbis, Z. (2014). Political and social divisions over climate change among young Queenslanders. *Environment and Planning A, 46*(7), 1638–1651.

UNESCO. (2012). *United Nations framework on climate change convention*. Retrieved from https://unfccc.int/resource/docs/2012/smsn/ngo/219.pdf

UNESCO. (2017). *UNESCO strategy for action on climate change*. Retrieved from https://unesdoc.unesco.org/ark:/48223/pf0000259255

United Nations International Children's Emergency Fund (UNICEF). (2014). The challenges of climate change: Children on the front line. *UNICEF Office of Research*. Retrieved from https://www.unicef-irc.org/publications/716-the-challenges-of-climate-change-children-on-the-front-line.html

Watts, N., Amann, M., Ayeb-Karlsson, S., Belesova, K., Bouley, T., Boykoff, M., . . . & Costello, A. (2018). The Lancet countdown on health and climate change: From 25 years of inaction to a global transformation for public health. *The Lancet, 391*(10120), 581–630.

Weissbecker, I., Sephton, S. E., Martin, M. B., & Simpson, D. M. (2008). Psychological and physiological correlates of stress in children exposed to disaster: Current research and recommendations for intervention. *Children Youth and Environments, 18*(1), 30–70.

Wong, K. K., Shi, J., Gao, H., Zheteyeva, Y. A., Lane, K., Copeland, D., . . . & Uzicanin, A. (2014). Why is school closed today? Unplanned K-12 school closures in the United States, 2011–2013. *PLoS One, 9*(12), e113755.

World Health Organization. (2021). *Status of meaningful adolescent and youth engagement (MAYE): Summary report of the results of an accountability survey submitted by signatories of the Global consensus statement on MAYE*. Retrieved from https://apps.who.int/iris/bitstream/handle/10665/349837/9789240037144-eng.pdf?sequence=1

2 The Impact of Indoor and Outdoor Heat Extremes on Schoolchildren

Brendon Hyndman, Adora Shortridge and Jennifer Vanos

Introduction

Across the world, droughts and extreme-heat wave events are becoming more common and intense (Guerreiro et al., 2018). The increasing occurrence is becoming so severe that models indicate a potential increase of almost 60,000 heat-associated deaths per year over three decades from 2025 across Europe (Ciscar et al., 2014). The global average air temperature has increased over 50 years (Alexander et al., 2006). Moreover, surface-temperature averages across the globe are expected to increase by two to four degrees Celsius by the beginning of the next century (Ngwenya et al., 2018). These trends of increased temperatures are expected to negatively impact land areas, which will impact vulnerable population groups, such as children, and increase the occurrence of heat illness (Ngwenya et al., 2018).

Urban growth is estimated to reach 6 billion urban dwellers by 2050, accompanied by large-scale urban development (Pisello et al., 2018). Such anthropogenic activities have increased urban temperatures, especially in cities where the summertime urban heat island (UHI) heightens the risk of extreme heat exposure to humans. Moreover, in the face of more frequent and severe heat waves linked to climate change (Mishra et al., 2015), growing thermal risks to humans are expected without appropriate adaptive strategies. High heat, especially when coupled with pre-existing health conditions (e.g., asthma) or lower fitness in children (e.g, Morrison, 2022) increases heat-health concerns. Heat also increases the levels of photochemical ozone (Zivin & Shrader, 2016) (see Chapter 3). Yet despite the widespread acknowledgment that extreme heat waves are expected to be more frequent, there is a lag in giving appropriate attention to extreme heat as a significant hazard (Ngwenya et al., 2018), especially within educational resources and holistically within school systems (Hyndman & Zundans-Fraser, 2021).

Globally, the cascading impacts of heat in schoolchildren range from slight illness and heat exhaustion to serious morbidity and mortality (Xu et al., 2014; Zivin & Shrader, 2016). Further, the association between high temperatures and adverse health outcomes is well established in developed countries, with adaptation efforts supporting decreased all-population mortality (Hondula et al., 2015); however, expanding research shows evidence of adverse heat effects in low- and middle-income countries (LMICs) (yet LMICs make up a small portion of heat-mortality research overall) (Green et al., 2019). Similarly, research on the exposure to heat and ensuing impacts on schoolchildren is less available in LMICs; hence, working to understand these impacts across regions – including the how, when, where and why heat exposures may be affecting child well-being at school – is imperative for improving infrastructure, education, policies and research on school heat using place-based research.

The lack of consistent or holistic policy attention to protect communities from heat (beyond athletes and sporting realms) could be attributed to the natural occurrence of extreme heat and belief systems towards acclimatisation and adaption (Adams et al., 2021; Hyndman & Zundans-Fraser, 2021). Yet the trends in extreme heat indicate that the ability to physiologically cope with heightened levels of intense heat that exceed our coping thresholds will increasingly put our populations at risk, creating a growing public health concern (Hyatt et al., 2010). There must be greater insight and attention from the public to prevent the impacts of heat exposure, and this prevention should start at the beginning of the lifespan, in schools (Hyndman & Zundans-Fraser, 2021). Focusing on better protecting and equipping schools to cope with extreme heat can ensure that impacts from increasing levels of heat are minimised in the future (Hoa et al., 2013).

Heat and Health Considerations

Research shows that extreme heat may negatively influence schoolchildren's educational performance, thermoregulation, thermal discomfort, and cause cognitive impairments (Hyndman, 2017a, 2017b; Park et al., 2021). If neglected, concerns about extreme heat can lead to heat illness, rashes, cramps, heat exhaustion and in the worst case, heat stroke or mortality in schoolchildren (Mangus & Canares, 2019) (see Figure 2.1). Most heat-health research has focused on heat impacts in adults, and while studies into the effects of heat in schoolchildren are emerging, there has been little focus on the intersectionality of acute and chronic heat on children, and how to comprehensively study the topic. Prevention of overexposure to extreme heat and sun, while also ensuring safe outdoor spaces for adequate play, is vital to promoting children's long-term health and reducing risk (Kennedy et al., 2021).

Heat extremes in schoolyards are amplified by the combination of the UHI effect and climate change (Kennedy et al., 2021), which, in tandem, increase a child's heat exposure and the outdoor and indoor cooling needs of schools. While climate change is affected by natural variability and anthropogenic emissions, urban areas may experience intensified heat and thus

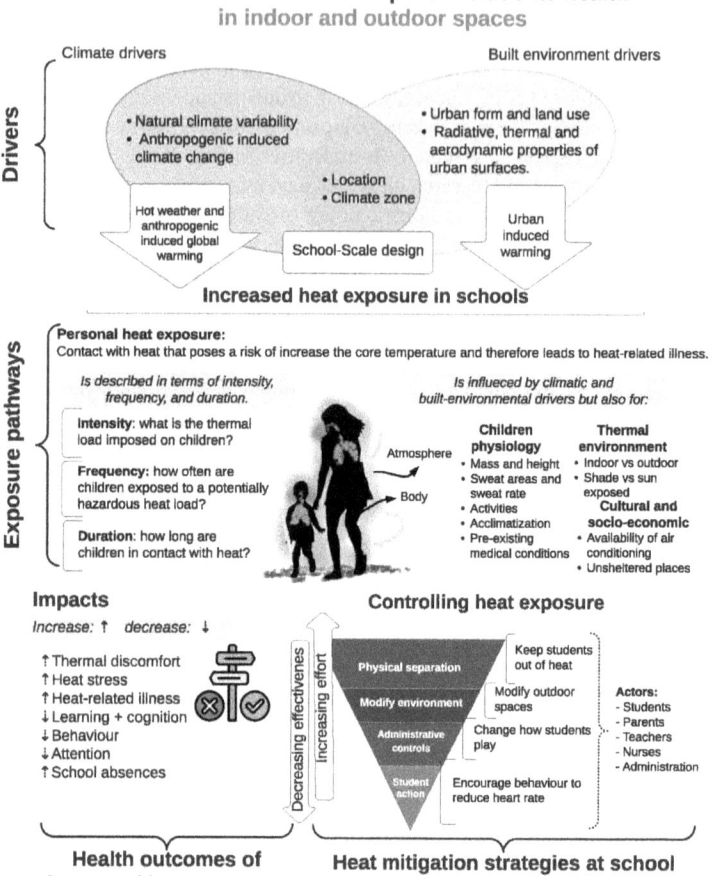

Figure 2.1 A conceptual diagram linking climate drivers and urban-induced heating to multiscale effects, outdoor and indoor heat, heat-exposure pathways, thermal discomfort, physical activity and impacts on health and learning

Note: A country's climate and cultural context influence the association between indoor/outdoor heat and a child's personal heat exposure. Social and behavioral contexts also influence exposure to outdoor/indoor heat and children's personal heat. Pathways of intervention systems affect thermal discomfort levels in children, physical activity intensity/length and impacts on learning and health from heat.

uncomfortable microclimates. For example, playgrounds often present some of the highest surface temperatures within an urban area due to artificial surfaces, thus increasing air temperatures, and many lack shade (Elgheznawy & Eltarabily, 2021; Olsen et al., 2019; Vanos et al., 2016; see Figure 2.2 and Chapter 6). Exposure to extreme heat and ultraviolet (UV) rays put children

Figure 2.2 An example of a group of schoolchildren huddled into a small, shaded area

Source: Image © J. Vanos for Arizona State University Research completed at Paideia Academies.

at acute risk of thermal-contact skin burns (Vanos et al., 2016), heat stress/ illnesses (lethargy, vomiting, headaches; Mangus & Canares, 2019) and sunburn (Dobbinson et al., 2014; Vanos et al., 2017b); natural and built shade use (Lanza & Durand, 2021) and other cooling amenities (Declet-Barreto et al., 2013) can reduce these concerns.

There has been some success in the United States with acclimatisation practices, policies and procedures to prepare high school student athletes with scaffolded heat exposure over time (Cooper et al., 2020). Acclimatisation can include physiological adaptations (e.g., enhanced thermoregulatory abilities such as vasodilation and sweating (Parsons, 2009), with further protection gained through behavioral interventions supporting safety (e.g., development of hydration practices, work-to-rest ratios and reducing sun exposure).

Developmental Risks on Schoolchildren

Quality outdoor school environments are vital to ensure that physical-activity participation is encouraged, alongside being a critical contextual realm to facilitate cognitive, social and affective development (Hyndman, 2017a, 2017b). For example, Remmers et al. (2017) found that children were significantly less physically active when air temperatures reached above 22°C. At least one-third of a child's daily physical activity is obtained during recess periods from scheduled classroom-based time, which occurs predominantly outdoors within school playgrounds (Ridgers et al., 2006).

In the United States, school recess periods have been previously recognised as possibly the greatest windows of time throughout a school year to impact schoolchildren's physical-activity participation (Robert Wood Johnson Foundation, 2007). Similarly, in Australia, Hyndman (2017a, 2017b) suggested that schoolchildren can engage in up to 4,200 school-recess-period opportunities in some contexts, representing a significant amount of exposure to developmental opportunities that can be facilitated or restricted. With the escalation of childhood lifestyle diseases (obesity, type 2 diabetes, cardiovascular disease) partly caused by a high proportion of schoolchildren across the world not meeting the recommended physical-activity guidelines (Guthold et al., 2018), there has been growing evidence pointing toward the importance of increasing schoolchildren engaging in outdoor-play activities over the past decade (Hyndman, 2017a, 2017b). Yet despite the many hours of ambient exposures that children receive during outdoor play, there is still a paucity of school-based data that has investigated extreme heat risks on children's health and education (Falk & Dotan, 2008; Hyndman, 2017a, 2017b).

Hyndman and Chancellor's (2015) Australian study discovered approximately 32% fewer males and almost 50% fewer females in an Australian study enjoyed "playing in the heat" compared to "playing in the sun." Yet despite this finding, the predominant focus of Australian outdoor-play policy has been on sun protection to prevent exposure to harmful UV rays (Hyndman &

Zundans-Fraser, 2021), rather than on the other potential negative impacts on play and health from extreme heat exposure. Of additional concern is that extreme weather events may prevent schoolchildren from developing positive physical-activity behaviors or reducing enjoyment, and evidence indicates that physical activity (Hayes et al., 2019) and enjoyment of activities (Ladwig et al., 2018) often track across the lifespan. The United Nations Convention on the Rights of the Child (2022) specifies that schoolchildren have a right to be protected from neglect (Item 19), have a right to a safe environment (Item 24), have a right to play (Item 31) and be protected from work that can be dangerous or bad for their education, development and health (Item 32). Considering the UN Rights of the Child, heat protection becomes even more vital.

Schoolchildren generally have similar risks in the onset of heat-related illness as adults (Mangus & Canares, 2019); however, specific physiologic, developmental and psychological or experiential differences unique to children are present regarding thermoregulation that are important to understand, which, if ignored, can create highly vulnerable situations. Dangerous heat-illness situations are more likely to present themselves during exercise in the heat (Mangus & Canares, 2019) due to age-dependent vulnerability factors, which include:

1 Children take longer to acclimatise to warm environments than adults, on average (Falk & Dotan, 2011);
2 Infants and young children have less effective behavioral thermoregulation than adults, who depend on supervisory control (Folkerts et al., 2020), hence lacking ability to respond to overheating (e.g., drink water, change environments);
3 Adolescents may be at higher risk for experiencing heat-related illness due to conditions such as obesity, sickle cell disease and trait, diabetes and cystic fibrosis (Bergeron, Devore & Rice, 2011; Howe & Boden, 2007);
4 Children perceive thermal comfort and sensation differently than adults (Ter Mors et al., 2011) and may not recognise the early signs of heat stress, which may predispose them to higher risk, particularly during outdoor play (Vanos et al., 2017a);
5 Children may be more susceptible to heat illness due to their higher body-mass-to-area ratio compared to adults, which increases convective heat gain under very high temperatures (Falk & Dotan, 2008);
6 On average, schoolchildren have lower sweat production (Morrison & Sims, 2014), limiting essential evaporative cooling to control body temperature (Gomes et al., 2013).

However, these susceptibilities in schoolchildren will depend on age, fitness, education and past experiences with heat symptoms, among other factors. With the many risks associated with schoolchildren being exposed to the negative impacts of extreme heat, hospitalisation and other illnesses have been recorded. Insights from Japan's Sporting Council in Asia unveiled that over a 32-year period during school hours, the death toll reached $N = 133$ from heat stroke via schoolchildren's engagement in sports such as track and field, judo, kendo, baseball, rugby, football and mountaineering (Hatori, 2013). In other parts of the world, such as Arizona in the United States, almost 300 schoolchildren were admitted to hospitals for emergency treatment for heat illness between 2015–2019 (ADHS, 2020a, 2020b). Nelson and colleagues (2011) report that almost half of the broader population that develops exertional heat illness are school-aged children and adolescents. Leithead and Lind (1964) historically identified that one or more of the following must have occurred for serious heat illness to eventuate: 1) lack of appreciation of the potential consequences from extreme heat (via supervision or specific individuals being exposed); 2) circumstances beyond an individual's control led to increased exposure to extreme heat; and 3) factors such as a lack of acclimatisation or dehydration were present. Given the previous concerns and that schoolchildren are often reliant on supervisors, are early in their education journey, and are less aware of heat exertion symptoms (Hyndman, 2017a, 2017b), protecting schoolchildren from heat extremes should be a priority.

Subtle behavioral considerations also exist, such as schoolchildren failing to recognise signs of dehydration during physical activities and thus not drinking enough water (Somboonwong et al., 2012). Not only can severe dehydration be fatal, it can have a negative flow-on impact on schoolchildren's classroom abilities, causing reduced cognition, concentration and memory retrieval (Benton & Burgess, 2009). Similar to outdoor exposure during recess breaks and in the school playground, the scheduling of physical education classes when heat extremes are present has also been recognised as problematic for schoolchildren's health. Doecke (1992) showcased data that found heat illnesses and impacts in schoolchildren peaked during the hottest months of the year, specifically dehydration, heat-related headaches/nausea, and sunburn. The children in the given study, spread across 17 Australian schools, were also found to be "listless" and had widespread negative perceptions towards undertaking physical activity and physical education in the tropic heat (Doecke, 1992).

Hyndman (2017a, 2017b) outlines problems with the lack of focus on protecting Australian schoolchildren from the heat because (1) learning is most attentive within the 20–24 degrees Celsius range (Earthman, 2002); (2) the mandatory requirements for schoolchildren to reach critical minimum thresholds of physical education time each week; (3) the crowded curriculum constraints on schoolteachers, reducing timetable flexibility; (4) much lower enjoyment of school play activities during weather extremes; (5) the schools in tropical climates exceed most wet bulb globe temperature (temperature/humidity combination) thresholds for safe physical-activity participation, despite over one million people in Australia living in tropical areas; and (6) schools need heat protection policy that aligns with school contexts, rather than drawing upon broader sporting guidelines. However, it should still be acknowledged that a lack of direct empirical and in situ studies on the impacts of extreme heat on children exist, particularly compared to adults and other vulnerable populations.

Improving coverage of both the school curriculum with heat-safety considerations (Hyndman, 2017a, 2017b) and teacher preparation to train teachers are also seen as important in adults making improved decisions relating to schoolchildren's play (Chancellor & Hyndman, 2017). Schäfer and Smith (1996) highlighted that just over 10% of judgments by adults relating to schoolchildren's play are mistakes. Without appropriate training, adults can then find it hard to determine what is developmentally appropriate according to play (Chancellor & Hyndman, 2017), and this can also relate to the various weather impacts on play, such as hot weather in schools.

Schoolchildren's Thermal Comfort

A key component of heat influences on schoolchildren is their "level of comfort." Over the past half-century, investigations into thermal-comfort studies have steadily progressed, with a growing focus on indoor school environments that go beyond adult-perception studies (Jiang et al., 2018; Domínguez-Amarillo et al., 2020). Thermal comfort is the condition of the mind that expresses satisfaction with the thermal environment and is thus a subjective evaluation (ANSI/ASHRAE, 2017). Thermal comfort has historically been challenging to determine due to the many different variables that impact comfort, including sociocultural (Brager & De Dear, 2003, Montazami et al., 2017) and the more commonly established physical variables (Vickers, 2017). The level of thermal comfort that people experience is impacted by many physical variables, including humidity, air temperature, level of physical activity, type of clothing, air velocities and the average radiant temperature (Parsons, 2009). Left unmonitored, poor thermal comfort can result from lack of airflow, high classroom-occupancy rates and excessive sunlight warming up learning spaces (Zomorodian et al., 2016). Similarly, it has been shown that indoor conditions such as high humidity, air and globe temperature, building or shade orientation, air quality and sunlight intensity can influence a child's learning environment (Noda et al., 2020). The use of comfort standards continues to evolve according to the many diverse variables that impact a child's thermal comfort, its subjective nature of measurement and the establishment of some measures being initially based upon adults (Teli et al., 2017; Vanos, 2015); hence, real-world assessments of children's thermal sensation, comfort and physiological responses are needed.

Most research focusing on thermal comfort in schools has been completed within tropic regions, yet with climate change, more focus will be required in other regions to accommodate schoolchildren (and teachers) (Rodríguez et al., 2021). For instance, slow changes in the climate system are being replaced by extreme heat waves that extend further into the shoulder seasons (Rodríguez et al., 2021). Thermal-comfort problems within school environments often relate to the differentials between students and teachers in thermal-comfort preferences and restrictive rules and regulations (Kim & De Dear, 2018). Hence, there are also concerns with children's thermal comfort, as children are often reliant on teachers being the gatekeepers to comfort decisions in school contexts (Kim & De Dear, 2018). For instance, within Indian schools, children showed a greater acceptance of indoor temperature fluctuations if they had the autonomy to modify ceiling fans and open windows (Jindal, 2018).

Within indoor spaces, the two established methods for determining thermal comfort include an "adaptive method," which suggests that people's comfort expectations can evolve depending on their awareness of their ability to modify the temperatures to improve the comfort within their own spaces (Rodríguez et al., 2021). The second method, which emerged from lab experiments with university-aged students, is based on the body's ability to thermoregulate (Rodríguez et al., 2021).

Further research will be essential to ensure there is more established, evidence-based insight into school-based thermal comfort, especially with children often preferring lower temperatures due to their thermal sensitivity to higher temperatures (Kim & De Dear, 2018). With reductions in schoolchildren's play within nature outdoors (Mustapa et al., 2015; Hyndman, 2019), there is also potential for school-playground designers to consider the weather and temperature buffering properties of including natural elements such as trees and garden features (Madden et al., 2018) (see Chapter 6). Improving our understanding of school-based thermal comfort will be critical, with children spending excessive time inside classrooms.

Indoor and Outdoor Heat Impacts Across International School Contexts

Researchers worldwide have studied extreme heat impacts on schoolchildren – from the desert to the tropics, from air-conditioned classrooms to cement buildings with windows and little airflow, and from a spectrum of qualitative to quantitative perspectives. Table 2.1 demonstrates the purpose and findings from a sample of studies relating to children's heat health and/or thermal comfort. The context of where these studies were performed is critical when considering mitigation/adaptation strategies. Because poor thermal conditions can impair learning and health (Saraiva et al., 2018), holistically including schoolchildren in thermal comfort decision-making is vital to maintain and optimise academic performance in various contexts and cultures.

The country's level of development influences several factors for indoor/outdoor heat impacts, including infrastructure, policy formality, environmental quality and thermal-comfort perceptions and sensations amongst the children. For example, clothing requirements for children in schools vary based on cultural context – students in Costa Rica, Africa and Iran have strict uniform requirements, and in Brazil clothing requirements are more relaxed (Table 2.1). Heat protection guidelines also differ. For example, Australia has a range of sporadic heat protection guidelines for schools that have been encouraged to be more consolidated for education purposes, often dominated by the generalised sporting guidelines. Canada has more formally developed policies for school-based heat protection, while the remaining countries listed (Table 2.1) have more informal or no policies regarding handling extreme heat in schools.

School infrastructure and environment also play a large role in students' thermal comfort, both in and out of the classroom. Classrooms studied in Brazil, Costa Rica and Australia contained air conditioners at some level. Schools in Africa contained no air conditioning and were comprised of "prefabricated asbestos sheeting with metal roofs or converted shipping containers" or had "no water supply, electricity ... or fans" (Bidassey-Manilal et al., 2016, p. 18; Dapi et al., 2010, p. 2).

As more insights are generated from the global literature, this can build awareness for global school communities of setting minimum heat-protective standards to ensure children's development at school can be optimised, both inside and outside the classroom. In addition to some of the protective strategies specified earlier such as through shade provision, hydration, education, policy provision and building community awareness, a multidimensional, preventive framework is an important approach to the complexity of the issue of heat protection across school communities (Hyndman, 2017a, 2017b). Hyndman (2017a, 2017b) packaged many of the researched and developed suggestions that have been circulating from organisations and research into a five-stage action framework, underpinned by the World Health Organization's Ottawa Charter for Health Promotion that included 1) Effective school-based policy; 2) Supportive Environment; 3) Training; 4) Prevention; 5) Community.

Shortridge et al. (2022) built upon the five action areas determined by Hyndman (2017a, 2017b) to ensure children's well-being could be protected relating to heat exposure in schools. From the interviews with key stakeholders, three major themes (and sub-themes) were found in school heat-readiness perceptions:

1 Barriers (*to prevention and protection*)
2 Awareness (*of heat dangers*)
3 Response (*to extreme heat*)

A Delphi survey resulted in 30 approved statements to be used in the HeatReady School Tool, which contains an evaluation rubric where the school can score their level of "readiness" and organise and plan their individual priorities and goals. All schools receive "HeatReady" packets, including the prioritisation tree to organise their progress towards the 30 recommendations over time (Figure 2.3; HUE Engage, 2022).

Table 2.1 Studies addressing heat protection and thermal comfort in schools (or as a model for schools) across diverse international contexts[2]

Country & Climate Context	Study Purpose	Findings or Recommendations Related to Children's Heat Health and/or Thermal Comfort	Reference
Australia	Literature reviews of various existing community/organisational policies and public perceptions to better inform future school heat protection provisions and policy improvements.	Recommend developing a more educational/school-specific heat protection policy outside of sporting guidelines.	Hyndman (2017a, 2017b) Hyndman and Zundans-Fraser (2021)
	To inform future research into student thermal comfort and cooling solutions for schools in Western Sydney and New South Wales.	Future research will need to address the built environment of schools, enhance collaboration across disciplines, test and implement policies and planning practices for cooling school playgrounds, and develop improved thermal-comfort models specifically for children.	Madden et al. (2018)
	To outline the notion and examples of "climate-smart" playgrounds; document surface, air and "feels like" temperatures in playgrounds; describe the process, outputs and outcomes of a playground transformation to create a "UV-smart Cool Playground."[1]	Developed ten recommendations that outline the processes to create, monitor and maintain climate-smart playgrounds that decrease overexposures to sun and heat.[1]	Pfautsch and Wujeska-Klause (2021)[1]
South Africa	To assess schoolchildren's (aged 14–17) perceived heat-health symptoms during school hours in the classroom.	For at least 1 hr on any study day, a large proportion of students felt tired (97.2%), had low concentration (96.8%) and felt sleepy (94.1%), with significant correlations between indoor temperatures and tiredness.[2]	Bidassey-Manilal et al. (2016)

Cameroon (Yaoundé and Douala)	To evaluate the impact of indoor heat on schoolchildren's (aged 12–16) health during school days, while also describing environmental conditions in schools. This study is also unique in measuring core body temperature.	There were significant correlations between indoor temperature and heat-stress symptoms.	Dapi et al. (2010)
United States (Texas, Arizona, California)	To test the performance of thermal-sensation output from the COMFA (COMfort FormulA) model on children (aged 9–13) playing in warm/hot outdoor environments in Texas.	The COMFA model adequately predicted schoolchildren's thermal sensations and heat balance, predicting thermal sensation with little to no error (0.2 and 0.0 scale error units in sun and shade, respectively). Shade significantly decreased the thermal perception and heat-stress risk in children and underlined the importance of accounting for changes in major heat contributors to the body (i.e., radiation, metabolism).	Vanos et al. (2017a)
	To improve understanding of heat perceptions, actions and heat-safety recommendations of key stakeholders in Phoenix, Arizona, and to identify themes from expert-stakeholder responses to gauge the effectiveness of school heat-preparedness levels.	Findings show that heat-safety resources are available but not fully utilised within the schools; extreme-heat readiness plans are needed that account for site-specific needs; students are negatively impacted by extreme heat both inside and outside the classroom. 30 final recommendations were developed as important school "HeatReady" actions.	Shortridge et al. (2022)
Costa Rica	To examine how reducing classroom air temperature in the tropics would affect pupils' thermal comfort and school performance.	The results showed improved schoolwork performance by tropically acclimated children when classroom temperatures were reduced from 30 to 25°C.	Porras-Salazar et al. (2018)

(Continued)

Table 2.1 (Continued)

Country & Climate Context	Study Purpose	Findings or Recommendations Related to Children's Heat Health and/or Thermal Comfort	Reference
Brazil	To identify the preferred and comfortable ranges of thermal and lighting parameters from the opinions of schoolchildren.	Classrooms had a mean air and radiant temperature of almost 27 degrees Celsius. Although the air-conditioning was used as a strategy to mitigate the discomfort caused by high temperatures, children's opinions about air temperature in the room showed discomfort due to both low (34%) and high temperatures (31%); almost half of the children would prefer classroom temperatures to be lower, and nearly all children preferred an air-conditioned environment.	Noda et al. (2020)
Iran	Identified the methods used to develop the adaptive thermal comfort equation relating neutral temperature to the outdoor climate.	Children sampled were sensitive to indoor temperature changes within a school day. A child's sensitivity to within-room temperature variation on a single day was higher than that over a longer period. Analysis revealed that schoolchildren adapt to outdoor temperature variations faster, but less completely, than adults.	Haddad et al. (2019)
Canada	To assess the literature and survey experts related to the contextual knowledge of thermal comfort in playgrounds as connected to design decision making.	Found overwhelming agreement from experts that thermal comfort should be an essential element in children's playgrounds, yet there was a strong consensus that the inclusion of thermal comfort factors in design has not been prioritised.[2]	Kennedy et al. (2021)

Source: [1]Seen as a useful public playground model with considerations schools could adopt; [2]see Chapter 6 for detailed information on climate-sensitive design related to heat and other extremes

Impact of Indoor and Outdoor Heat Extremes on Schoolchildren 31

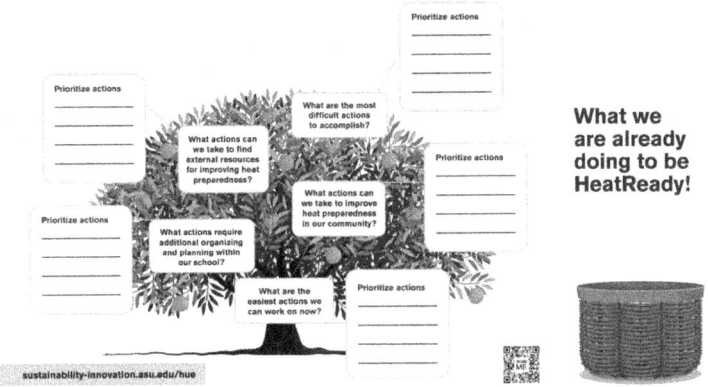

Figure 2.3 An organisation tool for schools to determine their level of heat readiness based on 30 recommendations

Note: Original image design by Arizona State University Global Institute of Sustainability. Schools place the different recommendations into a specific prioritised action or in the basket to showcase actions they are already taking to become heat ready. All HeatReady recommendations can be found in Shortridge et al. (2022)

Continuing to monitor the appropriateness of heat protection policies across jurisdictions is vital. For instance, careful review and modification of state heat protection policy for high school athletes in the United States has successfully reduced heat-exhaustion illnesses by between 35%–100% over seven years (Cooper et al., 2020). Additionally, applying lessons to playground models within and beyond school contexts in local communities has the potential to provide meaningful guidance for school heat safety.

Summary

Schools are important education hubs in our communities at the intersection of policies, procedures, contextual conditions, behaviors and networks of children, teachers, families and community representatives. Yet compared to many other health impacts on schools and despite the global data pointing to increased duration and intensity of extreme heatwaves, the negative consequences of extreme heat have received scarce attention beyond sporting organisations and athlete guidelines. Heat influences can be subtle through a child's discomfort when endeavoring to learn within scheduled classes, indirect through behavioral influences, and outright direct from the radiant or surface impacts of extreme heat both indoors and outdoors. Heat protection in schools remains an under-researched and overlooked domain relating to the development and well-being of our schoolchildren within both classrooms and during outdoor school endeavors. Most heat-related insights have emerged from science-focused disciplines (e.g., modelling climate data) and public health (e.g., hospital, illness, mortality statistics). Improved preparedness of education communities is vital to ensure there is improved heat-prevention training as well as appropriate communications and responses when extreme heat wave events impact our schooling systems. Although young people are some of the most vulnerable to the increasing occurrence of extreme heat waves, schoolchildren have been established as powerful supporters of protective changes against extreme weather events (UNICEF, 2021). It is now time for school systems to consider further protection against the detrimental influences of extreme heat on schoolchildren's development.

References

Adams, W. M., Hosokawa, Y., Casa, D. J., Périard, J. D., Racinais, S., Wingo, J. E., . . . & Walker, L. (2021). Roundtable on preseason heat safety in secondary school athletics: heat acclimatization. *Journal of Athletic Training, 56*(4), 352–361.

ADHS. (2020a). *Mortality and morbidity from exposure to excessive natural heat in Arizona 2008–2018.* Retrieved from https://pub.azdhs.gov/health-stats/report/heat/heat2018.pdf

ADHS. (2020b). *Arizona EPHT explorer – Heat stress illness, heat stress emergency department visits.* Retrieved from https://azdhs.gov/preparedness/epidemiology-disease-control/environmental-health/environmental-public-health-tracking/index.php

Alexander, L. V., Zhang, X., Peterson, T. C., Caesar, J., Gleason, B., Klein Tank, A. M. G., & Vazquez-Aguirre, J. L. (2006). Global observed changes in daily climate extremes of temperature and precipitation. *Journal of Geophysical Research: Atmospheres, 111*(D5).

ANSI/ASHRAE. (2017). *Standard 55–2017: Thermal environmental conditions for human occupancy.* Retrieved from https://www.ashrae.org/technical-resources/bookstore/standard-55-thermal-environmental-conditions-for-human-occupancy

Benton, D., & Burgess, N. (2009). The effect of the consumption of water on the memory and attention of children. *Appetite, 53*(1), 143–146.

Bergeron, M. F., DiLaura Devore, C., & Rice, S. G. (2011). Climatic heat stress and exercising children and adolescents. *Pediatrics, 128*(3), e741–e747.

Bidassey-Manilal, S., Wright, C. Y., Engelbrecht, J. C., Albers, P. N., Garland, R. M., & Matooane, M. (2016). Students' perceived heat-health symptoms increased with warmer classroom temperatures. *International Journal of Environmental Research and Public Health, 13*(6), 566.

Brager, G. S., & De Dear, R. J. (2003). Historical and cultural influences on comfort expectations. In *Buildings, culture and environment: Informing local and global practices* (pp. 177–201). Wiley.

Chancellor, B., & Hyndman, B. (2017). Adult decisions on students' play within primary school playgrounds. In *Contemporary school playground strategies for healthy students* (pp. 37–55). Springer.

Ciscar, J. C., Feyen, L., Soria, A., Lavalle, C., Raes, F., Perry, M., . . . & Ibarreta, D. (2014). Climate impacts in Europe. *The JRC PESETA II Project*. Munich Personal RePEc Archive. Retrieved from https://mpra.ub.uni-muenchen.de/55725/

Cooper, E. R., Grundstein, A. J., Miles, J. D., Ferrara, M. S., Curry, P., Casa, D. J., & Hosokawa, Y. (2020). Heat policy revision for Georgia high school football practices based on data-driven research. *Journal of Athletic Training*, 55(7), 673–681.

Dapi, L. N., Rocklöv, J., Nguefack-Tsague, G., Tetanye, E., & Kjellstrom, T. (2010). Heat impact on schoolchildren in Cameroon, Africa: Potential health threat from climate change. *Global Health Action*, 3(1), 5610.

Declet-Barreto, J., Brazel, A. J., Martin, C. A., Chow, W. T., & Harlan, S. L. (2013). Creating the park cool island in an inner-city neighborhood: Heat mitigation strategy for Phoenix, AZ. *Urban Ecosystems*, 16(3), 617–635.

Dobbinson, S., Jamsen, K., McLeod, K., White, V., Wakefield, M., White, V., . . . & Simpson, J. A. (2014). Maximising students' use of purpose-built shade in secondary schools: Quantitative and qualitative results of a built-environment intervention. *Health & Place*, 26, 136–142.

Doecke, P. (1992). *Geographical influences upon curriculum development*. Charles Darwin University. Retrieved from https://ris.cdu.edu.au/ws/portalfiles/portal/35461980/Thesis_CDU_6034_Doecke_P.pdf

Domínguez-Amarillo, S., Fernández-Agüera, J., González, M. M., & Cuerdo-Vilches, T. (2020). Overheating in schools: Factors determining children's perceptions of overall comfort indoors. *Sustainability*, 12(14), 5772.

Earthman, G. I. (2002). *School facility conditions and student academic achievement*. Retrieved from https://escholarship.org/uc/item/5sw56439

Elgheznawy, D., & Eltarabily, S. (2021). The impact of sun sail-shading strategy on the thermal comfort in school courtyards. *Building and Environment*, 202, 108046.

Falk, B., & Dotan, R. (2008). Children's thermoregulation during exercise in the heat – A revisit. *Applied Physiology, Nutrition, and Metabolism*, 33(2), 420–427.

Falk, B., & Dotan, R. (2011). Temperature regulation and elite young athletes. *The Elite Young Athlete*, 56, 126–149.

Folkerts, M. A., Gerrett, N., Kingma, B. R. M., Zuurbier, M., & Daanen, H. A. M. (2020). Care provider assessment of thermal state of children in day-care centers. *Building and Environment*, 179, 106915.

Gomes, L. H. L., Carneiro-Júnior, M. A., & Marins, J. C. B. (2013). Thermoregulatory responses of children exercising in a hot environment. *Revista Paulista de Pediatria*, 31, 104–110.

Green, H., Bailey, J., Schwarz, L., Vanos, J., Ebi, K., & Benmarhnia, T. (2019). Impact of heat on mortality and morbidity in low and middle income countries: A review of the epidemiological evidence and considerations for future research. *Environmental Research*, 171, 80–91.

Guerreiro, S. B., Dawson, R. J., Kilsby, C., Lewis, E., & Ford, A. (2018). Future heatwaves, droughts and floods in 571 European cities. *Environmental Research Letters*, 13(3), 034009.

Guthold, R., Stevens, G. A., Riley, L. M., & Bull, F. C. (2018). Worldwide trends in insufficient physical activity from 2001 to 2016: A pooled analysis of 358 population-based surveys with 19 million participants. *The Lancet Global Health*, 6(10), e1077–e1086.

Haddad, S., Osmond, P., & King, S. (2019). Application of adaptive thermal comfort methods for Iranian school children. *Building Research & Information*, *47*(2), 173–189.

Hatori, Y. (2013). Heat stroke in schools. *Japan Medical Association Journal*, *56*(3), 179–185.

Hayes, G., Dowd, K. P., MacDonncha, C., & Donnelly, A. E. (2019). Tracking of physical activity and sedentary behavior from adolescence to young adulthood: A systematic literature review. *Journal of Adolescent Health*, *65*(4), 446–454.

Hoa, D. T. M., Nguyet, D. A., Phuong, N. H., Phuong, D. T., Nga, V. T., Few, R., & Winkels, A. (2013). *Heat stress and adaptive capacity of low-income outdoor workers and their families in the city of Da Nang, Vietnam*. IIED. https://www.iied.org/10051iied

Hondula, D. M., Balling, R. C., Vanos, J. K., & Georgescu, M. (2015). Rising temperatures, human health, and the role of adaptation. *Current Climate Change Reports*, *1*(3), 144–154.

Howe, A. S., & Boden, B. P. (2007). Heat-related illness in athletes. *The American Journal of Sports Medicine*, *35*(8), 1384–1395.

HUE Engage (2022). *HeatReady schools*. Retrieved from https://engagehue.org/heatready-schools.

Hyatt, O. M., Lemke, B., & Kjellstrom, T. (2010). Regional maps of occupational heat exposure: past, present, and potential future. *Global Health Action*, *3*(1), 5715.

Hyndman, B. (2019). Let them play! Kids need freedom from play restrictions to develop. *The Conversation*. Retrieved from https://theconversation.com/let-them-play-kids-need-freedom-from-play-restrictions-to-develop-117586

Hyndman, B. (Ed.). (2017a). *Contemporary school playground strategies for healthy students*. Springer.

Hyndman, B. (2017b). 'Heat-Smart' schools during physical education (PE) activities: Developing a policy to protect students from extreme heat. *Learning Communities Journal: International Journal of Learning in Social Contexts (Special Edition)*, 56–72.

Hyndman, B., & Chancellor, B. (2015). Engaging children in activities beyond the classroom walls: A social – Ecological exploration of Australian primary school children's enjoyment of school play activities. *Journal of Playwork Practice*, *2*(2), 117–141.

Hyndman, B., & Zundans-Fraser, L. (2021). Determining public perceptions of a proposed national heat protection policy for Australian schools. *Health Promotion Journal of Australia*, *32*(1), 75–83.

Jiang, J., Wang, D., Liu, Y., Xu, Y., & Liu, J. (2018). A study on pupils' learning performance and thermal comfort of primary schools in China. *Building and Environment*, *134*, 102–113.

Jindal, A. (2018). Thermal comfort study in naturally ventilated school classrooms in composite climate of India. *Building and Environment*, *142*, 34–46.

Kennedy, E., Olsen, H., Vanos, J., Vecellio, D. J., Desat, M., Richters, K., . . . & Richardson, G. R. (2021). Reimagining spaces where children play: Developing guidance for thermally comfortable playgrounds in Canada. *Canadian Journal of Public Health*, *112*(4), 706–713.

Kim, J., & de Dear, R. (2018). Thermal comfort expectations and adaptive behavioural characteristics of primary and secondary school students. *Building and Environment*, *127*, 13–22.

Ladwig, M. A., Vazou, S., & Ekkekakis, P. (2018). "My best memory is when I was done with it": PE memories are associated with adult sedentary behavior. *Translational Journal of the American College of Sports Medicine, 3*(16), 119–129.

Lanza, K., & Durand, C. P. (2021). Heat-moderating effects of bus stop shelters and tree shade on public transport ridership. *International Journal of Environmental Research and Public Health, 18*(2), 463.

Leithead, C. S., & Lind, A. R. (1964). *Heat stress and heat disorders*. Cassell & CO Ltd.

Madden, A. L., Arora, V., Holmes, K., & Pfautsch, S. (2018). *Cool schools*. Western Sydney University. Retrieved from https://doi.org/10.26183/5b91d72db0cb7

Mangus, C. W., & Canares, T. L. (2019). Heat-related illness in children in an era of extreme temperatures. *Pediatrics in Review, 40*(3), 97–107.

Mishra, V., Ganguly, A. R., Nijssen, B., & Lettenmaier, D. P. (2015). Changes in observed climate extremes in global urban areas. *Environmental Research Letters, 10*(2), 024005.

Montazami, A., Gaterell, M., Nicol, F., Lumley, M., & Thoua, C. (2017). Impact of social background and behaviour on children's thermal comfort. *Building and Environment, 122*, 422–434.

Morrison, S. A. (2022). Moving in a hotter world: Maintaining adequate childhood fitness as a climate change countermeasure. *Temperature*, 1–19.

Morrison, S. A., & Sims, S. T. (2014). Thermoregulation in children: Exercise, heat stress & fluid balance. *Annales Kinesiologiae, 5*(1).

Mustapa, N. D., Maliki, N. Z., & Hamzah, A. (2015). Repositioning children's developmental needs in space planning: A review of connection to nature. *Procedia-Social and Behavioral Sciences, 170*, 330–339.

Nelson, N. G., Collins, C. L., Comstock, R. D., & McKenzie, L. B. (2011). Exertional heat-related injuries treated in emergency departments in the US, 1997–2006. *American Journal of Preventive Medicine, 40*(1), 54–60.

Ngwenya, B., Oosthuizen, J., Cross, M., Frimpong, K., & Chaibva, C. N. (2018). A review of heat stress policies in the context of climate change and its impacts on outdoor workers: Evidence from Zimbabwe. *International Journal of Social Ecology and Sustainable Development (IJSESD), 9*(1), 1–11.

Noda, L., Lima, A. V., Souza, J. F., Leder, S., & Quirino, L. M. (2020). Thermal and visual comfort of schoolchildren in air-conditioned classrooms in hot and humid climates. *Building and Environment, 182*, 107156.

Olsen, H., Kennedy, E., & Vanos, J. (2019). Shade provision in public playgrounds for thermal safety and sun protection: A case study across 100 play spaces in the United States. *Landscape and Urban Planning, 189*, 200–211.

Park, R. J., Behrer, A. P., & Goodman, J. (2021). Learning is inhibited by heat exposure, both internationally and within the United States. *Nature Human Behaviour, 5*(1), 19–27.

Parsons, K. (2009). Maintaining health, comfort and productivity in heat waves. *Global Health Action, 2*(1), 2057.

Pfautsch S., Wujeska-Klause A. (2021). *Guide to climate-smart playgrounds – Research findings and application* (p. 60) Western Sydney University. https://doi.org/10.26183/2bgz-d714

Pisello, A. L., Saliari, M., Vasilakopoulou, K., Hadad, S., & Santamouris, M. (2018). Facing the urban overheating: Recent developments. Mitigation potential and sensitivity of the main technologies. *Wiley Interdisciplinary Reviews: Energy and Environment, 7*(4), e294.

Porras-Salazar, J. A., Wyon, D. P., Piderit-Moreno, B., Contreras-Espinoza, S., & Wargocki, P. (2018). Reducing classroom temperature in a tropical climate improved the thermal comfort and the performance of elementary school pupils. *Indoor Air, 28*(6), 892–904.

Remmers, T., Thijs, C., Timperio, A., Salmon, J. O., Veitch, J., Kremers, S. P., & Ridgers, N. D. (2017). Daily weather and children's physical activity patterns. *Medicine & Science in Sports & Exercise, 49*(5), 922–929.

Ridgers, N. D., Stratton, G., & Fairclough, S. J. (2006). Physical activity levels of children during school playtime. *Sports Medicine, 36*(4), 359–371.

Robert Wood Johnson Foundation. (2007). *Recess rules: Why the undervalued playtime may be America's best investment for healthy kids and healthy schools report*. Robert Wood Johnson Foundation.

Rodríguez, C. M., Coronado, M. C., & Medina, J. M. (2021). Thermal comfort in educational buildings: The classroom-comfort-data method applied to schools in Bogotá, Colombia. *Building and Environment, 194*, 107682.

Saraiva, T. S., De Almeida, M., Bragança, L., & Barbosa, M. T. (2018). Environmental comfort indicators for school buildings in sustainability assessment tools. *Sustainability, 10*(6), 1849.

Schäfer, M., & Smith, P. K. (1996). Teachers' perceptions of play fighting and real fighting in primary school. *Educational Research, 38*(2), 173–181.

Shortridge, A., VI, W. W., White, D. D., Guardaro, M. M., Hondula, D. M., & Vanos, J. K. (2022). HeatReady schools: A novel approach to enhance adaptive capacity to heat through school community experiences, risks, and perceptions. *Climate Risk Management*, 100437.

Somboonwong, J., Sanguanrungsirikul, S., & Pitayanon, C. (2012). Heat illness surveillance in schoolboys participating in physical education class in tropical climate: An analytical prospective descriptive study. *BMJ Open, 2*(4), e000741.

Teli, D., Bourikas, L., James, P. A., & Bahaj, A. S. (2017). Thermal performance evaluation of school buildings using a children-based adaptive comfort model. *Procedia Environmental Sciences, 38*, 844–851.

Ter Mors, S., Hensen, J. L., Loomans, M. G., & Boerstra, A. C. (2011). Adaptive thermal comfort in primary school classrooms: Creating and validating PMV-based comfort charts. *Building and Environment, 46*(12), 2454–2461.

United Nations Convention on the Rights of the Child. (2022). Retrieved from www.unicef.org.au/our-work/information-for-children/un-convention-on-the-rights-of-the-child

UNICEF. (2021). *The climate crisis is a child rights crisis: Introducing the children's climate risk index*. Retrieved from https://www.unicef.org/reports/climate-crisis-child-rights-crisis

Vanos, J. K. (2015). Children's health and vulnerability in outdoor microclimates: A comprehensive review. *Environment International, 76*, 1–15.

Vanos, J. K., Herdt, A. J., & Lochbaum, M. R. (2017a). Effects of physical activity and shade on the heat balance and thermal perceptions of children in a playground microclimate. *Building and Environment, 126*, 119–131.

Vanos, J. K., McKercher, G. R., Naughton, K., & Lochbaum, M. (2017b). Schoolyard shade and sun exposure: Assessment of personal monitoring during children's physical activity. *Photochemistry and Photobiology, 93*(4), 1123–1132.

Vanos, J. K., Middel, A., McKercher, G. R., Kuras, E. R., & Ruddell, B. L. (2016). Hot playgrounds and children's health: A multiscale analysis of surface temperatures in Arizona, USA. *Landscape and Urban Planning, 146*, 29–42.

Vickers, N. J. (2017). Animal communication: When i'm calling you, will you answer too?. *Current Biology, 27*(14), R713–R715.

Xu, Z., Sheffield, P. E., Su, H., Wang, X., Bi, Y., & Tong, S. (2014). The impact of heat waves on children's health: A systematic review. *International Journal of Biometeorology, 58*(2), 239–247.

Zivin, J. G., & Shrader, J. (2016). Temperature extremes, health, and human capital. *The Future of Children*, 31–50.

Zomorodian, Z. S., Tahsildoost, M., & Hafezi, M. (2016). Thermal comfort in educational buildings: A review article. *Renewable and Sustainable Energy Reviews, 59*, 895–906.

3 The Impact of Air Quality on Schoolchildren

Giovanni Di Virgilio, Melissa Hart, Angela Maharaj and Donna Green

Approximately 93% of children globally are exposed daily to air that is sufficiently polluted, that it puts their health and development at risk (WHO, 2018). In 2020, a UK coroner made legal history by ruling that air pollution was a partial cause of death in an asthmatic nine-year-old girl due to sustained exposure to nitrogen dioxide and particulate matter from traffic emissions (Laville, 2020). This ruling has been hailed as a turning point for public health and regulation in industrialised nations as it enables explicit recognition of the health impacts of air pollution. Whilst this case was not related to the child's school, it has raised the stakes on all institutions with a duty of care for minors to re-examine their exposure to outdoor and indoor air pollution.

Criteria air pollutants are commonly monitored and regulated owing to their potential to cause adverse health impacts. These pollutants include $PM_{2.5}$ and PM_{10} (fine particulate matter ≤ 2.5 and ≤ 10 μm in aerodynamic diameter) (Roberts et al., 2019; Zhang et al., 2019), nitrogen oxides (NO_x), carbon monoxide (CO), ozone (O_3) and sulphur dioxide (SO_2) (Buka et al., 2006). Compared to healthy adults, groups such as the elderly (Chu et al., 2018), people with pre-existing respiratory conditions (Haikerwal et al., 2016) and a range of other comorbidities are at increased risk from elevated air pollution. Schoolchildren are also vulnerable due to continued physical development (Kim, 2004), rapid breathing rate, high physical activity, more extended periods outdoors, and smaller body size (Dixon, 2002). Even short-term, infrequent exposure to air pollutants can have serious health impacts on children (e.g., Vardoulakis et al., 2020) and their cognitive development (Costa et al., 2019). A more significant concern is a range of long-term impacts, including a greater risk of heart disease, respiratory diseases (Gauderman et al., 2004) and damage to the nervous system (Sram et al., 2017) that are also linked to chronic exposure to air pollution at lower levels (Hayes et al., 2020).

Outdoor Air-Pollution Impacts on Schoolchildren

The varying exposure of school children to air pollution at school is a growing policy issue (Mohai et al., 2011; Wolfe et al., 2020). Children globally spend approximately 30% of their waking time within a school environment (OECD, 2014), with students typically spending more than six hours daily in and around school buildings. Exposure to air pollution whilst engaged in school-related activity is associated with decelerated cognitive development (Rivas et al., 2018). School students also have higher asthma morbidity from exposure to air pollutants in the school environment (Carrion-Matta et al., 2019). Moreover, children are regularly exposed to high levels of air pollution from traffic emissions during their journeys to and from school with rush hour concentrations of NO_2 several times the background levels of the rest of the day (Varaden et al., 2019).

Air pollution caused by natural disasters and extreme weather (such as wildfires, haboobs and dust storms), some of which are likely exacerbated by climate change; add to these health impacts on schoolchildren. Approximately 7.4 million children are affected by smoke emissions from wildfires in North America each year (Rappold et al., 2017). School closures due to wildfires either in terms of direct risks or smoke emissions being common during fire seasons (Chalupka & Anderko, 2019). The recent 2018 Camp Fire in California caused considerable damage to school infrastructure, forcing school closures (Schulze et al., 2020). Even moderate wildfires can have harmful effects on children's health. Aguilera et al. (2021) found that $PM_{2.5}$ emissions from wildfires during 2011–2017 in San Diego County, California was ten times more harmful on children's respiratory health than $PM_{2.5}$ emitted from other sources. The impacts of wildfire smoke emissions are not unique to North America and affect fire-prone regions globally (Filkov et al., 2020). For example, Indonesia's 2015 fire season resulted in the closure of schools and affected more than 5 million school children (Bank, 2015). Further, in 2021, many European nations were battling fires near built-up regions of Greece and Turkey (Commission, 2021), which led to widespread impacts on local communities. Exposure to smoke emissions from wildfires and smoke from prescribed burns (or managed burning of forest products) designed to reduce the risk of wildfires occurring, is associated with serious health impacts. Multiple studies focused on adult populations have shown that hospitalisations for respiratory diseases consistently increase with exposure to smoke from wildfires (Alman et al., 2016; Black et al., 2017; Shusterman et al., 1993). Fine particulate emissions from wildfires are linked to adverse health impacts (Cascio, 2018), with mortality rates increasing on fire days with poor air quality (Johnston et al., 2011; Morgan et al., 2010). However, health impacts from wildfire smoke can occur from exposures well below the long-standing, mandated (e.g., the World Health Organisation – WHO) 24-hour threshold for $PM_{2.5}$ of 25 µg/m³. For example, an increase of 10 µg/m³ in a two-day moving average of fine particulate matter is associated with an increase of 0.68% in daily all-cause mortality (Liu et al., 2019). This association is stronger in regions with lower average $PM_{2.5}$ levels and higher average temperatures (Shaposhnikov et al., 2014). However, it is problematic that there is a relative paucity of studies intentionally focusing on the health impacts of wildfire smoke on children (Holm et al., 2021).

The health impacts of wildfire smoke also result from many more compounds in addition to the pollutants typically monitored by regulatory air-quality networks. Wildfire smoke contains several toxins and carcinogens such as formaldehyde, acrolein, hydrogen cyanide and mercury (Desservettaz et al., 2019; Guérette et al., 2018; Howard & Huston, 2019). These airborne toxins are not measured at air-quality monitoring stations and are largely unregulated, but can have adverse health impacts even at low concentrations. These gases fall into the toxicological classes of upper and lower respiratory tract disorders, eye irritation, disruption of oxygen transport and carcinogens (MacSween et al., 2020). The combined effect of breathing in these gases and fine particles is likely to put further stress on the body.

Internationally, the frequency and duration of wildfires are projected to increase by the end of the century (Flannigan et al., 2013) as climate change drives fire weather conditions away from the expected range of internal variability (Abatzoglou et al., 2019). For example, fire seasons are projected to occur earlier each year in Australia, with severe wildfires becoming more frequent (Di Virgilio et al., 2019; Dowdy et al., 2019). Consequently, fire-prone regions globally are likely to experience more frequent severe wildfires, and more children are thus likely to be exposed to wildfire smoke in the future.

Indoor Air-Pollution Impacts

Indoor air quality is also directly linked to adverse health effects in schoolchildren (Tran et al., 2020), although there is limited evidence of these associations in a school environment beyond the analysis of ventilation rates and carbon dioxide levels (e.g., Stabile et al., 2017). Indoor air quality is affected by building materials and maintenance that, when inadequate, can result in damp and mould spores, and poor choice of cleaning products that can create short-term spikes in volatile organic compounds. Inadequate ventilation, air-conditioning rates and overcrowded classrooms contribute to a high buildup of carbon dioxide, which has been shown to reduce student performance (Toftum et al., 2015; Wargocki et al., 2020) and cause health effects such as headaches, nausea, fatigue and increased school absences. High levels of particulate matter and high temperatures in the microenvironment (see Chapter 2) reduce school achievement (Toftum et al., 2015) and adversely affect health.

Outdoor sources that can affect indoor air quality include road traffic (Perera, 2017), fossil fuel combustion, and other anthropogenic activities such as industrial processes. For instance, nitrogen dioxide from anthropogenic sources outside of the classroom can exacerbate the severity of virus-induced asthma (Chauhan et al., 2003) and generally increase schoolchildren's susceptibility to infections. The indoor microenvironment of schools is also heavily influenced by the ventilation type and exchange rate, with indoor air quality often being closely related to outdoor air quality (Cooper et al., 2020). Carrion-Matta et al. (2019) sampled 32 north American inner-city schools and found that classroom average indoor concentrations of $PM_{2.5}$ (5.2 µg/m³) were lower than average outdoor concentrations (6.5 µg/m³). Principal sources of indoor $PM_{2.5}$ were secondary pollution (41%) and road traffic (17%), biomass burning (15%), soil dust (6%) and marine aerosols (4%). Similarly, principal sources of outdoor $PM_{2.5}$ across all seasons were secondary pollution (41%) and road traffic (26%), followed by biomass burning (17%), soil dust (7%), road dust (3%) and marine aerosols (1%). Classroom ventilation can frequently offer children inadequate protection from outdoor pollutants, especially soot and NO_2 (Wichmann et al., 2010).

Indoor air quality and student academic performance in the school classroom is directly associated with ventilation rates (Haverinen-Shaughnessy et al., 2015). Improving air quality in classrooms improves progress in maths and reading (Haverinen-Shaughnessy et al., 2015). In Austria, higher in-classroom PM and CO_2 concentrations were associated with reduced cognitive performance in school (Hutter et al., 2013). CO_2 levels are associated with lower annual attendance, lower test scores in reading, writing and arithmetic in Scottish schools (Gaihre et al., 2014) as well as reductions in short-term attention performance in German (Twardella et al., 2012) and Portuguese schools (Ferreira & Cardoso, 2014).

Current Policy and Mitigation Actions

Regarding air-quality standards and legislation, the WHO recently revised its Air Quality Guidelines (AQGs) due to increasing evidence showing how air pollution affects different aspects of human health. The 2021 AQG concentrations are substantially lower than the previous AQGs issued by the WHO in 2005 (World Health, 2021). The recommended average annual upper limit for $PM_{2.5}$ has been reduced by half from 10 to 5 µg/m³. The AQG for NO_2 has been reduced by 75%. A recommended summertime mean concentration has been proposed for O_3, which exacerbates diseases like asthma and chronic obstructive pulmonary disease (COPD). Revised AQGs are also proposed for CO, PM_{10}, and SO_2. Although AQGs are not legally binding, like all WHO guidelines, AQGs provide policymakers with evidence-based tools to help guide national and state legislation and policies to reduce air-pollutant concentrations and thus decrease the disease burden that results from exposure to air pollution. Many countries have historically set their own guidelines following WHO AQGs, and continuing this tradition would surely bode well for the citizens of many nations. For instance, the WHO estimates that almost 80% of global deaths related to $PM_{2.5}$ exposure could be avoided if current air-pollution levels are reduced to those proposed in the updated AQG (World Health, 2021).

In addition to air-pollution concentration guidelines, several specific policies and mitigation actions can be implemented to reduce schoolchildren's exposure to poor air quality. For instance, where feasible, traffic may be routed away from schools to reduce pollutant concentrations at the schools (Rafiepourgatabi et al., 2021), especially during morning and afternoon school drop-off and collections. Such actions can also be supplemented with "safe school pathways" to encourage and facilitate active means of travel such as walking and cycling. Cleaning inside the school buildings after school hours can reduce children's exposure to certain pollutants, such as fine/ultrafine particles (Rivas et al., 2018). Where feasible, new schools should not be built adjacent to major roads, given these are a principal source of indoor and outdoor air pollution in schools. In terms of school-building design, the indoor school environments should prioritise a transition from combustion heating, as it contributes to poor indoor air quality in classrooms (Paton-Walsh et al., 2019). The design and implementation of improved ventilation is also essential given inadequate ventilation increases exposure to indoor pollutants (Lee & Chang, 2000).

Leadership from state- or national-level governments on air-quality policy and assistance in implementing air-quality improvements can improve schoolchildren's health outcomes. In a review of 50 North American states and the District of Columbia, Jones et al. (2015) found that state-level assistance concerning indoor air policy was positively associated with implementing policies and practices by school districts that were conducive to air-quality improvement. For instance, such districts were more likely to require schools to periodically inspect heating, ventilation and air-conditioning systems, look for sources of contamination, deal with condensation and mould and reduce possible sources of indoor particulate matter. Conversely, such measures were less likely in school districts without state-level leadership and assistance on air quality.

The Need for Real-Time, Distributed Air Quality and Meteorology Data Networks

Whilst policies and positive interventions such as those described previously can effectively mitigate exposure to pollution in schools from sources such as road traffic, they are less effective against more transient and acute air-pollution sources such as wildfires, dust storms and agricultural sources. As described previously, wildfires are becoming increasingly common due to anthropogenic climate change. Moreover, planning timely, locally relevant improvements to air quality or mitigating exposure to pollutant sources such as wildfires requires the continuous monitoring of air quality and concurrent meteorology across the urban airshed and surrounding regions (Di Virgilio et al., 2021). However, many locations affected by pollution from wildfire smoke, as well as anthropogenic sources like traffic emissions, are not equipped with accurate air quality or meteorology sensors. This issue can hamper timely, locally relevant planning regarding daily activities to manage air-pollution exposure, which is particularly important for vulnerable groups such as children.

The collection and dissemination of quality-assured, high-temporal resolution observations of air quality and meteorology data is fundamental to informing policy on mitigating children's exposure to air pollution during school time. As shown in section 3, such data could contribute to early warning networks for impending poor air-quality events. There is a clear and urgent need for such networks to be introduced.

The following section introduces innovative observational networks developed to monitor the range of air pollutants that can impact children. We focus on a citizen-science air-quality monitoring network recently initiated at five primary schools and one university in Sydney, Australia, demonstrating how accurate, real-time data can inform resilience planning to respond to air pollution. This citizen-science network was highly effective in showing in *real time* how changes in regional and local meteorology interact with pollutant sources to create complex spatiotemporal variation in the timing, duration and severity of air-pollution impacts during the Black Summer wildfires of 2019–2020 (Giovanni Di Virgilio et al., 2021). The knowledge gained from this citizen-science project on the pollutant–meteorology covariate relationships that were assessed helped reduce schoolchildren's exposure to air pollution. This analysis also helped to develop air-quality forecasting and pollution-exposure mitigation procedures. Finally, we review how building design, enhanced protective procedures and revised policies can improve indoor air quality at schools.

Real-Time, Distributed Air-Quality Monitoring Networks

In many cities, regulatory networks provide the main source of information on local meteorological and air-quality conditions. In Sydney, an Air Quality Monitoring Network (AQMN) operated by the New South Wales Department of Planning and Industry (DPIE) has historically been the main source of information on air quality. The DPIE AQMN provides broad coverage across Sydney (Figure 3.1). DPIE sensors are sited following the requirements of Australian Standard AS/NZS 3580.1.1 2016. Among other specifications, these regulations identify the need to install a monitoring station to provide accurate data on various air pollutants, including $PM_{2.5}$, PM_{10}, CO, O_3, SO_2 and NO_X for every 25,000 people. However, as with any regulatory-grade network, coverage across urban areas can continually be expanded, and notable gaps in AQMN coverage include the rural–urban transition where there is a substantial rapid urban development. Importantly, Sydney's population is projected to increase (~20%) to over 6 million by 2027, with much of this expansion occurring at the rural–urban transition in western Sydney (Australian Bureau of Statistics, 2017). These demographic changes will likely increase the exposure of many thousands more people to unsafe levels of a range of air pollutants (M. A. Hart et al., 2021).

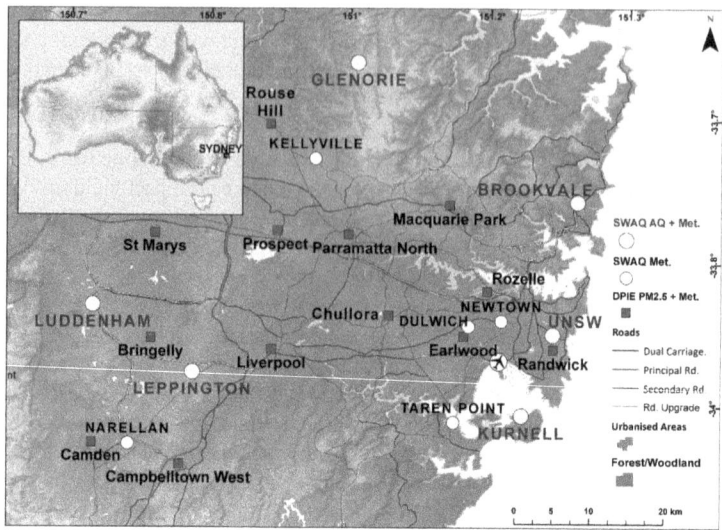

Figure 3.1 The geography of Sydney and the locations of the Schools Weather and Air Quality sensors sited at primary schools in Sydney and the University of New South Wales (UNSW)

Note: Regulatory sensors in the NSW Government (DPIE) Air Quality Monitoring Network (AQMN) are also shown (only DPIE sensors referred to by the present chapter are labelled – see www.dpie.nsw.gov.au/air-quality/air-quality-data-services for further details of the entire DPIE network). SWAQ meteorology-only sensors are also shown

The Schools Weather and Air Quality network (SWAQ) is a citizen-science project initiated in Sydney, New South Wales in September 2019, which provides a quality-controlled source of observational data on local air pollution and meteorology to the present (September 2021 at the time of writing). The SWAQ network comprises ten meteorological stations, of which five also include air-quality stations, at school locations around Sydney. The joint air quality and meteorology sensors are sited in public primary schools in the suburbs of Brookvale, Glenorie, Kurnell, Leppington, Luddenham along with a station at the University of New South Wales (UNSW) (Figure 3.1). SWAQ uses Vaisala AQT420 sensors to measure CO, O_3, SO_2, NO_2 (ppm), $PM_{2.5}$ and PM_{10} (µg/m³). Vaisala WXT536 sensors measure the near-surface air temperature (°C), air pressure (mbar), relative humidity (%), wind direction (°), wind speed (m/s), and rainfall (mm). All sensors record and transmit at 20-minute intervals owing to power constraints. Sensors are powered by Vaisala QMP201CSUB solar panel units, complete with battery backup, and data transmission is performed by MOG100 devices (see the manufacturer of these devices for further details: www.vaisala.com/). Sensors were sited

The Impact of Air Quality on Schoolchildren 45

Figure 3.2 Schools Weather and Air Quality (SWAQ) Vaisala AQT420 air-quality sensor and WXT536 meteorology sensor located at a Sydney primary school in 2019, complete with SWAQ logo

following World Meteorological Organisation (WMO) guidelines for urban areas (Oke, 2006) and at two-meter height. Monitoring stations (see example in Figure 3.2) are located at varying elevations within semirural, residential and commercial areas. The SWAQ data are available to schoolchildren and teachers via the project website at www.swaq.org.au for use in curriculum-aligned science activities, and are published by researchers for broad use (M. Hart et al., 2021; Ulpiani et al., 2022).

The location choice of the SWAQ sensors was deliberate to cover areas not well serviced by the existing government network, including at rural–urban transitions and areas of rapid urban development, noting that urbanisation at the rural–urban fringe can increase exposure to the risks associated with wildfires (Knorr et al., 2016). For this reason, SWAQ data can supplement existing government-reference-station data to explore the duration, scale and covariates of events such as severe wildfires. That SWAQ sensors are located at schools is significant given that children are at greater risk from elevated air pollution than the general population. SWAQ data thus offer researchers, policy-makers and citizens a valuable and timely new data source that can be used together with DPIE data to investigate phenomena such as the air-quality impacts of socioeconomic changes and extreme events.

Case Study I: Black Summer

Australia is one of several regions globally to frequently experience severe wildfires, most recently the devastating fires during the summer of 2019–2020. Wildfires on the scale of Black Summer have no historically recorded precedent in Australia, burning twice the total area of previous wildfire seasons (Morgan et al., 2020). The fires peaked from December 2019–January 2020 and caused 429 smoke-related deaths (Johnston et al., 2020), burnt over 18 million hectares and destroyed 3,113 homes (Filkov et al., 2020) and killed three billion animals (van Eeden et al., 2020). There was ample dry, combustible vegetation because 2019 had been Australia's warmest and driest year on record (Bureau of Meteorology, 2019).

In the southeastern Australian state of New South Wales (NSW), daily mean $PM_{2.5}$ exceeded the 25 µg/m³ national standard at one or more Sydney or regional population centres on 118 days in 2019, versus 52 days in 2018 (NSW Government, 2020). Focusing on the impacts of Black Summer on Sydney schools as recorded by the SWAQ sensors, which are predominantly located in semirural or suburban regions, on several occasions during the fires, hourly $PM_{2.5}$ concentrations spiked to over 400 µg/m³ for up to three consecutive hours (Di Virgilio et al., 2021). Similar exceedances frequently occurred for consecutive days through Black Summer's peak. Such was the widespread extent and ferocity of the fires that the hazardous air pollution filled the entire Sydney metropolitan area and multiple states across southeastern Australia and other Pacific nations (NASA, 2020). In this respect, these events sharply contrast with the historical pattern of wildfire air-pollution impacts in Australia, which generally tended to be sporadic, shorter-term (runs of days to a week) spikes in $PM_{2.5}$ in more localised regions (Walter et al., 2020). Nevertheless, the onset, duration and severity of air pollution events during these fires showed considerable spatiotemporal variation for locations in both the

SWAQ and DPIE networks. For instance, a geographic sequence of air-pollution impacts was observed across Sydney, which may reflect the transport of smoke from a source fire by the passage of synoptic features, including the associated wind changes, and the interaction of these processes with local meteorological factors (Di Virgilio et al., 2021).

During Black Summer, SWAQ sensors showed that diurnal changes in $PM_{2.5}$ typically started rapidly increasing at schools during the early mornings, but peaked at different times, ranging from late morning to early afternoon, dependent on the school in question. This pattern of changes in $PM_{2.5}$ is more nuanced than previous findings of pollution from wildfires for specific periods, which typically indicate that $PM_{2.5}$ concentrations were lower at most locations in Sydney during the mornings and higher during the afternoons (Ulpiani et al., 2020; Vardoulakis et al., 2020). It is essential to consider how the timing of occurrence of elevated $PM_{2.5}$ varies with location, both in terms of facilitating preparations to minimise exposure, but also because the toxicity of smoke particles can increase markedly in the hours after they are first emitted as they undergo oxidation in the atmosphere (Wong et al., 2019). This finding highlights the importance of sub-hourly to hourly air-pollutant measurements for locally relevant resilience planning, noting that even exposure for a few hours to relatively low concentrations of $PM_{2.5}$ can have significant health risks (Zhao et al., 2020).

Notably, SWAQ sensors recorded coinciding peaks in diurnal variation in normalised $PM_{2.5}$ *and* normalised air temperature at all schools in this network (Figure 3.3). Elevated temperatures and air pollution can individually have health impacts on children and other vulnerable groups. However, there is evidence that when increases in both temperature and air pollution are combined, the health impacts may be synergistic. Recently, Patel et al. (2019) found a 6.6% joint additive effect of exposure to high concentrations of $PM_{2.5}$ and heat waves on emergency-department admissions.

The diurnal patterns of temperature and $PM_{2.5}$ noted during Black Summer illustrate the important point that air-quality impacts from different sources do not occur in isolation. Instead, pollutant severity levels are strongly dependent upon concurrent meteorology. We therefore need to understand how different meteorological factors covary with, and moderate, wildfire emissions, and pollutant emissions more generally. This understanding can, in turn, inform the mitigation of air-quality impacts as they pertain to vulnerable groups like schoolchildren and the broader population. This theme is further illustrated by 20-minute-interval pollutant and meteorology observations recorded at SWAQ schools throughout Black Summer, for instance, for variation in $PM_{2.5}$, CO, air pressure, relative humidity, wind speed and temperature at Luddenham Primary School on 26 November (Figure 3.4). On this day, wildfires were raging around Sydney, with $PM_{2.5}$ and CO being two main pollutants emitted by fires. There is one marked increase in $PM_{2.5}$ at 09:00 AEST lasting approximately one hour, and then another much larger increase in $PM_{2.5}$ that

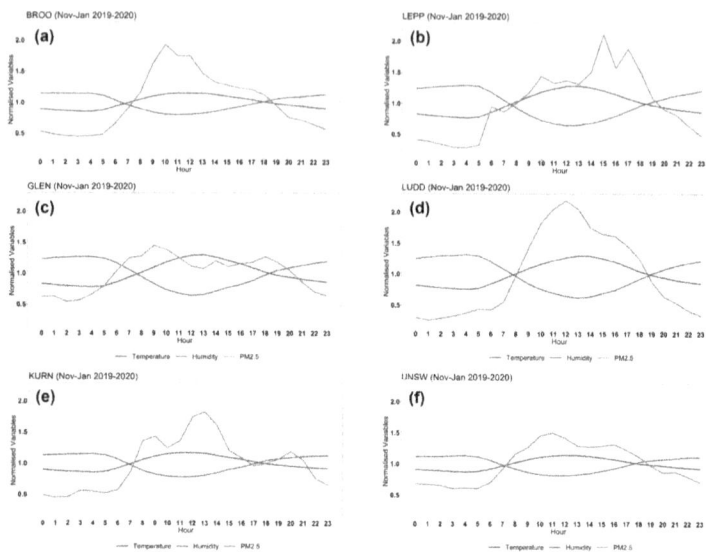

Figure 3.3(a-f) Diurnal variation in normalised $PM_{2.5}$, temperature and relative humidity at five Sydney schools during Black Summer

Source: BROO = Brookvale; GLEN = Glenorie; KURN = Kurnell; LEPP = Leppington; LUDD = Luddenham; and UNSW = University of New South Wales

starts at 14:00 AEST and lasts until approximately 20:00. Both $PM_{2.5}$ events are preceded by a steady reduction in air pressure. There is also a steady reduction in relative humidity from over 80% to around 50% during the early morning at the approximate onset of the first spike in $PM_{2.5}$, with further reductions in humidity that last for the rest of the day. Wind direction is variable but generally shows a mixture of north and northwesterly flows during the morning, before showing a more westerly orientation in the afternoon. Near-surface air temperature starts increasing at the approximate start of the first increase in $PM_{2.5}$, and then peaks at approximately 10:00 and remains high until the early evening. This sequence of changes is reflected in the synoptic weather patterns of this day. At 05:00 AEST, there are westerly winds over southeast Australia, transporting hot, dry air from inland Australia over this region, representing typically dangerous wildfire weather conditions. At around 11:00 AEST, pressure and humidity fall, and winds freshen from the northwest as a cold front passes. After the front passes at around 17:00 AEST, and pressure rises, relative humidity is low, and winds shift direction, becoming westerly. The corresponding situation for CO is also shown in Figure 3.4,

The Impact of Air Quality on Schoolchildren   49

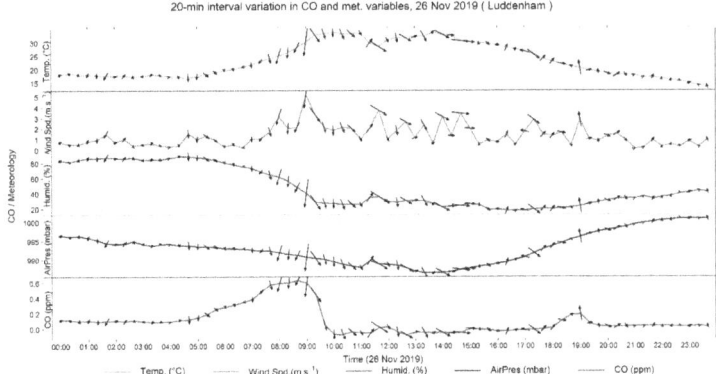

Figure 3.4 (top) Time series of 20-min-interval temperature (°C), wind speed (m/s), relative humidity (%), air pressure (hPa), and PM$_{2.5}$ (μg/m^3) at SWAQ-Luddenham on 26 November 2019; (bottom) variation in meteorological and CO (ppm) observations at SWAQ-Luddenham during 26 November 2019

noting the larger/longer duration increase in CO during the morning versus a more muted CO event later in the day.

The variations in pollutants and local meteorological factors described previously may reflect the transport of smoke from a fire by the evolution of synoptic systems, including the associated wind changes, and the interaction of these processes with local meteorological factors. Long-range transport of emissions from wildfires along a front has been noted in North America by using satellite remote sensing and modelling approaches (Mathur, 2008; Morris et al., 2006). In previous research using data from the SWAQ sensors, Di Virgilio et al. (2021) found a statistically significant nonlinear relationship between variation in temperature, humidity, wind speed and PM$_{2.5}$ concentrations that may, in part, reflect the passage of cold frontal systems, as well as prefrontal troughs. Such systems can have varying effects on fire behaviour and air quality, dependent upon how these systems develop with time across southeastern Australia. This information could be useful in developing warning systems for impending air-quality events at schools, thus offering valuable information for primary carers to plan for such events and supervise children accordingly. It is important to consider how the timing of pollutant occurrences varies with location, both in terms of facilitating preparations to minimise exposure, but also because the toxicity of smoke particles can increase markedly in the hours after they are first emitted as they undergo oxidation in the atmosphere (Wong et al., 2019). This process also reinforces the importance of widespread, sub-hourly to hourly pollutant and meteorology measurements for locally relevant resilience planning, both for schools and the community more broadly. We note that even exposure to low concentrations of $PM_{2.5}$ for a matter of hours can have health risks (Zhao et al., 2020). Although there are cost, technical and logistical challenges to implementing such distributed networks, the real-time information they provide is essential. As networks like SWAQ demonstrate, it is financially viable to place such citizen-science networks in schools, ideally on a citywide basis, using low-to-mid cost sensors that provide scientifically rigorous data (Di Virgilio et al., 2021).

Case Study II: Indoor Monitoring in Australia

Indoor air quality is largely unmonitored and unregulated in Australia. Given the significant percentage of time Australians spend indoors exposed to unknown concentrations of air pollutants, this is an important public health concern that needs immediate attention. The lack of indoor air-quality standards for non-domestic spaces stands out from our generally heavily regulated indoor environment, for example, compared to the annual checking and tagging of electronic goods, or regular checks and replacement of fire or sprinkler systems in these shared indoor spaces. With no national, state or territory guidance, it has fallen to individual building or facility managers to develop ad hoc ventilation measures to enhance the natural and mechanical purification of indoor air.

The COVID-19 pandemic has raised concerns over this lack of regulation for indoor air monitoring and regulation, and recently there has been a great deal of interest in local indoor air-quality monitoring – especially tied to SMART buildings that can be designed to redirect airflow through existing ventilation systems to introduce cleaned, or fresh, air, into rooms requiring more regular air change. Retrofitting existing HVAC or AC systems with MERV-13 filtration with UV sterilisation or specifying these air purification options for new builds are actions that are increasingly being sought (Zosky et al., 2021). Some shared spaces have a disproportionate number of vulnerable people. Schools, early learning centres, aged care homes and hospitals fit this category. Guiding how best to monitor, ventilate and maintain safer levels of air pollution in these shared spaces is vitally important.

Managing and maintaining air quality in schools is receiving increasing attention in Australia. One significant issue currently unresolved is the dilemma of conflicting risk-management advice for days of high bushfire or hazard reduction smoke, when advice is to keep windows closed. Closing windows has the potential to increase the transmission of airborne virus particles (and concentrate other air pollutants such as carbon dioxide). In the short term, installation of HEPA-grade air purifiers is the only practical solution to address both very significant air-quality concerns. Longer-term approaches that could retrofit or install A/C systems with filtration would enable more systematic approaches to managing air quality, however, they would still be operating in an effectively "unregulated" space. Hence, indoor air-quality regulations and monitoring are central to resolving this air-quality issue.

The Impact of Air Quality on Schoolchildren 51

The Clean Air Schools project at UNSW is installing 200 paired indoor and outdoor monitors in 100 schools around Greater Sydney to identify the gradient of air pollution between the playground exposure and the classroom exposure. Clarity Nodes that have been calibrated for $PM_{2.5}$, NO_2 and CO_2 against government reference monitors have been used to collect a year's worth of data identifying levels of smoke and traffic pollution that schoolchildren are exposed to. This goes in concert with local meteorological readings, and intervention studies (for example, opening/closing the windows near a monitor to see if there are any beneficial effects for air quality, or the use of HEPA air purifiers), as well as relocating indoor monitors inside school buildings to identify if there are any "cleaner" air locations on-site, and can inform the development of policy to protect the wider school community.

Key Challenges and Opportunities

Improved Scientific Understanding

The onset, duration and severity of air-pollution events at schools shows complex patterns of spatiotemporal variation. These patterns reflect not just the timing of emissions, but also the modulation of emissions by local meteorological variation, the evolution of synoptic processes and interactions between these factors. Understanding air-pollution meteorology is vital to managing air-quality impacts experienced by schoolchildren going to/from school and whilst at school, and if they are being homeschooled.

Continuous, Widespread Monitoring Required

A widespread rollout of low-to-mid-cost outdoor and indoor sensors to monitor are necessary for schools, and these can complement existing regulatory-grade networks operated by governments. Such networks facilitate the previously mentioned scientific endeavour and provide the essential raw data for the "early warning networks" needed to inform the management of schoolchildren's exposure to pollution events from diverse sources. If such networks are combined with an improved understanding of meteorology–pollutant associations (i.e., as demonstrated via the previous case studies and previous research), these can inform the design of future school mitigation/management policies and also the formulation of new, locally relevant AQIs/AQGs.

Air-Quality Standards

To protect the health of vulnerable groups like schoolchildren, as well as public health more generally, the AQGs and standards need to be revised regularly according to the latest World Health Organization (WHO) recommendations. As described previously, the WHO AQGs have recently been revised, and several key pollutants (e.g., $PM_{2.5}$) have received substantial reductions in the exposure guidelines. We also note that even before this recent revision by the WHO, some jurisdictions (e.g., some within Australia) were not fully compliant with the WHO guidelines for some pollutants (e.g., ozone).

As a more general guiding principle, standards should be based on health guidelines over pragmatic considerations for air quality in a particular city/locality. This process will allow for targets to improve air quality. Arguably, given that, as stated previously, even short-term exposure to $PM_{2.5}$ can be harmful, which can be particularly pertinent to vulnerable groups such as schoolchildren, standards and baselines may need to consider higher-frequency time intervals than daily intervals.

Public Communication and Education

All levels of government should enhance collaboration to develop nationally consistent public messaging on air pollution, including consistent categorisation, and public health advice, and ideally, this should include tailoring advice to the benefit of at-risk groups such as schoolchildren, e.g., such that the messaging is accessible, easy to understand and ideally compelling (e.g., swaq.org.au/explore). Some considerations for improved, accessible messaging (noting that adherence to WMO guidelines is important) include but are not limited to:

 i Data on which the public-facing information is based ought to use consistent calculations, e.g., by using consistent averaging periods, air-quality information (AQI) calculations, etc.;
 ii Develop research-based national guidelines on providing information on appropriate air-quality education activities to minimise harm, including on the use of personal protective equipment (PPE);
 iii Develop a research-based national, strategic air-quality education program to facilitate informed and timely decision-making by the public and especially vulnerable groups like schoolchildren, enabling preventative actions either in response to exposure to air pollution, or to minimise/avoid exposure in the first place.
 iv Continue to invest in the further research and development of technology to minimise exposure to air pollution (e.g., smoke forecasting systems) building on work already undertaken; provide training in the use of these systems and support their widespread use and adoption by multiple user groups.
 v Disseminate information via easy-to-use, visually compelling and informative media that are readily accessible to children and frequented by them, such as popular online sources.

References

Abatzoglou, J. T., Williams, A. P., & Barbero, R. (2019). Global emergence of anthropogenic climate change in fire weather indices. *Geophysical Research Letters*, *46*(1), 326–336. https://doi.org/10.1029/2018gl080959

Aguilera, R., Corringham, T., Gershunov, A., & Benmarhnia, T. (2021). Wildfire smoke impacts respiratory health more than fine particles from other sources: Observational evidence from Southern California. *Nature Communications*, *12*(1), 1493.

Alman, B. L., Pfister, G., Hao, H., Stowell, J., Hu, X., Liu, Y., & Strickland, M. J. (2016). The association of wildfire smoke with respiratory and cardiovascular emergency department visits in Colorado in 2012: A case crossover study. *Environmental Health*, *15*(1), 64. https://doi.org/10.1186/s12940-016-0146-8

Australian Bureau of Statistics. (2017). *Population projections, Australia, 2017*. Retrieved from www.abs.gov.au/ausstats

Bank, T. W. (2015). *Indonesia's fire and haze crisis*. Retrieved from www.worldbank.org/en/news/feature/2015/12/01/indonesias-fire-and-haze-crisis

Black, C., Tesfaigzi, Y., Bassein, J. A., & Miller, L. A. (2017). Wildfire smoke exposure and human health: Significant gaps in research for a growing public health issue. *Environmental Toxicology and Pharmacology*, *55*, 186–195. https://doi.org/10.1016/j.etap.2017.08.022

Buka, I., Koranteng, S., & Osornio-Vargas, A. R. (2006). The effects of air pollution on the health of children. *Paediatrics & Child Health*, *11*(8), 513–516. Retrieved from https://pubmed.ncbi.nlm.nih.gov/19030320

Bureau of Meteorology. (2019). *Annual climate statement 2019*. Retrieved from www.bom.gov.au/climate/current/annual/aus/

Carrion-Matta, A., Kang, C.-M., Gaffin, J. M., Hauptman, M., Phipatanakul, W., Koutrakis, P., & Gold, D. R. (2019). Classroom indoor $PM_{2.5}$ sources and exposures in inner-city schools. *Environment International*, *131*, 104968. https://doi.org/10.1016/j.envint.2019.104968

Cascio, W. E. (2018). Wildland fire smoke and human health. *Science of the Total Environment*, *624*, 586–595. https://doi.org/10.1016/j.scitotenv.2017.12.086

Chalupka, S., & Anderko, L. (2019). Climate change and schools: Implications for children's health and safety. *Creative Nursings*, *3*, 249–257. https://doi.org/10.1891/1078-4535.25.3.249

Chauhan, A. J., Inskip, H. M., Linaker, C. H., Smith, S., Schreiber, J., Johnston, S. L., & Holgate, S. T. (2003). Personal exposure to nitrogen dioxide (NO_2) and the severity of virus-induced asthma in children. *Lancet*, *361*(9373), 1939–1944. https://doi.org/10.1016/s0140-6736(03)13582-9

Chu, H. Y., Xin, J. Y., Yuan, Q., Zhang, X., Pan, W., Zeng, X. Y., . . . Wang, M. L. (2018). Evaluation of vulnerable $PM_{2.5}$-exposure individuals: A repeated-measure study in an elderly population. *Environmental Science and Pollution Research*, *25*(12), 11833–11840. https://doi.org/10.1007/s11356-018-1412-9

Commission, E. (2021). *Forest fires: EU helps Italy, Greece, Albania and North Macedonia to fight devastating fires*. Retrieved from file:///I:/UNSW/CCRC/SWAQ/book/references/Forest_fires__EU_helps_Italy__Greece__Albania_and_North_Macedonia_to_fight_devastating_fires_.pdf

Cooper, N., Green, D., Guo, Y., & Vardoulakis, S. (2020). School children's exposure to indoor fine particulate matter. *Environmental Research Letters*, *15*(11), 115003. https://doi.org/10.1088/1748-9326/abbafe

Costa, L. G., Cole, T. B., Dao, K., Chang, Y.-C., & Garrick, J. M. (2019). Developmental impact of air pollution on brain function. *Neurochemistry International, 131,* 104580. https://doi.org/10.1016/j.neuint.2019.104580

Desservettaz, M., Phillips, F., Naylor, T., Price, O., Samson, S., Kirkwood, J., & Paton-Walsh, C. (2019). Air quality impacts of smoke from hazard reduction burns and domestic wood heating in western Sydney. *Atmosphere, 10*(9), 557.

Di Virgilio, G., Evans, J. P., Blake, S. A. P., Armstrong, M., Dowd, A. J., Sharples, J., & McRae, R. (2019). Climate change increases the potential for extreme wildfires. *Geophysical Research Letters, 46*(14), 8517–8526. https://doi.org/10.1029/2019gl083699

Di Virgilio, G., Hart, M. A., Maharaj, A. M., & Jiang, N. (2021). Air quality impacts of the 2019–2020 Black Summer wildfires on Australian schools. *Atmospheric Environment, 261,* 118450. https://doi.org/https://doi.org/10.1016/j.atmosenv.2021.118450

Dixon, J. K. (2002). Kids need clean air: air pollution and children's health. *Family Community Health, 24*(4), 9–26. https://doi.org/10.1097/00003727-200201000-00004

Dowdy, A. J., Ye, H., Pepler, A., Thatcher, M., Osbrough, S. L., Evans, J. P., . . . McCarthy, N. (2019). Future changes in extreme weather and pyroconvection risk factors for Australian wildfires. *Scientific Reports, 9*(1), 10073. https://doi.org/10.1038/s41598-019-46362-x

Ferreira, A. M., & Cardoso, M. (2014). Indoor air quality and health in schools. *Jornal Brasileiro de Pneumologia, 40*(3), 259–268. https://doi.org/10.1590/s1806-37132014000300009

Filkov, A. I., Ngo, T., Matthews, S., Telfer, S., & Penman, T. D. (2020). Impact of Australia's catastrophic 2019/20 bushfire season on communities and environment. Retrospective analysis and current trends. *Journal of Safety Science and Resilience, 1,* 44–56. https://doi.org/https://doi.org/10.1016/j.jnlssr.2020.06.009

Flannigan, M., Cantin, A. S., de Groot, W. J., Wotton, M., Newbery, A., & Gowman, L. M. (2013). Global wildland fire season severity in the 21st century. *Forest Ecology and Management, 294,* 54–61. https://doi.org/10.1016/j.foreco.2012.10.022

Gaihre, S., Semple, S., Miller, J., Fielding, S., & Turner, S. (2014). Classroom carbon dioxide concentration, school attendance, and educational attainment. *Journal of School Health, 84*(9), 569–574. https://doi.org/10.1111/josh.12183

Gauderman, W. J., Avol, E., Gilliland, F., Vora, H., Thomas, D., Berhane, K., . . . Peters, J. (2004). The effect of air pollution on lung development from 10 to 18 years of age. *New England Journal of Medicine, 351*(11), 1057–1067. https://doi.org/10.1056/NEJMoa040610

Government, N. (2020). *NSW annual air quality statement 2019.* New South Wales Government. Retrieved from www.environment.nsw.gov.au/topics/air/air-quality-statement

Guérette, E. A., Paton-Walsh, C., Desservettaz, M., Smith, T. E., Volkova, L., Weston, C. J., & Meyer, C. P. (2018). Emissions of trace gases from Australian temperate forest fires: Emission factors and dependence on modified combustion efficiency. *Atmospheric Chemistry and Physics, 18*(5), 3717–3735.

Haikerwal, A., Akram, M., Sim, M. R., Meyer, M., Abramson, M. J., & Dennekamp, M. (2016). Fine particulate matter ($PM_{2.5}$) exposure during a prolonged wildfire period and emergency department visits for asthma. *Respirology, 21*(1), 88–94. https://doi.org/10.1111/resp.12613

Hart, M. A., Cooper, N., Green, D., & Lipson, M. (2021). The synergistic impacts of urban air pollution compounding our climate emergency. In R. Chen & A. G. McGregor (Eds.), *Urban climate science for planning healthy cities*. Springer International Publishing.

Hart, M. A., Maharaj, A., Di Virgilio, G., & Ulpiani, G. (2021). Schools weather and air quality (SWAQ) – Quality controlled urban dataset – Sydney (NSW). Version 1.0.0. *Terrestrial Ecosystem Research Network (TERN)*. Dataset. Retrieved from https://doi.org/10.5281/zenodo.5016296

Haverinen-Shaughnessy, U., Shaughnessy, R. J., Cole, E. C., Toyinbo, O., & Moschandreas, D. J. (2015). An assessment of indoor environmental quality in schools and its association with health and performance. *Building and Environment, 93*, 35–40. https://doi.org/10.1016/j.buildenv.2015.03.006

Hayes, R. B., Lim, C., Zhang, Y. L., Cromar, K., Shao, Y. Z., Reynolds, H. R., . . . Thurston, G. D. (2020). $PM_{2.5}$ air pollution and cause-specific cardiovascular disease mortality. *International Journal of Epidemiology, 49*(1), 25–35. https://doi.org/10.1093/ije/dyz114

Holm, S. M., Miller, M. D., & Balmes, J. R. (2021). Health effects of wildfire smoke in children and public health tools: A narrative review. *Journal of Exposure Science & Environmental Epidemiology, 31*(1), 1–20. https://doi.org/10.1038/s41370-020-00267-4

Howard, C., & Huston, P. (2019). Climate change and infectious diseases: The solutions: The health effects of climate change: Know the risks and become part of the solutions. *Canada Communicable Disease Report, 45*(5), 114.

Hutter, H. P., Haluza, D., Piegler, K., Hohenblum, P., Fröhlich, M., Scharf, S., . . . Moshammer, H. (2013). Semivolatile compounds in schools and their influence on cognitive performance of children. *International Journal of Occupational Medicine and Environmental Health, 26*(4), 628–635. https://doi.org/10.2478/s13382-013-0125-z

Johnston, F. H., Borchers-Arriagada, N., Morgan, G. G., Jalaludin, B., Palmer, A. J., Williamson, G. J., & Bowman, D. M. J. S. (2020). Unprecedented health costs of smoke-related $PM_{2.5}$ from the 2019–20 Australian megafires. *Nature Sustainability*. https://doi.org/10.1038/s41893-020-00610-5

Johnston, F. H., Hanigan, I., Henderson, S., Morgan, G., & Bowman, D. (2011). Extreme air pollution events from bushfires and dust storms and their association with mortality in Sydney, Australia 1994–2007. *Environmental Research, 111*(6), 811–816. https://doi.org/10.1016/j.envres.2011.05.007

Jones, S., Doroski, B., & Glick, S. (2015). Association between state assistance on the topic of indoor air quality and school district-level policies that promote indoor air quality in schools. *The Journal of School Nursing: The Official Publication of the National Association of School Nurses, 31*. https://doi.org/10.1177/1059840515579082

Kim, J. J. (2004). Ambient air pollution: Health hazards to children. *Pediatrics, 114*(6), 1699–1707. https://doi.org/10.1542/peds.2004-2166

Knorr, W., Arneth, A., & Jiang, L. (2016). Demographic controls of future global fire risk. *Nature Climate Change, 6*(8), 781–785. https://doi.org/10.1038/nclimate2999

Laville, S. (2020). Air pollution a cause in girl's death, coroner rules in landmark case. *The Guardian*. Retrieved from https://www.theguardian.com/environment/2020/dec/16/girls-death-contributed-to-by-air-pollution-coroner-rules-in-landmark-case

Lee, S. C., & Chang, M. (2000). Indoor and outdoor air quality investigation at schools in Hong Kong. *Chemosphere*, *41*(1), 109–113. https://doi.org/10.1016/S0045-6535(99)00396-3

Liu, C., Chen, R., Sera, F., Vicedo-Cabrera, A. M., Guo, Y. M., Tong, S. L., . . . Kan, H. D. (2019). Ambient particulate air pollution and daily mortality in 652 cities. *New England Journal of Medicine*, *381*(8), 705–715. https://doi.org/10.1056/NEJMoa1817364

MacSween, K., Paton-Walsh, C., Roulston, C., Guérette, E. A., Edwards, G., Reisen, F., . . . & Kubistin, D. (2020). Cumulative firefighter exposure to multiple toxins emitted during prescribed burns in Australia. *Exposure and Health*, *12*, 721–733.

Mathur, R. (2008). Estimating the impact of the 2004 Alaskan forest fires on episodic particulate matter pollution over the eastern United States through assimilation of satellite-derived aerosol optical depths in a regional air quality model. *Journal of Geophysical Research: Atmospheres*, *113*(D17). https://doi.org/https://doi.org/10.1029/2007JD009767

Mohai, P., Kweon, B. S., Lee, S., & Ard, K. (2011). Air pollution around schools is linked to poorer student health and academic performance. *Health Affairs*, *30*(5), 852–862. https://doi.org/10.1377/hlthaff.2011.0077

Morgan, G. W., Sheppeard, V., Khalaj, B., Ayyar, A., Lincoln, D., Jalaludin, B., . . . Lumley, T. (2010). Effects of bushfire smoke on daily mortality and hospital admissions in Sydney, Australia. *Epidemiology*, *21*(1), 47–55. https://doi.org/10.1097/EDE.0b013e3181c15d5a

Morgan, G. W., Tolhurst, K. G., Poynter, M. W., Cooper, N., McGuffog, T., Ryan, R., . . . Davey, S. M. (2020). Prescribed burning in south-eastern Australia: History and future directions. *Australian Forestry*, *83*(1), 4–28. https://doi.org/10.1080/00049158.2020.1739883

Morris, G. A., Hersey, S., Thompson, A. M., Pawson, S., Nielsen, J. E., Colarco, P. R., . . . Witte, J. C. (2006). Alaskan and Canadian forest fires exacerbate ozone pollution over Houston, Texas, on 19 and 20 July 2004. *Journal of Geophysical Research: Atmospheres*, *111*(D24). https://doi.org/10.1029/2006JD007090

NASA. (2020). *NASA earth observing system data and information system (EOSDIS)*. NASA.

OECD. (2014). *How long do students spend in the classroom?* OECD.

Oke, T. R. (2006). *Initial guidance to obtain representative meteorological observations at urban sites*. Retrieved from www.wmo.int/pages/prog/www/IMOP/publications/IOM-81/IOM-81-UrbanMetObs.pdf

Patel, D., Jian, L., Xiao, J. G., Jansz, J., Yun, G., & Robertson, A. (2019). Joint effect of heatwaves and air quality on emergency department attendances for vulnerable population in Perth, Western Australia, 2006 to 2015. *Environmental Research*, *174*, 80–87. https://doi.org/10.1016/j.envres.2019.04.013

Paton-Walsh, C., Rayner, P., Simmons, J., Fiddes, S. L., Schofield, R., Bridgman, H., . . . Zhang, Y. (2019). A clean air plan for Sydney: An overview of the special issue on air quality in New South Wales. *Atmosphere*, *10*(12), 774. Retrieved from www.mdpi.com/2073-4433/10/12/774

Perera, F. P. (2017). Multiple threats to child health from fossil fuel combustion: Impacts of air pollution and climate change. *Environmental Health Perspectives*, *125*(2), 141–148. https://doi.org/https://doi.org/10.1289/EHP299

Rafiepourgatabi, M., Woodward, A., Salmond, J. A., & Dirks, K. N. (2021). The impact of route choice on active commuters' exposure to air pollution: A systematic review. *Frontiers in Sustainable Cities, 2*(69). https://doi.org/10.3389/frsc.2020.565733

Rappold, A. G., Reyes, J., Pouliot, G., Cascio, W. E., & Diaz-Sanchez, D. (2017). Community vulnerability to health impacts of wildland fire smoke exposure. *Environmental Science & Technology, 51*(12), 6674–6682. https://doi.org/10.1021/acs.est.6b06200

Rivas, I., Querol, X., Wright, J., & Sunyer, J. (2018). How to protect school children from the neurodevelopmental harms of air pollution by interventions in the school environment in the urban context. *Environment International, 121*, 199–206. https://doi.org/https://doi.org/10.1016/j.envint.2018.08.063

Roberts, S., Arseneault, L., Barratt, B., Beevers, S., Danese, A., Odgers, C. L., . . . Fisher, H. L. (2019). Exploration of NO_2 and $PM_{2.5}$ air pollution and mental health problems using high-resolution data in London-based children from a UK longitudinal cohort study. *Psychiatry Research, 272*, 8–17. https://doi.org/10.1016/j.psychres.2018.12.050

Schulze, S. S., Fischer, E. C., Hamideh, S., & Mahmoud, H. (2020). Wildfire impacts on schools and hospitals following the 2018 California camp fire. *Natural Hazards, 104*, 901–925.

Shaposhnikov, D., Revich, B., Bellander, T., Bedada, G. B., Bottai, M., Kharkova, T., . . . Pershagen, G. (2014). Mortality related to air pollution with the Moscow heat wave and wildfire of 2010. *Epidemiology, 25*(3), 359–364. https://doi.org/10.1097/ede.0000000000000090

Shusterman, D., Kaplan, J. Z., & Canabarro, C. (1993). Immediate health effects of an urban wildfire. *The Western Journal of Medicine, 158*(2), 133–138. Retrieved from https://pubmed.ncbi.nlm.nih.gov/8434462

Sram, R. J., Veleminsky, M., Jr., Veleminsky, Sr. M., & Stejskalová, J. (2017). The impact of air pollution to central nervous system in children and adults. *Neuroendocrinology Letters, 38*(6), 389–396.

Stabile, L., Dell'Isola, M., Russi, A., Massimo, A., & Buonanno, G. (2017). The effect of natural ventilation strategy on indoor air quality in schools. *Science of the Total Environment, 595*, 894–902. https://doi.org/10.1016/j.scitotenv.2017.03.048

Toftum, J., Kjeldsen, B. U., Wargocki, P., Menå, H. R., Hansen, E. M. N., & Clausen, G. (2015). Association between classroom ventilation mode and learning outcome in Danish schools. *Building and Environment, 92*, 494–503. https://doi.org/10.1016/j.buildenv.2015.05.017

Tran, V. V., Park, D., & Lee, Y.-C. (2020). Indoor air pollution, related human diseases, and recent trends in the control and improvement of indoor air quality. *International Journal of Environmental Research and Public Health, 17*(8), 2927. Retrieved from www.mdpi.com/1660-4601/17/8/2927

Twardella, D., Matzen, W., Lahrz, T., Burghardt, R., Spegel, H., Hendrowarsito, L., . . . Fromme, H. (2012). Effect of classroom air quality on students' concentration: Results of a cluster-randomized cross-over experimental study. *Indoor Air, 22*(5), 378–387. https://doi.org/10.1111/j.1600-0668.2012.00774.x

Ulpiani, G., Hart, M.A., Di Virgilio, G., Maharaj, A.M., Lipson, M.J., and Potgieter, J. (2022). A citizen centred urban network for weather and air quality in Australian schools. *Scientific Data 9*, 129. https://doi.org/10.1038/s41597-022-01205-9

Ulpiani, G., Ranzi, G., & Santamouris, M. (2020). Experimental evidence of the multiple microclimatic impacts of bushfires in affected urban areas: The case of Sydney during the 2019/2020 Australian season. *Environmental Research Communications, 2*(6), 065005. https://doi.org/10.1088/2515-7620/ab9e1a

van Eeden, L., Nimmo, D., Mahony, M., Herman, K., Ehmke, G., Driessen, J., . . . Dickman, C. (2020). *Australia's 2019–2020 bushfires: The wildlife toll – Interim report*. Retrieved from www.wwf.org.au/ArticleDocuments/353/Animals%20Impacted%20Interim%20Report%2024072020%20final.pdf.aspx?OverrideExpiry=Y:

Varaden, D., Leidland, E., & Barratt, B. (2019). *The breathe London wearables study engaging primary school children to monitor air pollution in London*. Environmental Research Group and Kings College London.

Vardoulakis, S., Jalaludin, B. B., Morgan, G. G., Hanigan, I. C., & Johnston, F. H. (2020). Bushfire smoke: Urgent need for a national health protection strategy. *Medical Journal of Australia, 212*(8), 349–353. e341. https://doi.org/10.5694/mja2.50511

Walter, C. M., Schneider-Futschik, E. K., Knibbs, L. D., & Irving, L. B. (2020). Health impacts of bushfire smoke exposure in Australia. *Respirology, 25*(5), 495–501. https://doi.org/10.1111/resp.13798

Wargocki, P., Porras-Salazar, J. A., Contreras-Espinoza, S., & Bahnfleth, W. (2020). The relationships between classroom air quality and children's performance in school. *Building and Environment, 173*, 106749. https://doi.org/10.1016/j.buildenv.2020.106749

WHO. (2018). *More than 90% of the world's children breathe toxic air every day [Press release]*. Retrieved from www.who.int/news/item/29-10-2018-more-than-90-of-the-worlds-children-breathe-toxic-air-every-day

Wichmann, J., Lind, T., Nilsson, M. A. M., & Bellander, T. (2010). $PM_{2.5}$, soot and NO_2 indoor – outdoor relationships at homes, pre-schools and schools in Stockholm, Sweden. *Atmospheric Environment, 44*(36), 4536–4544. https://doi.org/https://doi.org/10.1016/j.atmosenv.2010.08.023

Wolfe, M. K., McDonald, N. C., Arunachalam, S., Baldauf, R., & Valencia, A. (2020). Impact of school location on children's air pollution exposure. *Journal of Urban Affairs, 17*. https://doi.org/10.1080/07352166.2020.1734013

Wong, J. P. S., Tsagkaraki, M., Tsiodra, I., Mihalopoulos, N., Violaki, K., Kanakidou, M., . . . Weber, R. J. (2019). Effects of atmospheric processing on the oxidative potential of biomass burning organic aerosols. *Environmental Science & Technology, 53*(12), 6747–6756. https://doi.org/10.1021/acs.est.9b01034

World Health Organization. (2021). *WHO global air quality guidelines: Particulate matter ($PM_{2.5}$ and PM_{10}), ozone, nitrogen dioxide, sulfur dioxide and carbon monoxide*. World Health Organization.

Zhang, Z. L., Dong, B., Li, S. S., Chen, G. B., Yang, Z. G., Dong, Y. H., . . . Guo, Y. M. (2019). Exposure to ambient particulate matter air pollution, blood pressure and hypertension in children and adolescents: A national cross-sectional study in China. *Environment International, 128*, 103–108. https://doi.org/10.1016/j.envint.2019.04.036

Zhao, B., Johnston, F. H., Salimi, F., Kurabayashi, M., & Negishi, K. (2020). Short-term exposure to ambient fine particulate matter and out-of-hospital cardiac arrest: A nationwide case-crossover study in Japan. *The Lancet Planetary Health, 4*(1), e15–e23. https://doi.org/10.1016/S2542-5196(19)30262-1

Zosky, G. R., Porta Cubus, A., Morgan, G., Tham, R., Heyworth, J., Marks, G. B., . . . Jalaludin, B. (2021). Centre for Air pollution, energy and health Research (CAR) position paper: There is no "safe" level of air pollution. *Implications for Australian Policy*. https://doi.org/10.25959/100.00036248

4 The Influences of Extreme Cold and Storms on Schoolchildren

Brendon Hyndman and Brenton Button

Cold is defined as a "relatively low temperature," which is often perceived as "uncomfortable" (Merriam-Webster, 2014). It can be difficult in cold climates with low sunlight and temperatures, and with high rainfall, to provide school settings with satisfying experiences (Watchman et al., 2020). Very little is known about the impact of cold weather extremes or winters on schoolchildren (Brooks et al., 2017). Within schools, children are especially vulnerable to the impacts of cold temperatures (Rasi et al., 2017) and important outdoor-recreation time can be reduced if the outdoors are deemed unfavourable by school gatekeepers. Extremely cold climates and winter conditions are characterised by aspects such as prolonged periods of temperatures that are equal or less than 0 degrees Celsius (or 32 Fahrenheit) for at least two months (Pressman & Mänty, 1988). Other perceptions of extremely cold climates can be attributed to the amount of snowfall. The most common elements associated with wintry conditions include subfreezing temperatures, regular snow precipitation, reduced levels of daylight/sunshine and prolonged periods of low temperatures (Stout et al., 2018).

In global regions such as in Canada in North America, and Finland in Europe, there are major challenges for well-being, especially during winter. Such northern-latitude regions can pose even greater challenges than those caused by heat (Rasi et al., 2017; Chen et al., 2016). Historically, it has been well documented that there should be as much protection from the outdoor elements as possible through architecture, to shield or filter undesirable cold conditions (Pressman, 1985; Olgyay, 2016). Yet it is also important to not overprotect people from nature, as we are all built to live in tandem with nature and we often thrive from natural interactions (Pressman, 1985). This is especially vital for children who are establishing habits they carry with them across the lifespan. Despite freezing temperatures in Finland, cold and fresh air is considered healthy (Rasi et al., 2017). It has been reported that approximately 96% of Finnish adults will spend time outdoors engaged in recreation (Sievanen & Neuvonen, 2011), which has been found to assist with emotional well-being (Pasanen et al., 2014). Moreover, children engaging in regular "outdoor" activities has been linked to improved physical-activity participation, less incidences of being overweight, increased independent mobility and improved mental health (Tillmann et al., 2018). Finland is an example of one of the extremely cold climates with temperatures staying consistently below 0 degrees Celsius throughout winter, with average temperatures below 15 degrees Celsius in the coldest month of the northern region. Despite some adaption to cold climates (Näyhä, 2005), cold exposure has detrimental impacts on health, with regular connections being made between extreme cold and mortality across a host of studies (Xu et al., 2012; Vardoulakis et al., 2014; Guo et al., 2014). Some of the health difficulties experienced from the cold include peripheral-circulation concerns (which can lead to frostbite) and respiratory difficulties or diseases (Xu et al., 2014). Frostbite in childhood can also lead to impaired finger development (Ervasti et al., 1993). A study from Finland identified that as temperature levels decreased, so did schoolchildren's outdoor recreational time (Rasi et al., 2017). The study investigated the schoolchildren's perceptions and discovered that every child reported having reddened cheeks, and there were occasions where the children experienced pain and numbness in the cheeks. Moreover, the cold air resulted in many of the children experiencing a runny nose or respiratory difficulties, or experiencing pain and numbness on their ears or toes. In such conditions, the primary school children would run, skate, cycle, ski, sled and undertake snowmobiling (Rasi et al., 2017). Interestingly, despite the freezing temperatures and symptoms, this did not stop the Finnish primary school children from engaging in outdoor recreation activities. This is especially important, for the health benefits from children's outdoor, unstructured play. The authors suggest that adults and play gatekeepers should monitor schoolchildren's clothing and ensure there are spaces for the children to dry clothes and change clothing if these become damp (Rasi et al., 2017). Despite a greater prevalence of focus on extreme heat impacts, there are regions in the world such as Ontario in Canada and Finland in Europe, which require significant mitigation from extreme cold weather exposure for continued participation in developmental activities. In such climates, it will be important to consider inclusions within the school curricula and professional-development programs.

In Canada, children attend school from September to June and are exposed to winter conditions for most large segments of the school year. It has been established that wintry conditions can shorten the duration of outdoor school activities (Ergler et al., 2013). Moreover, the physical-activity participation of children is greater in the warmer months in Canada (Bélanger et al., 2009). A series of related studies by Button and colleagues have gone a step further and examined how daily weather changes can impact children's physical activity across the whole day. In one study they examined how weather patterns impacted both light physical activity and moderate-to-vigorous physical activity. The study found that for each increase in 1°C, there was on average a 1.33-minute increase in moderate-to-vigorous physical activity, but the temperature had no effect on light physical activity. In this study average daily temperatures ranged from −11°C to 18°C. The study also found that on days with rain (Figure 4.1), children had an average of 23 fewer minutes of moderate-to-vigorous physical activity and 50 fewer minutes of light physical activity when compared to days without rain. Snow was found to have no impact on moderate-to-vigorous physical activity or light physical activity (Button et al., 2021). The researchers suggested that snow allows children to participate in certain activities like sliding, riding a snow machine or ice skating, while rain affords fewer opportunities. Finally, the research team found that weather had no significant impact on daily sedentary time (Button et al., 2020a). This series of studies highlights the often-overlooked impacts of weather patterns on children's activity, especially cooler weather.

It has been suggested that more comfortable outdoor-recreation participation by schoolchildren could be prolonged by almost six weeks by considering ways to improve comfort levels in the outdoor environment (Li, 2019), such as capturing more sunlight, alongside more opportunities to adapt to the outside climate, rather than full protection through heating systems. Artificially maintained temperatures should be avoided to prevent discomfort when occupants will expect outdoor temperatures to reflect indoor comfort levels. It has also been recognised that "Light can affect human behaviour, mood and health via pathways other than the visual system" (Figueiro, 2013). Historically, design strategies to protect schoolchildren from the outdoor cold have included use of windows to capture sunlight, and shielding ventilation from cold, harsh winds (Matus, 1988). Modern adaptations include a reliance on heating systems, which can be problematic for the environment if there is too much reliance. Suggestions for school design include ensuring there is a connection between the natural elements between indoor and outdoor spaces throughout the year (Pressman & Mänty, 1988).

Storms and Unplanned School Closures

There are many extreme weather events that have an impact on schoolchildren. Cyclones or hurricanes and tornadoes are major extreme weather events and these storms can include a combination of impact from rainfall, snow and winds on school systems. The negative impact on school systems is what is referred to as "unplanned school closures." Although unplanned school closures can be related to infectious diseases, the lens of this chapter is based around when the level of extreme weather becomes so severe that a wide range of schools are forced to close, negatively interrupting schoolchildren's learning and development (Hyndman, 2017).

Until the last decade, there had been limited international evidence outlining the causes, components and frequencies of unplanned school closures from extreme storm events, despite the widespread impact of such extreme storms on schoolchildren and their respective school communities. Most of the research that had previously been conducted relating to school closures had been related to the prevention of contagious diseases, such as influenza (Wu et al., 2010). Closing schools as a community strategy to prevent the progression of severe influenza cases had been common with socially dense school contexts and to prevent schoolchildren returning contagious diseases to their households (WHO, 2006; Markel, 2007). Reflecting the COVID-19 pandemic of 2020, school closures were prominent within the United States during 2009 due to a pandemic. Despite this, there has been very little research capturing the impact of extreme weather events on school closures in the United States, despite snow storms being highly prevalent (Wong et al., 2014). As pandemics are becoming more common, school closures from extreme weather events will be able to follow suit by leading to strategies to continue to accommodate schoolchildren's learning experiences and schoolteachers' class-delivery methods. The common reasons for school closures have been categorised as being due to weather/natural disasters, illness, school-building issues, violence, teacher strikes and a death of a member of the school community (Wong et al., 2014). Yet it has been established that both extreme weather events (e.g., rain/snow/wind storms, or temperature extremes) and natural disasters (e.g., flooding, cyclones, bushfires, tornadoes) have been almost as common for school closures as pandemics. Over the past decade it has become clear that contagious diseases are not the only common cause of unplanned school closures. From 2011 to 2013 in the United States, Wong and colleagues (2014) recognised that almost 30 million schoolchildren were negatively impacted from unplanned school closures. Moreover, extreme weather was attributed to 79% of the total 21,000 unplanned school closures across the United States over that two-year period. There is very little research to demonstrate the impact on academic performance from unplanned school closures, yet research reports have shown that state-based assessment scores have been lower in areas where schools have been forced to close their campuses due to extreme snowfall, in comparison to other periods when the schools have not had to close (Marcotte & Hemelt, 2008).

Both Australia and the United States provide strong examples of extreme weather events, due to their large sizes and contrasting extremes across expansive regions. Although mostly known for its dry and hot climate, there have been cases in Australia with over 40 schools being shut down due to snowstorms across the state of New South Wales. Such icy conditions have caused hazards on the roads, with many vehicle collisions occurring, which has compromised the safety of children arriving to school. Common in the United States, snowstorms have been characterised by ice, snow, strong winds and heavy rain. In addition to safety impacts on schoolchildren commuting to school, the impact of road closures from heavy snowfall can simply prevent children attending school entirely (Meddows, 2015).

In 2017, all southeastern schools in the Australian state of Queensland and many schools across the top of the state of New South Wales were closed due to the uncharacteristic southern trajectory of Cyclone Debbie (including the ex-cyclonic impact) (Burke & Schipp, 2017). This cyclone's southern trajectory of movement away from the tropical region hit large population areas in Australia, causing large-scale destruction and the closure of over 2,000 schools. The eye of the cyclone passed over Brisbane, one of Australia's largest cities with gusts of over 100km from the cyclone, alongside major flooding and power outages (Burke & Schipp, 2017). Such uncharacteristic weather extremes continue to emerge with increased frequency across the globe (Cai et al., 2015), which creates a growing need to protect our most vulnerable populations; that includes protecting disruption from children's attendance at school.

Across other parts of the globe, such as Southeast Asia (Parvin et al., 2022; Bernabe et al., 2021) and Africa (Mudavanhu, 2014), flooding from extreme storms are a major disrupter for schooling systems. In a study across 30 schools in Bangladesh (Asia), Parvin and colleagues (2022) identified that there was little understanding relating to disaster mitigation in about half of the schoolchildren; it was suggested that there needs to be improved knowledge and understanding of the impacts of extreme storms and to ensure the determinants on schoolchildren's preparedness, such impacts, are better adhered to by policy makers. The United Nations specify that if people are better informed and motivated, this can reduce educational vulnerability to extreme weather events (United Nations, 2015), including training, participation, sharing and educative opportunities. Similarly, research from India found that storms significantly disrupt children's education (Bernabe et al., 2021). In the regions that were exposed to the most powerful winds, it was predicted using national data that almost 7% of children were less likely to reach levels of education beyond secondary schooling and almost 10% would be educationally lagging. The researchers calculated that the schoolchildren that were educationally behind in those regions would also have a lower probability of securing post-school employment. Across the world in Zimbabwe, Africa, flood intensities and frequencies also pose a threat to school attendance and educative opportunities (Mudavanhu, 2014). Mudavanhu (2014) identified that regular flooding results in substantial absenteeism, poor syllabus continuation from teachers (leading to impaired academic performance), loss of teaching personnel and children's hours of learning. Suggestions to improve school capabilities from the impact of floods included improved building standards, resources, better considerations of geographical school locations and school terrains. For instance, there were school buildings developed in regularly flooded wetland contexts or close to rivers. The findings reinforced earlier research that found that extreme weather events led to poor academic performances and teachers having challenges to continue meeting syllabus objectives.

In the Caribbean (Spencer et al., 2016) and the United States (Ward et al., 2008), the impacts of hurricanes have also been detrimental to schoolchildren's educational attainment. A 17-year study of over 800 schools in the Caribbean demonstrated that there were significant, negative effects on schoolchildren's academic performance if a hurricane struck when schools were in session. Interestingly, progress in the humanities subjects appeared to be unaffected (Spencer et al., 2016). The long-term impacts of Hurricane Katrina in the United States were also established to have had a negative educational impact on schoolchildren, with around 80,000 schoolchildren displaced, and disruptions evident from the aftermath of the storm with increased incidence of anxiety, disruptive behaviours and slow adjustments back to school (Ward et al., 2008). These are all examples of extremely high-risk weather events, so the protective considerations to maintain school-based developmental activities would not be advised. Yet the research conducted of the impacts from these extreme storms on education systems suggest that more can be done related to preparing for "Plan B" with schooling approaches via alternative locations and providing effective guides towards educational recovery. For instance, ensuring schoolchildren can have access to educational opportunities as soon as is feasible, to return the children to learning routines and reduce anxieties from being physically separated from peers.

Although most of the impacts upon school systems from extreme storms are due to closure during the extreme weather events (Miller & Hui, 2022) from wind damage to the school or excess flooding, there has been some evidence of the negative impacts of lightning strikes from storms on schoolchildren. It is common practice for schools to avoid outdoor activities if a storm is about to arrive, yet there have been cases of dozens of schoolchildren becoming injured and even killed by a lightning strike at a soccer game (Dollinger, 1985). Lightning strikes are very sporadic and randomised during extreme thunderstorms, and although occurrences of injury to people have decreased over the decades, fatalities and injuries are still common from children riding their bikes, out fishing and sheltering under trees (Curran et al., 2000). Although lightning strikes can still be considered by schools for weather-protection practices, predicting the range of lightning strikes with handheld detection devices during athletic events has been deemed to have high levels of variability (DeCaria et al., 2011). Of additional concern is the extreme weather phenomena of tornadoes. For instance, in the United States it has been reported over multiple decades that there can be approximately 1,300 tornadoes per year that occur across the regions of many school communities (NOAA, 2013), especially between March to June (NOAA, 2013). Oklahoma is a state situated in what is known as "Tornado Alley." Among the structures and buildings that have been negatively impacted by the regular tornado occurrences over the decades in Oklahoma (~62 reported per year) have been a combination of $N = 7$ elementary and high schools, and more recently four schools were damaged in the Little Axe area of Oklahoma in May, 2011 (Iyer, 2020). Warnings of tornado occurrences for communities (including schools) are provided by radar instruments or via trained experts in tornado spotting (NOAA, 2013). In 2008, Simmons and Sutter reported that the average amount of time between a tornado reporting and warning was

11 minutes. The process of alerting involves a variety of stakeholders and steps that include storm/weather personnel, emergency services, public service officers and schools themselves. As recognised earlier in the chapter, the power of such extreme storms results in not only the closure of schools, but forced relocations for schoolchildren from learning contexts and daily routines they are used to (Miller & Hui, 2022).

Another type of storm that has caused school closures in Australia have been bushfires or firestorms. In recent years, there have been regular catastrophic fire conditions that have resulted in widespread school closures across Australian states. The purpose of the closures was intended to be for when fire conditions are catastrophic and to ensure families are able to enact their bushfire plans and prepare their properties for such conditions (Perpitch, 2016; ABC, 2019). Political leaders can announce a "state of emergency" to close schools due to bushfire conditions, unless schools are highly equipped with comprehensive bushfire plans (McGowan et al., 2019). Despite these examples, there is very little research on the number of unplanned school closures that take place or the learning impact that occurs within school systems.

Are Schoolchildren Losing Out From School Closures on Their Development?

Attendance at school is well established to be paramount for children to get the most out of their education. Yet it is clear that due to extreme storms impacting on school closures, some children can have on-campus learning opportunities compromised. The positive news is that research has demonstrated that if an absence from school is an authorised instance (e.g., due to an extreme storm event), the impact on their development will be less than if the absence from school is not authorised with little reasoning or explanation from the child. This is due to unauthorised absences generally characterising trends of a single student's misbehaviour and disengagement, or reflecting parents' negative attitudes towards education that schoolchildren can inherit and demonstrate in their schooling. Although further research is required to establish if the reasoning for such impacts are from teachers progressing with class objectives if a single student is absent, compared to school closures impacting an entire class simultaneously.

We know from early-childhood settings that preschool attendance is an enormous indicator on a child's development (Schurer et al., 2018). With so much consultation and consideration from world-leading experts and practitioners for the development of curricula to scaffold skills for children, there is no doubt that schools need to be prepared to mitigate any unplanned disruptions to their development trajectory. The curriculum is designed to ensure schoolchildren are learning what is vital for their lifelong development. Essentially, the level of negative impact on a child's educational development and performance will be attributed to the amount of time that the child is absent from school and how regularly this disruption occurs. If the storm event is catastrophic, schools will need improved contingency plans for children to be able to work from home.

Research by Zubrick (2014) demonstrates that if absences occur by schoolchildren on a regular basis, this will have a negative impact on reading, writing and numerical performances. Similarly, Hancock and colleagues (2013) outline in their research that schoolchildren who are absent for more than one-tenth of school days in a calendar year or ten days within a school term will subsequently be vulnerable to reduced academic achievement. As normalised absence rates sit at around 7%, it is clear that additional, unplanned absences could result in many schoolchildren being vulnerable to educational risk. Yet unplanned developments in 2020 may have assisted schools to be able to better cope with children not attending campus and not being disadvantaged if they are unable to physically reach campuses due to extreme storm events. Schools are now better able to adapt to ensure that not being on campus does not mean not being able to engage in classes and continue to learn.

The international COVID-19 crisis that occurred in 2020 may have helped fast-track the ability of school systems to be able to cater for children that have been forced to work from home. Although not a weather extreme, the characteristics of the COVID-19 virus to force unplanned school closures also forced schoolteachers to adapt and innovate through online methods. The same procedures can now be adopted if school campuses are not safe for children to attend.

Disrupting Play Behaviours and the School Day

Although school closures from extreme weather are significant measures, there are other disruptions that have been captured that can negatively impact schoolchildren. Studies of hundreds of primary (elementary) children have recognised that the schoolchildren are more likely to not participate in or have lower enjoyment for participating in active play and physical education activities from wet and cold weather (Hyndman & Chancellor, 2015). The impact of wet weather and cold temperatures could make it more difficult for schoolchildren to comply with physical-activity recommendations, developed to ensure children are meeting adequate physical-activity levels to prevent ill health (Turrisi et al., 2021).

A study by Button et al. (2020b) examined the impact of weather on physical activity during recess and curriculum time. Recess is when children go outside and are granted freedom in the activities that they pick and choose as long as they fall within the general school rules. During recess time, for each 1°C increase in maximum daily temperature, children were getting almost 14 more seconds of physical activity. During recess, children were expected to go outside, but there was still a decrease in physical activity as the temperature dropped. This suggests that aspects of the colder weather were hampering children's physical activity. Physical activity during curriculum time is normally teacher-led and undertaken with peers, often via health and physical education classes. During curriculum time, children had almost 11 fewer minutes of moderate-to-vigorous physical activity on days with rain than days without rain. The authors suggested that on days without rain, teachers might be more willing to extend recess or take children outside at the end of the day (Button et al., 2020b). Another way poor weather can affect children's physical activity is by influencing transportation to school. A child's journey to and from school provides an opportunity for children to be active each day by either walking, biking or wheeling to school. Despite the benefits of active travel, the number of children who actively travel to school continues to decline (Rothman et al., 2018; Figure 4.1). A study by Mitra and Faulkner (2012) and Oliver et al. (2014) found that weather was not associated with travel modes to school. However, work by Button et al. (2020c) found that children indicated that it could be too cold to walk, and during winter, the lack of properly maintained sidewalks made it difficult and frustrating to walk to school. With active play and movement being critical for schoolchildren to engage in, schools need to ensure there are spaces and regulations within their environments to ensure children can continue to participate in and enjoy their school-based physical activities (Harrison et al., 2011). There are also considerations for schoolteachers who can become stressed in making decisions during wet weather and will need to be able to monitor safety aspects if there

Figure 4.1 An example of a pupil actively travelling to school during snow conditions

The Influences of Extreme Cold and Storms on Schoolchildren 69

Figure 4.2 An example of surfacing that can result in lost traction for recreational activities

is play occurring on surfaces that have lost traction from the rain (Chancellor & Hyndman, 2017a, 2017b; Figure 4.2).

Despite such benefits to engaging in outdoor, active play, children are spending less time outdoors than previous generations (Tandon et al., 2012). It is clear that when outdoor conditions are not favourable, such as from cold weather, children's opportunities to engage in outdoor play are reduced (Mitra & Faulkner, 2012). Adverse seasonal conditions such as cold weather also receive little attention in the research literature, which has been attributed to such conditions being "non-modifiable" (Mitra & Faulkner, 2012). Teachers have been recognised as allocating significantly less time outdoors during cooler months across the school year in Slovene and Norwegian schools (Kos & Jerman, 2013). Scholars have called for further research to determine how gatekeepers believe cold weather impacts on decisions around outdoor play (Copeland et al., 2011; Chancellor & Hyndman, 2017a, 2017b). A study into gatekeepers' beliefs around cold weather in Minnesota schools in the United States identified that there needs to be improved outdoor-play policies according to weather extremes (Hughes et al., 2017). There was a range of inconsistencies reported with minimum temperatures aligned with cold-weather policies ranging significantly across institutions. Yet rather than looking to continue outdoor play and providing improved comfort within the outdoor elements (Figure 4.3), many of the schools had temperature-specific

Figure 4.3 Schoolchildren continuing to play outside, despite a flooded play area

policies that triggered school cancellations in northern Minnesota – although it should be acknowledged that there are a diverse range of factors that impact on cold-weather policies and procedures, including school expectations, the people involved, the spaces, the actual weather conditions (which can vary) and general beliefs and attitudes towards cool weather (Hughes et al., 2017). This reinforces the consideration for school communities to adapt policies according to their school-based needs or that a consistent policy would need to be created that can provide a foundation/base for schools to be able to adapt (Hyndman & Zundans-Fraser, 2020).

Over 35 years ago, Hollenhorst and Ewert (1985) noted that outdoor play would be impacted by adult gatekeepers' beliefs that impact their decision making, and this has recently been reinforced by Chancellor and Hyndman (2017a, 2017b). Chancellor and Hyndman (2017a, 2017b) suggest more formalised training for schoolteachers around school-contextual decision making during outdoor play within teacher-training programs. The untrained beliefs of adults could contribute to potentially compromising decisions on how children should be playing within cold weather conditions. The Minnesota study by Hughes and colleagues revealed that in the majority, adult gatekeepers' beliefs around children's play within cold weather were mainly positive. Moreover, the study suggested that although weather-related policies were lacking in many of the educational institutions, the gatekeepers were confident, willing and encouraging of outdoor play. Similar to the Finland (Rasi et al., 2017) and Quebec (Watchman et al., 2020) contexts outlined, addressing barriers

The Influences of Extreme Cold and Storms on Schoolchildren 71

Figure 4.4 A child wearing weather-equipped boots continues to play in a flooded play space

to outdoor play within extreme cold weather can ensure schoolchildren's opportunities for outdoor play in cold weather can be maximised (Figure 4.4).

What Are the Solutions to Be Able to Mitigate Extreme Cold Weather and Storm Events on School Activities?

The 2020 COVID-19 pandemic has taught the world that we need to be able to accommodate new platforms and online mechanisms to engage with our school systems, classes and educational protocols. For instance, Forsyth County Schools in the United States utilises specially designed online-learning management systems, with instructions posted at the beginning of a school day (and prior to a school-closure day); schoolchildren commence working through lessons on the weather-impacted school day and completion of scheduled work is not linked to student attendance (Forsyth, 2022).

Moving forward to what schools will need to consider as we delve deeper into the 21st century, scholars indicate that there needs to be:

1 Further scholarship into the differential between actual risks during outdoor play during extreme cold weather and education gatekeepers' perceptions.
2 Both indoor-and-outdoor-play and physical-activity opportunity allocations should be maintained as much as possible within school communities;

therefore additional comfort (e.g., access to warm clothing, shelter, smart board activity strategies) need to be considered for schoolchildren during days of extreme cold. For instance, Reznik et al. (2015) have found positive improvements from inside-play initiatives such as with an audio CD and teachers facilitating education-focused aerobic activities.
3 Professional development needs to be organised for schoolteachers, parents, principals, education assistants and schoolchildren to ensure that play decision making is optimised and that play during cold weather can be safely integrated into curricula learning opportunities. Such a whole-school professional-development approach can ensure schoolchildren stay active during extreme weather events. All stakeholders can ensure that cold, rain and snow weather should be approached with enthusiasm and supportive clothing.
4 Consider what has been proposed to protect schoolchildren from extreme weather with whole-school approaches (Hyndman, 2017), such as optimising communication channels to parents during extreme cold/storm weather events, displaying reminder/guidance signs and posters for schoolchildren and accurate temperature gauges to guide gatekeeper decision making around outdoor play.

Although there are instances in which extreme weather reaches avoidable thresholds, scholars propose (Hyndman, 2017; Jacobs et al., 2019) that cancelling or abandoning school play opportunities should be considered as a last resort for school systems due to the benefits of outdoor play on children's development. Jacobs and colleagues (2019) identified that there are wide inconsistencies across jurisdictions into what schools see as a threshold for cancelling school recess time. Schools must consider how they can support children's play as a major priority. Providing such essential strategies, resources and programs can help to ensure that children have "access to and benefit from a wide range of stimulating and challenging outdoor play experiences" in cold weather (Little & Wyver, 2008, p. 39). Such support will allow schoolchildren to have the opportunities to accumulate and enact practical understandings of how to negotiate within their contexts across seasons.

References

Australian Broadcasting Corporation (ABC). (2019). *More than 100 SA schools to close in catastrophic fire conditions*. Retrieved from www.abc.net.au/news/2019-11-19/sa-schools-to-close-amid-catastrophic-fire-conditions/11718984

Bélanger, M., Gray-Donald, K., O'Loughlin, J., Paradis, G., & Hanley, J. (2009). Influence of weather conditions and season on physical activity in adolescents. *Annals of Epidemiology, 19*(3), 180–186.

Bernabe, A., Diop, B., Pelli, M., & Tschopp, J. (2021). *Childhood exposure to storms and long-term educational attainments in India*. Retrieved from https://conference.iza.org/conference_files/ClimateChange_2021/tschopp_j30206.pdf

The Influences of Extreme Cold and Storms on Schoolchildren 73

Brooks, A. M., Ottley, K. M., Arbuthnott, K. D., & Sevigny, P. (2017). Nature-related mood effects: Season and type of nature contact. *Journal of Environmental Psychology*, *54*, 91–102.

Burke, L., & Schipp, D. (2017). Schools closed, evacuations ordered as 'nightmare' Debbie stalks south. Retrieved from www.news.com.au/technology/environment/schools-closed-as-brisbane-and-sydney-brace-for-fall-as-cyclone-debbies-aftereffects-get-disastrous/news-story/9f025c16d4be60ddaa330e09c73a6f96

Button, B. L., Clark, A. F., Martin, G., Graat, M., & Gilliland, J. A. (2020b). Measuring temporal differences in rural Canadian children's moderate-to-vigorous physical activity. *International Journal of Environmental Research and Public Health*, *17*(23), 8734.

Button, B. L., Martin, G., Clark, A. F., Graat, M., & Gilliland, J. A. (2020a). Examining factors of accelerometer-measured sedentary time in a sample of rural Canadian children. *Children*, *7*(11), 232.

Button, B. L., Shah, T. I., Clark, A. F., Wilk, P., & Gilliland, J. A. (2021). Examining weather-related factors on physical activity levels of children from rural communities. *Canadian Journal of Public Health*, *112*(1), 107–114.

Button, B. L., Tillmann, S., & Gilliland, J. (2020c). Exploring children's perceptions of barriers and facilitators to physical activity in rural Northwestern Ontario, Canada. *Rural and Remote Health*, *20*(3), 5791–5791.

Cai, W., Wang, G., Santoso, A., McPhaden, M. J., Wu, L., Jin, F. F., . . . & Guilyardi, E. (2015). Increased frequency of extreme La Niña events under greenhouse warming. *Nature Climate Change*, *5*(2), 132–137.

Chancellor, B., & Hyndman, B. (2017a). Adult Decisions on Students' Play Within Primary School Playgrounds. In *Contemporary school playground strategies for healthy students* (pp. 37–55). Springer.

Chancellor, B., & Hyndman, B. (2017b). The rush to judgement: Mapping moral geographies of the primary school playground. *Global Studies of Childhood*, *7*(1), 38–50.

Chen, H., Wang, J., Li, Q., Yagouti, A., Lavigne, E., Foty, R., . . . & Copes, R. (2016). Assessment of the effect of cold and hot temperatures on mortality in Ontario, Canada: A population-based study. *CMAJ Open*, *4*(1), E48.

Copeland, K. A., Sherman, S. N., Khoury, J. C., Foster, K. E., Saelens, B. E., & Kalkwarf, H. J. (2011). Wide variability in physical activity environments and weather-related outdoor play policies in child care centers within a single county of Ohio. *Archives of Pediatrics & Adolescent Medicine*, *165*(5), 435–442.

Curran, E. B., Holle, R. L., & López, R. E. (2000). Lightning casualties and damages in the United States from 1959 to 1994. *Journal of Climate*, *13*(19), 3448–3464.

DeCaria, A. J., Wimer, J. W., Fijalkowski, H. M., Miziorko, M. R., & Limbacher, J. A. (2011, January). Detection efficiencies and range accuracies of three portable lightning detectors compared with the National Lightning Detection Network. *Presented at the 91st Annual Meeting of the American Meteorological Society*. Seattle, Washington.

Dollinger, S. J. (1985). Lightning-strike disaster among children. *British Journal of Medical Psychology*, *58*(4), 375–383.

Ergler, C. R., Kearns, R. A., & Witten, K. (2013). Seasonal and locational variations in children's play: Implications for wellbeing. *Social Science & Medicine*, *91*, 178–185.

Ervasti, O., Hassi, J., & Manelius, J. (1993). Frostbite-induced changes in bones and joints. *Duodecim; Laaketieteellinen Aikakauskirja*, *109*(1), 60–63.

Figueiro, M. G. (2013). An overview of the effects of light on human circadian rhythms: Implications for new light sources and lighting systems design. *Journal of Light & Visual Environment, 37*(2–3), 51–61.

Forsyth County Schools. (2022). *Teaching & learning parent help guide.* Retrieved from www.forsyth.k12.ga.us/Page/46646

Guo, Y., Gasparrini, A., Armstrong, B., Li, S., Tawatsupa, B., Tobias, A., . . . & Williams, G. (2014). Global variation in the effects of ambient temperature on mortality: A systematic evaluation. *Epidemiology, 25*(6), 781.

Hancock, K. J., Shepherd, C. C., Lawrence, D., & Zubrick, S. R. (2013). Student attendance and educational outcomes: Every day counts. *Canberra: Department of Education, Employment and Workplace Relations.* Retrieved from https://www.telethonkids.org.au/globalassets/media/documents/research-topics/student-attendance-and-educational-outcomes-2015.pdf

Harrison, F., Jones, A. P., Bentham, G., van Sluijs, E. M., Cassidy, A., & Griffin, S. J. (2011). The impact of rainfall and school break time policies on physical activity in 9–10 year old British children: A repeated measures study. *International Journal of Behavioral Nutrition and Physical Activity, 8*(1). https://ijbnpa.biomedcentral.com/articles/10.1186/1479-5868-8-47

Hollenhorst, S., & Ewert, A. (1985). *Importance-performance evaluation: A method of discerning successful program components.* American Camping Association Convention. https://files.eric.ed.gov/fulltext/ED264068.pdf

Hughes, A. C., Zak, K., Ernst, J., & Meyer, R. (2017). Exploring the intersection of beliefs toward outdoor play and cold weather among Northeast Minnesota's formal education and non-formal EE communities. *International Journal of Early Childhood Environmental Education, 5*(1), 20–38.

Hyndman, B. (2017). Does bad weather affect student performance in school. *The Conversation.* Retrieved from https://theconversation.com/does-bad-weather-affect-student-performance-in-school-75461

Hyndman, B., & Chancellor, B. (2015). Engaging children in activities beyond the classroom walls: A social – Ecological exploration of Australian primary school children's enjoyment of school play activities. *Journal of Playwork Practice, 2*(2), 117–141.

Hyndman, B., & Zundans-Fraser, L. (2020). Determining public perceptions of a proposed national heat protection policy for Australian schools. *Health Promotion Journal of Australia, 32*(1), 75–83. https://doi.org/10.1002/hpja.327

Iyer, R. N. (2020). *Natural disaster shocks: Does household response impact children's educational achievement.* Georgetown University.

Jacobs, L. E., Hansen, A. Y., Nightingale, C. J., & Lehnard, R. (2019). What is "too cold?" Recess and physical education weather policies in Maine elementary schools. *Maine Policy Review, 28*(1), 49–58.

Kos, M., & Jerman, J. (2013). Provisions for outdoor play and learning in Slovene preschools. *Journal of Adventure Education & Outdoor Learning, 13*(3), 189–205.

Li, Y., Song, Y., Cho, D., & Han, Z. (2019). Zonal classification of microclimates and their relationship with landscape design parameters in an urban park. *Landscape and Ecological Engineering, 15*(3), 265–276.

Little, H., & Wyver, S. (2008). Outdoor play: Does avoiding the risks reduce the benefits? *Australasian Journal of Early Childhood, 33*(2), 33–40.

Marcotte, D. E., & Hemelt, S. W. (2008). Unscheduled school closings and student performance. *Education Finance and Policy*, *3*(3), 316–338.

Markel, H., Lipman, H. B., Navarro, J. A., Sloan, A., Michalsen, J. R., Stern, A. M., & Cetron, M. S. (2007). Nonpharmaceutical interventions implemented by US cities during the 1918–1919 influenza pandemic. *JAMA*, *298*(6), 644–654.

Matus, A. (1988). Microtubule-associated proteins: Their potential role in determining neuronal morphology. *Annual Review of Neuroscience*, *11*(1), 29–44.

McGowan, M, Cox, L., Zhou, N., & Davidson, H. (2019). NSW fires: Almost 600 schools closed today amid catastrophic bushfire conditions. *The Guardian*. Retrieved from www.theguardian.com/australia-news/2019/nov/11/nsw-fires-premier-declares-state-of-emergency-amid-most-devastating-bushfires-ever-seen

Meddows, D. (2015). NSW Snowstorm: Road closures, school closures, flooding alerts. *The Daily Telegraph*. Retrieved from www.dailytelegraph.com.au/news/nsw-snowstorm-road-closures-school-closures-flooding-alerts/news-story/8486e6b51f6833af805decd35f4d1deb

Merriam-Webster. (2014). *Definition of cold*. Retrieved from https://www.merriam-webster.com/dictionary/cold

Miller, R. K., & Hui, I. (2022). Impact of short school closures (1–5 days) on overall academic performance of schools in California. *Scientific Reports*, *12*(1), 1–13.

Mitra, R., & Faulkner, G. (2012). There's no such thing as bad weather, just the wrong clothing: Climate, weather and active school transportation in Toronto, Canada. *Canadian Journal of Public Health*, *103*(3), S35-S41.

Mudavanhu, C. (2014). The impact of flood disasters on child education in Muzarabani District, Zimbabwe. *Jàmbá: Journal of Disaster Risk Studies*, *6*(1), 8.

National Oceanographic and Atmospheric Administration (NOAA): US Department of Commerce. (2013). *Storm prediction center*. Retrieved from www.spc.noaa.gov/faq/

Näyhä, S. (2005). Environmental temperature and mortality. *International Journal of Circumpolar Health*, *64*(5), 451–458.

Olgyay, V. (2016). *Design with climate: Bioclimatic approach to architectural regionalism-new and expanded edition*. Princeton university press.

Oliver, M., Badland, H., Mavoa, S., Witten, K., Kearns, R., Ellaway, A., ... & Schluter, P. J. (2014). Environmental and socio-demographic associates of children's active transport to school: a cross-sectional investigation from the URBAN Study. *International Journal of Behavioral Nutrition and Physical Activity*, *11*(1), 1–12.

Parvin, G. A., Takashino, N., Islam, M. S., Rahman, M. H., Abedin, M. A., & Ahsan, R. (2022). Disaster-induced damage to primary schools and subsequent knowledge gain: Case study of the Cyclone Aila-Affected community in Bangladesh. *International Journal of Disaster Risk Reduction*, *72*, 102838.

Pasanen, T. P., Tyrväinen, L., & Korpela, K. M. (2014). The relationship between perceived health and physical activity indoors, outdoors in built environments, and outdoors in nature. *Applied psychology: Health and Well-being*, *6*(3), 324–346.

Perpitch, N. (2016). Schools closed, fire crews on standby with catastrophic conditions forecast. *Australian Broadcasting Corporation*. Retrieved from www.abc.net.au/news/2016-11-15/catastrophic-fire-risk-closes-wa-schools/8025074

Pressman, N. (Ed.). (1985). *Reshaping winter cities: Concepts, strategies and trends*. University of Waterloo Press.

Pressman, N., & Mänty, J. (Eds.). (1988). *Cities designed for winter*. Department of Architecture, Tampere University of Technology.

Rasi, H., Kuivila, H., Pölkki, T., Bloigu, R., Rintamäki, H., & Tourula, M. (2017). A descriptive quantitative study of 7-and 8-year-old children's outdoor recreation, cold exposure and symptoms in winter in Northern Finland. *International Journal of Circumpolar Health, 76*(1), 1298883.

Reznik, M., Wylie-Rosett, J., Kim, M., & Ozuah, P. O. (2015). A classroom-based physical activity intervention for urban kindergarten and first-grade students: A feasibility study. *Childhood Obesity, 11*(3), 314–324.

Rothman, L., Macpherson, A. K., Ross, T., & Buliung, R. N. (2018). The decline in active school transportation (AST): A systematic review of the factors related to AST and changes in school transport over time in North America. *Preventive Medicine, 111*, 314–322.

Schurer, S., Nutton, G., Mckenzie, J., Su, J. Y., & Silburn, S. (2018). Preschool participation, school attendance and academic achievement. In *Early pathways to school learning: Lessons from the NT data linkage study* (pp. 111–128). Menzies School of Health Research.

Sievanen, T., & Neuvonen, M. (2011). Recreational use of nature 2010. *Working Papers of the Finnish Forest Research Institute*. Retrieved from https://jukuri.luke.fi/handle/10024/536119

Spencer, N., Polachek, S., & Strobl, E. (2016). How do hurricanes impact scholastic achievement? A Caribbean perspective. *Natural Hazards, 84*(2), 1437–1462.

Stout, M., Collins, D., Stadler, S. L., Soans, R., Sanborn, E., & Summers, R. J. (2018). "Celebrated, not just endured:" Rethinking winter cities. *Geography Compass, 12*(8), e12379.

Tandon, P. S., Zhou, C., Sallis, J. F., Cain, K. L., Frank, L. D., & Saelens, B. E. (2012). Home environment relationships with children's physical activity, sedentary time, and screen time by socioeconomic status. *International Journal of Behavioral Nutrition and Physical Activity, 9*(1), 1–9.

Tillmann, S., Tobin, D., Avison, W., & Gilliland, J. (2018). Mental health benefits of interactions with nature in children and teenagers: A systematic review. *Journal of Epidemiology and Community Health, 72*(10), 958–966.

Turrisi, T. B., Bittel, K. M., West, A. B., Hojjatinia, S., Hojjatinia, S., Mama, S. K., . . . & Conroy, D. E. (2021). Seasons, weather, and device-measured movement behaviors: A scoping review from 2006 to 2020. *International Journal of Behavioral Nutrition and Physical Activity, 18*(1), 1–26.

United Nations International Strategy for Disaster Reduction [UNISDR], Hyogo Framework for Action. (2005/2015). *Building the resilience of nations and communities to disasters*. United Nations.

Ward, M. E., Shelley, K., Kaase, K., & Pane, J. F. (2008). Hurricane Katrina: A longitudinal study of the achievement and behavior of displaced students. *Journal of Education for Students Placed at Risk, 13*(2–3), 297–317.

Watchman, M., Demers, C. M., & Potvin, A. (2020). Biophilic school architecture in cold climates. *Indoor and Built Environment, 30*(5), 585–605.

Wong, K. K., Shi, J., Gao, H., Zheteyeva, Y. A., Lane, K., Copeland, D., . . . & Uzicanin, A. (2014). Why is school closed today? Unplanned K-12 school closures in the United States, 2011–2013. *PLoS One, 9*(12), e113755.

World Health Organisation (WHO). (2006). Nonpharmaceutical interventions for pandemic influenza, national and community measures. *Emerging Infectious Diseases, 12*(1), 88.

Wu, J. T., Cowling, B. J., Lau, E. H., Ip, D. K., Ho, L. M., Tsang, T., . . . & Riley, S. (2010). School closure and mitigation of pandemic (H1N1) 2009, Hong Kong. *Emerging Infectious Diseases, 16*(3), 538.

Vardoulakis, S., Dear, K., Hajat, S., Heaviside, C., Eggen, B., & McMichael, A. J. (2014). Comparative assessment of the effects of climate change on heat-and cold-related mortality in the United Kingdom and Australia. *Environmental Health Perspectives, 122*(12), 1285–1292.

Xu, Z., Etzel, R. A., Su, H., Huang, C., Guo, Y., & Tong, S. (2012). Impact of ambient temperature on children's health: A systematic review. *Environmental Research, 117*, 120–131.

Xu, Z., Hu, W., Su, H., Turner, L. R., Ye, X., Wang, J., & Tong, S. (2014). Extreme temperatures and pediatric emergency department admissions. *Journal Epidemiol Community Health, 68*(4), 304–311.

Zubrick, S. (2014). School attendance: Equities and inequities in growth trajectories of academic performance. *Australian Council for Educational Research (ACER): Research Conference.* Retrieved from https://research.acer.edu.au/cgi/viewcontent.cgi?referer=&httpsredir=1&article=1221&context=research_conference

5 Public Perceptions of Weather-Protection Strategies for Schools

Brendon Hyndman

With the increases expected in more high-intensity, frequent extreme weather events, scholars report on the importance of ensuring that more preventive work is undertaken within communities to define and solve weather problems and to promote more widespread change (Rudel, 2019). To date, many of the responses that are undertaken to protect communities from extreme weather are reactive in nature, with considerations of what to do if communities are exposed to extreme weather, and recovery focuses, rather than preventive initiatives (Giordono et al., 2020). There are many considerations when it comes to weather protection for our local communities, and one of the big debates is related to broader accountability versus alignment to contextual conditions (Giordono et al., 2020). Other challenges in implementing protective weather policies within communities include institutional capacities for implementation and sustainability initiatives (Mullin & Rubado, 2017). Yet many policy scholars acknowledge that the key to implementing any community policies is to build upon a "window of opportunity" when extreme weather events occur, which is more likely to lead to consensus and support for policy change (Crow et al., 2018).

There are many stakeholders across communities that develop concerns about a multitude of factors that can impact on the livelihoods of citizens, and this results in widespread discussions, policy and changed proposals with mixed results (Giordono et al., 2020). Unfortunately, it is the personal harms that are identified from various events that result in the most urgent changes and support for the modification of policies related to adverse weather extremes (Zanocco et al., 2018). It has been recognised that drawing upon the collective beliefs of a population can play a vital role in being able to positively impact on policy outcomes and discourses (McAdam, 2017). Geordono and colleagues (2020) suggest that drawing upon dialogue relating to extreme weather events plays a significant role in policy change, yet is one of multiple considerations. It is also suggested that the lowest amount of policy initiatives relating to extreme weather events included policies to protect from risks and resources dedicated to community capacity building.

To be able to effectively introduce policies, mobilising the public is crucial to ensure there is sufficient support for the implementation of policies. Although the majority of policies that are introduced into society come about from linear interaction between both political decision makers and discipline leaders (Huang et al., 2016), there are strong benefits to initially outlining policy considerations into the public area. For instance, if there is strong backing for the components of a policy, this can help gather momentum, support, advocacy, fast-track information to the public and determine any areas of public concern to ensure any policy is accommodating to what the public believes is needed (Huang et al., 2016). This approach to firstly engaging with the public is known as a "bottom-up approach," which can be a more lengthy and drawn-out process in comparison to a fast-paced policy enactment without any broader initial consultation. By firstly gaining broader perceptions that could inform a future policy, this can help provide time for the public to consider the range of scientific issues that could be involved in any future implementation and help facilitate people's "informed citizenry" (Sinatra & Hofer, 2016). Zivin and Shrader (2016, p. 34) state "it's clear that public policy can and must help minimise the damage to children's health caused by climate change."

What Research Has Considered Weather-Protection Policy for Schools?

Despite the research into adverse weather events and local communities, very few scholars have produced research into the considerations of school weather-protection policy. Research has emerged from the United States that explored the implementation of policies to protect school communities from cold weather extremes (Jacobs et al., 2019). The study investigated existing policies, collected surveys/interviews from principals and weather data that uncovered the large inconsistencies in how schools protect students and teachers from adversely cold conditions across the US state of Maine (Jacobs et al., 2019). Large amounts of cancelled recess time due to the weather were also discovered, yet there was little understanding or tracking of this process of cancelling recess due to the weather. The data analysed by the researchers suggested that clearer, more consistent cutoffs for cancelling recess and understanding of weather data needed to be developed. For instance, schools in one side of the state had set a higher-than-optimal minimum-temperature and wind-chill reading, which resulted in children missing excessive amounts of recess time.

The authors found that schoolchildren could be engaging in much more important, unstructured development time during recess if schools simply lowered their recess-cancellation cutoffs by 10 degrees Fahrenheit. There was a differential in the cutoff temperature in which schools cancelled recess time across the state by up to 20 degrees Fahrenheit. This study reinforced the argument towards a more consistent policy message in this particular instance. Jacobs and colleagues (2019) identified an importance of administrators within schools having a better understanding of how many outdoor days students could be missing out on. The authors additionally pointed to how the inconsistent beliefs and intentions of school leaders could drastically impact the outdoor time experienced by school students. Educators were encouraged to have a stronger role in monitoring their cancellation data to develop students' health and provide encouragement towards this important developmental time.

Across many international jurisdictions, sun-protection policies have gained widespread coverage in order to protect the rising occurrence of skin cancers (WHO, 2022). The World Health Organisation (2022) details a range of recommendations that include the wearing of protective clothing, use of sunscreen, avoiding artificial tanning practices, monitoring the UV index and limiting midday sun exposure. For example, within Australia, state and nationwide surveys have shown that strong advocacy for the provision of sun protection has enhanced sun-protection practices with the use of sunglasses, sunscreen and shade via its national "Sunsmart Policy" (Sharplin et al., 2013). Yet more recently Hyndman (2017a, 2017b) reinforced the importance of another major health and learning risk from extreme heat impacts on students and teachers. It was acknowledged that sporting organisations often provide some heat-protection guidelines for the broader population, but there was nothing specific to ensure appropriate heat-protection considerations within many schooling contexts. This was despite wide-ranging impacts on students from heat-related illness from exposure to extreme heat. With students across the world failing miserably to meet global physical-activity recommendations to meet health outcomes, Hyndman (2017a, 2017b) suggested that better protection and supportive considerations for school students' outdoor physical activities is one method that could help encourage improved participation during physical education and recess activities, especially in tropical areas. A similar problem established on the other side of the world related to the problematic policy support to protect students from extreme cold exposure in the United States (Jacobs et al., 2019).

What Should Be Considered in a Weather-Protection Policy?

Given that one of the major concerns of the impact of extreme weather is on schoolchildren's health, which can subsequently have an impact on learning (if health is impaired), it has been acknowledged that a holistic health framework is important to ensure all levels of the school community are activated. For instance, the World Health Organisation's Ottawa Charter (1986) refers to five key action areas: (1) building school policy to promote health (scheduling and resource adaptions to support protection); (2) facilitating supportive environments (displaying information to help support, such as guideline posters); (3) ensuring the community can be empowered with the strategy (gaining community feedback, developing communication methods); (4) ensuring community skills are enhanced in the health area (to help prepare children at home); and (5) having a preventive approach (monitoring the strategy and integrating into class-based learning approaches). A published media article utilising the Ottawa Charter with aligned considerations for weather protection was the facilitator and prompt for public comments, which forms the basis of this chapter. The aim of this chapter was to investigate considerations perceived by the public for future implementation of weather-protection policy for schools via an online public social media forum.

Data Collection and Analyses

After University Human Research Ethics approval was obtained, public considerations relating to the protection of schoolchildren from extreme weather were drawn from publicly available comments on a national-news media article. The media article outlined protection-policy components that should be considered by governments for protecting schools from extreme weather events, which were framed with the five World Health Organisation's Ottawa Charter action areas for health protection. The article coincided with an extreme heat wave event, yet the public voiced a number of consideration relating to protecting school communities from a range of extreme weather. Each of the necessary steps for utilising public data were met and detailed within the ethics documentation. In addition to meeting university guidelines, the data-collection steps involved showcasing that the comments were public in nature, the compliance with the social media platform terms and conditions were for the use of public commentary and that the content within the comments being determined were not sensitive in nature (Townsend & Wallace, 2017). Moreover, these initial steps in meeting the protocol of utilising public data were reinforced by the de-identification of any names from the posts relating to protecting school communities from extreme weather. A total of $N = 612$ comments from the general public were captured relating to extreme weather protection in schools.

The open-ended comments captured during the investigation were analysed via the application of NVivo (version 12) qualitative analysis software to facilitate the identification of key themes (NVivo Qualitative Data Analysis Software, 2015). The analyses of the public comments involved firstly becoming familiar with and immersed in the survey data via a system of reading, highlighting and making notes on the data (Grbich, 2012). Given the holistic considerations required to protect schoolchildren and educators' health in the school communities, a multi-level social–ecological model (Golden & Earp, 2012) was adopted for the varying layers of influence deemed as being important policy considerations by the general public. A final step in the analytical process consisted of a review of the data by applying the "nodes most frequently codes" NVivo function to ensure all common themes were captured.

Social–Ecological Model

Social–ecological models have emerged from public health and psychology disciplines (Wattchow et al., 2016). The social–ecological model is important to be able to determine the broader, external impacting factors on a behaviour, such as the contextual conditions surrounding an individual by examining multiple surrounding dimensions (Bronfenbrenner, 1979). Since the 1970s, many versions of the social–ecological model have been unearthed that help discover the multitude of influences on an individual (Wattchow et al., 2016).

The public responses to the potential of a national weather-protection policy were investigated by applying the social–ecological model, which could then be utilised as the conceptual framework to determine the multiple dimensions of influence on schooling behaviours at the individual, social, physical-environment and policy levels (Wattchow et al., 2016). The individual level emphasises aspects within an individual such as beliefs, expectations, intentions, actions, characteristics and histories. The social level is based around the connected relationships surrounding an individual such as family, friends, peers, teachers, students and other supportive networks (Wattchow et al., 2016). The physical-environment level considers the physical contexts surrounding an individual that can hinder or facilitate certain behaviours (Wattchow et al., 2016). The policy/organisational influences consider aspects such as guidelines, regulations, rules, policies and procedures that influence a behaviour. These are often developed by an organisation. When considering all of these influences on behaviours, powerful insights can be generated to comprehensively consider all angles of influence that can be addressed (Wattchow et al., 2016). In simple terms, this can be described as a "person-contextual fit," which can facilitate the solutions to educational dilemmas of high complexity (e.g., diverse weather impacts on health and learning in schools) (Wattchow et al., 2016). By applying the social–ecological model as the conceptual framework, this ensures the broad influences on extreme weather protection in schools can be fully understood. This also can help with ensuring appropriate school solutions can be developed and unveiled to teachers and students to improve their contextual circumstances (Wattchow et al., 2016).

Social–Ecological Perceptual Insights

The multiple dimensions of the social–ecological model provide a holistic framework to determine the varying public considerations towards weather-protection policy for schools. The NVivo qualitative analysis software was applied to determine the themes, which were then mapped accordingly. Themes were determined according to four dimensions of influence in schools: individual, social, physical environment and policy/organisational.

Individual Levels of Influence

From the analyses, three main individual-level themes emerged from the public perceptions in relation to considering a weather-protection policy; including (1) protection for health, (2) protection for learning and (3) the balance between adaption and support. The public expressed many concerns relating to not sufficiently protecting students from extreme weather and the negative health implications this can result in: "My son had back-to-back PE in the middle of the day on one of the hottest days on record. His first day back after suffering heat-related absent seizures, and the teacher didn't let him take a break." Others reported poor protective school experiences on their health, such as, "My son is fair skinned, he burns on the short walk to school. If he was sent out to play sports on a 40 degree Celsius day, I would be livid!" and "I was a teacher aide supervising students in a tin shed 2pm in the afternoon and I went home with heat stroke. At the end of the day I reported it to the principal, and wasn't asked to work at that school again. It's like suck it up." There were regular comparisons to the workforce and those who are less trained in dealing with extreme weather and temperatures: "Do not forget the young 17-year-old tradesman that died last year due to a blasé attitude to the dangers of excessive heat."

There was debate relating to whether schoolchildren should simply "adapt" to adverse weather extremes during their schooling activities, to resemble the school activities of the past generations or provide increased protection: "It's easy to say get over it but are kids really going to be able to learn?"; "Our ancestors went to school in a room shed on the edge of the desert and survived, so will our children"; and, "All you older people banging on about how you battled through. Look at the statistics. It is hotter now than it was back in your day. Policies need to be made for current conditions and future projections, not the past." The arguments against simply letting children try to cope, adapt and put up with extreme conditions were related to workforce policies that protect employees from adverse conditions and how schools are now much more informed with modern opportunities to optimise learning conditions: "Nobody will argue children deserve optimum learning conditions to learn to their potential, I hope"; "So everyone who usually works in buildings with appropriate heating and cooling . . . you would be fine about turning these off and just opening the windows when there are weather extremes?"; "How can they (students) learn when they are sweltering or shivering?"; "How cruel and ridiculous to expect kids to learn and teachers to teach in that atmosphere"; and, "I think learning can continue, as long as there are modern, supportive considerations." Moreover, others referred to how contingencies may need to be considered for those that do not even make it to school: "I live in Canada and snow days happen each Winter because it's too snowy and icy to get to work/school. It's really unproductive, need strategies to make the time more productive on those days"; and how things are different now than in the past: "Lucky for us, we are in the 21st century with electricity!"

Trends in the analyses appeared towards the public perceiving that there needed to be more accountability for schools to implement protective practices for learning and not rely on their own belief systems to make decisions subjectively: "I want a policy that ensures my little girl who is just starting school, can be a productive learner and be safe." Others were aware of the overlooked nature of how adverse weather extremes can impact on learning: "I think you can see the point – learning in general needs an environment that is protective from weather extremes." There were also many reports of the intersection between schoolchildren's health and learning: "Stale, hot air results in reduced attention, misbehaviour and tiredness"; "Being physically comfortable with child's health supported helps facilitate learning."

Interpersonal (Social) Levels of Influence

The analyses from the public perceptions of the interpersonal influences relating to a weather-protection policy for schools revealed themes such as the dependence of children on adults and a differential in resources between adults and children. There was general support from the public in relation to a weather-protection policy to prevent a differential between school conditions and other workplace conditions, e.g., the protective resources for adults when compared with schoolchildren. The comparisons with workplace conditions for employees were strongly reported: "Bet politicians and bureaucrats in their departmental air-conditioned offices would not remain at work at their desks if they didn't have air conditioning and the temps were soaring to 35 to 40 degrees!" and "No other public servants have to work in weather extremes, and if the government cares about kids learning then they should want the kids to be comfortable."

Additionally, the introduction of a school weather-protection policy was supported due to the public perceiving the children to be dependent on adults within schools for protective provisions: "They're underdeveloped humans, how do you expect them to match full adult capacity with their resilience to weather extremes?" and "Children do suffer more."

Physical-Environment Levels of Influence

The analyses revealed that the physical-environment levels of influence were the most prevalent from the public's perceptions regarding the provision of weather-protection policy for schools. The major themes that emerged included funding constraints, the building designs in schools and the importance of policy benchmarking. It was evident from the public posts that the ability to ensure the provision of protective resources in schools was challenging due to the costs and other competing priorities for funding: "Turn off the smart board laptops . . . I'd much rather my son look at a blackboard with chalk, to save money for weather protection. Problem solved"; "The department does not contribute a cent to weather protection. It is up to the school to fund it"; and "It's time governments started to install solar panels – you would have a warm/cool place to learn and spend time when the weather is extreme . . . you would power the whole school; relieving themselves of power bills after about 5–6 years." Similar frustrations were expressed in the prioritisation of funding: "Schools need to put the duty of care to the children first, before paying out for non-essential things like smart boards. You can teach without a smart board, but a teacher that has fainted, can't teach." Differentials were reported between the protective provisions within staff offices within schools and the students' classrooms: "Our small school had to foot the entire power bills without any extra allocations, that's what stopped the protection. Rest assured, the offices and principal have it. I feel for the classroom teachers." There were also suggestions to be fully holistic with investments with school weather protection with links to health services, emergency responses, disaster budgets and other services.

There were also differentials reported with the type of school in which the students were attending. For instance, it was reported in the public posts that "half the classrooms in public schools head no air conditioning and in some parts of the city, it is just 30 percent"; "It's more likely to be underfunded public schools with out of date infrastructure, which have the most problems." Drastic comparisons were also made with both government offices having protective comforts and even prison systems having widespread heating and cooling protections, compared to public schools.

Other members of the public reported concerns with the building designs in their schools: "It's made even worse by the fact that most schools are brick and cement ovens with very little air flow. We really need to invest in building schools that are engineered to suit our climate so that we don't have to rely so much on technology"; "The insulation is a hindrance, trapping the heat in. Half the issue is most schools are so old, no thought was taken to the building designs for weather protection or air flow"; and "I can't believe there are classrooms without adequate cooling and heating, that is unacceptable. I think there needs to be an investigation by journalists and the government needs to step in." Frustration was evident from a number of members of the public in their posts: "Why is it so difficult in this modern age to install protective equipment in schools for adverse weather such as ceiling fans, extractor vents, evaporative fooling systems and other technologies to improve working spaces? I cannot believe there is still a debate about whether to provide supportive classrooms"; and "There needs to be compulsory shading for the playgrounds! Our schools is pleading to our local member to help us raise enough money for shading. It should be automatic, not a luxury our council struggles to raise money for!" The benchmarking of other jurisdictions were suggested as important to be looked at: "The northern hemisphere has really cold temperatures, sometimes ice and snow. When schools are built there, governments factor in the costs of protective systems, not to do so, is against the law"; and "How ridiculous (not prioritising weather protection in schools) – how do you think progressive places like Hong Kong, Singapore and Dubai cope?" References were made to European policies from decades ago that let schoolchildren go home when the temperatures reached 25–30 degrees Celsius. There was also reference to how there is policy in some parts of the world to prevent the dangers by simply not letting a child attend school: "More danger in simply leaving your house"; how Europe, the United States and Canada have "cold-weather/extreme-weather policies, yet other jurisdictions do not" and how in the past, there were policies designed "to send kids home early if the temperature exceeded a certain threshold."

Policy/Organisational Levels of Influence

The public perceptions revealed sporadic support and criticism if weather-protection provisions were solely left to schools, rather than having a broader expectation and policy guidelines. Some of the public referred to the importance of the "Principal's need to be trusted to make decisions that are in the best interests of their students" and to "prevent excess regulations in schools," yet others referred to the difficulties of inconsistent provisions from school leadership, such as how resources are used to protect students in schools: "it is unclear whether to wear a hat, hold an umbrella, play in the middle of the day in the sun, utilise libraries or other areas that are protected from extreme weather during lunch time activities." For instance, in one school the uniform expectations were deemed to be unhelpful on an excessively hot day: "the heads of school (at the assembly) were trying to discipline kids for having their shirts untucked, their neck ties and collars unbuttoned"; and how some schools were too focused on the provision of hats: "the heat is worse now than 10 years ago, hats only do so much." It was reported that when there was the provision of caps in some schools, the quality needed to be addressed: "the dodge caps aren't great for sun protection!" There was agreement that flexible scheduling was important to ensure that the most at-risk activities to extreme weather could be buffered: "I am concerned at the number of high schools, who make kids undertake physical education when the weather is at its worst, there is no flexibility with the timetabling"; and "change the sporting calendar to reflect the change in seasons and sun exposure."

Situating the Findings

With widespread expectation that there will be increases in the occurrence of adverse weather events (Giordono et al., 2020), it is important to investigate public perceptions relating to the implementation of policy to protect our school communities (Huang & Feeney, 2016). Although developing broader weather-protection policies to make schools more accountable is important, there can still be some challenges in ensuring that institutional capacity to implement initiatives is addressed (Mullin & Rubado, 2017). As scholars note that policy implementation is most successful when there is alignment with "windows of opportunity" that arise from extreme weather events (Crow et al., 2018), the global patterns of weather extremes continue to accumulate, which presents an important time to protect some of our most vulnerable members of our communities: schoolchildren. The present chapter fills a void in the literature by showcasing insights and considerations via public perceptions into the implementation of weather-protection policy. By underpinning the chapter with a social–ecological model framework, it has the potential to holistically capture multiple angles of insights for future consideration and implementation for education systems.

It was revealed through the data analyses that the public's perceptions had appropriate alignment with each of the social–ecological-model levels of influence. The broad themes that emerged from the public perceptions indicated that there was overall support for the implementation of a broader, consistent policy for weather protection in schools due to the potential negative implications from weather extremes on health and learning, alongside perceived lower support compared with adult workplaces. There was also support evident for weather-protection policy to make schools more accountable, informed, improve school design/uniform expectations and to ensure weather protection had greater prioritisation across educational contexts. Despite the perceived potential for weather-protection policy across schools, there were a number of queries raised from the public relating to whether such policy would prevent the development of childhood resilience and adaption (e.g., previous generations survived). These public insights have the potential to guide future policy implementation in ensuring the multiple levels of influence on a schooling system are considered.

The detrimental intrapersonal influences from being exposed to heat waves have been commonly established in the literature: including dehydration, heat stress, heat stroke, hospitalisation increases and even cases of mortality (Zivin & Shrader, 2016; Hyndman & Zundans-Fraser, 2021), and these concerns resulted in many public posts to have more established policy in place to protect students and teachers (e.g., hydration support, classroom climate control, scheduling of activities). Yet with a growing "over-protection" culture emerging across educational contexts, protecting students' health and learning actually generated debate in many of the parents. It was clear that a number of the public posts were from those from earlier generations that did not have access to the modern technologies and advanced insights of the modern age, and that was the contextual arrangement they were used to in school. The debate raises considerations for future policy provision to build awareness of what "level of risk" is healthy for schoolchildren. There have been growing reports of helicopter parenting and cotton wool kids (Hyndman & Telford, 2015) being harmful in preventing children being exposed to the many variables in their play environments, and children overcoming small levels of risk that they can control has been deemed healthy for their learning trajectories and self-efficacy (Brussoni et al., 2015). Yet it is also acknowledged in the literature that children are less able to self-regulate and make positive health decisions relating to extreme heat influences. It should be acknowledged that calculating whether to jump off a rock, climb a structure or leap across monkey bars is quite different to being exposed to extreme temperatures on the body's physiological systems, and some children can be unaware of the signs of dehydration (Somboonwong et al., 2012). In relation to the development of and compliance with weather-related policies, recent research out of Arizona, USA suggests an importance of "heat acclimatization" for college sports athletes (e.g., football) (Kerr et al., 2019). Like other international jurisdictions, there appears to be a gap between education–school-context specific guidelines, compared to general sporting advice for athletes (Hyndman, 2017a, 2017b). Yet acclimatisation-guideline considerations are an area for consideration in climates in which there will be little respite from extreme heat.

Some of the parents referred to international policies of the past that allowed students to not attend school when temperatures reached a certain threshold, yet others reported how detrimental this would be to parents' employment. There is a growing push to use modern advancements to ensure school students are more protected through a range of supportive considerations (e.g., timetabling, hydration access, knowledge development, infrastructure) to ensure children do not need to be prevented from engaging in outdoor activities (Hyndman & Zundans-Fraser, 2021). The lack of consistency that emerged from the various jurisdictions in which the public resided reinforced Jacobs and colleagues' (2019) findings of how unhelpful it can be to leave policy decisions relating to extreme weather to an individual school's determination. Jacobs et al. (2019) also discovered how there could be an excess of unnecessary cancelling of school-recess time, depending on what temperature was determined as being the specific "cut-off." With schoolchildren having the opportunity to engage in over 4,000 recess periods during their schooling in some jurisdictions or having almost no recess time in others (Hyndman, 2017a, 2017b), ensuring that physical activities can continue to be engaged with (and/or better supported) will be important for children's development. Low levels of enjoyment have also been self-reported by elementary school children for playing during hot or cold conditions, so this provides emphasis on doing more to support children's play according to the weather (Hyndman & Chancellor, 2015). Continued research is warranted into the types and levels of risk that schoolchildren are exposed to, and to establish improved public understanding of a spectrum or scale of risks that are appropriate and not appropriate for exposure in schools.

There was less prevalence of themes from the public in relation to social levels of influence, and one of the reasons could be that weather impacts are often mostly seen through the lens of being part of the "environment"; the study was focused on people's individual perceptions and it related to protective policy. Carter (2017) details that social influences within school contexts are challenging to make predictions or gather clear insights on. Yet one clear social influence that emerged in the study was how policy and procedures seem to be clearer in the general workforce for adults. There has been greater attention of research into climate impacts on the workforce, such as extreme heat having negative influences on workplace productivity (Zander et al., 2015). Many of the public posts pointed to the differentials between children in school and adults in the workplace, and it was clear there was frustration that schools may not be guided to the same levels of accountability and performance in relation to adverse weather. It was outlined that within schools there can be a differential in cooling/heating support between staff offices and classrooms and in other professions compared with schools. The lack of public funding was seen as a major contributor to the absence of weather-protection support mentioned by the public in the schooling sector. Xu and colleagues (2012) mention that children are categorised as a vulnerable group, and just like in the workforce, there is also a need for children to be productive with their learning and development. With adults regularly being the gatekeepers to funding considerations within schools, an important factor to develop children's health is for school leaders to gain insight from children's voices when allocating funds to promote their health (Honkanen et al., 2018). By addressing the insights of schoolchildren, this reduces the difference between what adults think children want and need compared to what is reality (Hyndman, 2016).

Similar to findings identified by Chancellor (2013) and Hyndman and Chancellor (2017), a key concern perceived by the public was the lack of updates to modern facilities and improved focuses on the outdoor contexts beyond classroom walls, especially within public schools. More comprehensive audits are required to identify the appropriateness of weather-protection provisions across schooling systems (see Chapter 6). Consistent debate on whether air-conditioning and heating systems should be included within schools was a major theme from the public posts. Although the heating and cooling effects on schoolchildren's health and development were well recognised, there were concerns relating to the expenses of such provisions. There were suggestions that money could be saved for schools to enhance weather-protection practices by improving insulation within classes, and providing longer-term solar-electricity provisions. Solar electricity was described as being important with excess electricity usage seen as a major contributor to the global trends with extreme weather. The increased provision of renewable, lower-cost energy solutions could be a major solution to the rollout of heating and cooling systems to protect schoolchildren and for teachers to continue developmental activities during days of adverse weather (Niemelä et al., 2016), and warrants further research. As the development of weather-protection policies in schools is an area of emerging research (Jacobs et al., 2019; Hyndman & Zundans-Fraser, 2021), there need to be improvements in international benchmarking and reporting of school weather-protection policies. The public referred to international jurisdictions that are very successful with their air-conditioning rollouts and international policies from the past. Such continued insights are vital (Altinok et al., 2018) to enhance our population's understanding of additional evidence and considerations, especially with inequalities with policy provisions across different countries and disciplinary sectors being identified as prevalent (Hyndman, 2017a, 2017b; Jacobs et al., 2019; Hyndman & Zundans-Fraser, 2021).

The most dominant policy/organisation-level theme related identified in the study related to the provisions and expectations for school uniforms and the alignment with suitability according to weather extremes. Within Australia, the restrictions of school uniforms on outdoor play, physical activities and physical education have been well documented. The findings align with previous reports that parents and teachers support moves away from traditional, restrictive uniforms to those that can be more comfortable to engage in outdoor activities (McCarthy et al., 2020; Reidy, 2021). Teachers, schoolchildren and parents have been found to be supportive of physically active-focused clothes which often have more breathable, flexible materials and are more comfortable (McCarthy et al., 2020) during activities. Modifying uniforms according to weather variables was also included as part of a multistep heat-protection policy proposed by Hyndman and Zundans-Fraser (2021) relating to increasing schoolchildren's comfort when engaging in activities during heat waves. The proposed policy was based upon merging guidelines from different sectors and disciplines into a package aligned to the education sector.

This chapter contributes unique public and scholarly insights into the under-researched area of weather-protection policy provision within schools, conceptually framed by the social–ecological model. A variety of supportive themes were identified from the public relating to the provision of more widespread weather-protection policy provisions that included protecting schoolchildren (and teachers) from the negative implications from weather extremes on health and learning, alongside perceived lower support compared to other workplaces. There was also support evident for weather-protection policy to make schools more accountable, informed, improve school design/uniform expectations and to ensure weather protection had greater prioritisation across educational contexts. Despite the perceived potential for weather-protection policy across schools, there were a number of queries raised from the public relating to whether such policy would prevent the development of childhood resilience and adaption (e.g., previous generations survived). Overall, the chapter's insights suggest there is merit for pursuing more comprehensive and broader consideration of weather-protection policy to support the school system, teachers and schoolchildren.

References

Altinok, N., Angrist, N., & Patrinos, H. A. (2018). Global data set on education quality (1965–2015). *World Bank Policy Research Working Paper 8314*. Retrieved from https://papers.ssrn.com/sol3/papers.cfm?abstract_id=3256551

Bronfenbrenner, U. (1979). *The ecology of human development: Experiments by nature and design*. Harvard university press.

Brussoni, M., Gibbons, R., Gray, C., Ishikawa, T., Sandseter, E. B. H., Bienenstock, A., . . . & Tremblay, M. S. (2015). What is the relationship between risky outdoor play and health in children? A systematic review. *International Journal of Environmental Research and Public Health, 12*(6), 6423–6454.

Carter, I. (2017). *Human behavior in the social environment: A social systems approach*. Routledge.

Crow, D. A., Albright, E. A., Ely, T., Koebele, E., & Lawhon, L. (2018). Do disasters lead to learning? Financial policy change in local government. *Review of Policy Research, 35*(4), 564–589.

Giordono, L., Boudet, H., & Gard-Murray, A. (2020). Local adaptation policy responses to extreme weather events. *Policy Sciences, 53*(4), 609–636.

Golden, S. D., & Earp, J. A. L. (2012). Social ecological approaches to individuals and their contexts: Twenty years of health education & behavior health promotion interventions. *Health Education & Behavior, 39*(3), 364–372.

Grbich, C. (2012). *Qualitative data analysis: An introduction*. Sage.

Honkanen, K., Poikolainen, J., & Karlsson, L. (2018). Children and young people as co-researchers – researching subjective well-being in residential area with visual and verbal methods. *Children's Geographies, 16*(2), 184–195.

Huang, W. L., & Feeney, M. K. (2016). Citizen participation in local government decision making: The role of manager motivation. *Review of Public Personnel Administration, 36*(2), 188–209.

Chancellor, B. (2013). Primary school playgrounds: Features and management in Victoria, Australia. *International Journal of Play, 2*(2), 63–75.

Hyndman, B. (Ed.). (2017a). *Contemporary school playground strategies for healthy students*. Springer.

Hyndman, B. (2017b). 'Heat-Smart' schools during physical education (PE) activities: Developing a policy to protect students from extreme heat. *Learning Communities Journal: International Journal of Learning in Social Contexts (Special Edition), 21*, 56–72.

Hyndman, B., & Chancellor, B. (2015). Engaging children in activities beyond the classroom walls: A social – ecological exploration of Australian primary school children's enjoyment of school play activities. *Journal of Playwork Practice, 2*(2), 117–141.

Hyndman, B., & Chancellor, B. (2017). Are secondary school environments conducive for active play opportunities? An objective assessment across Australian secondary school playgrounds. *International Journal of Play*, *6*(1), 40–52.

Hyndman, B., & Zundans-Fraser, L. (2021). Determining public perceptions of a proposed national heat protection policy for Australian schools. *Health Promotion Journal of Australia*, *32*(1), 75–83.

Hyndman, B. P. (2016). A qualitative investigation of Australian youth perceptions to enhance school physical activity: The Environmental Perceptions Investigation of Children's Physical Activity (EPIC-PA) study. *Journal of Physical Activity & Health*, *13*(5), 543–550.

Hyndman, B. P., & Telford, A. (2015). Should educators be'wrapping school playgrounds in cotton wool'to encourage physical activity? Exploring primary and secondary students' voices from the school playground. *Australian Journal of Teacher Education (Online)*, *40*(6), 60–84.

Jacobs, L. E., Hansen, A. Y., Nightingale, C. J., & Lehnard, R. (2019). What is "too cold?" Recess and physical education weather policies in Maine elementary schools. *Maine Policy Review*, *28*(1), 49–58.

Kerr, Z. Y., Scarneo-Miller, S. E., Yeargin, S. W., Grundstein, A. J., Casa, D. J., Pryor, R. R., & Register-Mihalik, J. K. (2019). Exertional heat-stroke preparedness in high school football by region and state mandate presence. *Journal of Athletic Training*, *54*(9), 921–928.

McAdam, D. (2017). Social movement theory and the prospects for climate change activism in the United States. *Annual Review of Political Science*, *20*, 189–208.

McCarthy, N., Hope, K., Sutherland, R., Campbell, E., Hodder, R., Wolfenden, L., & Nathan, N. (2020). Australian primary school principals', teachers', and parents' attitudes and barriers to changing school uniform policies from traditional uniforms to sports uniforms. *Journal of Physical Activity and Health*, *17*(10), 1019–1024.

Mullin, M., & Rubado, M. E. (2017). Local response to water crisis: Explaining variation in usage restrictions during a Texas drought. *Urban Affairs Review*, *53*(4), 752–774.

Niemelä, T., Kosonen, R., & Jokisalo, J. (2016). Cost-optimal energy performance renovation measures of educational buildings in cold climate. *Applied Energy*, *183*, 1005–1020.

NVivo Qualitative Data Analysis Software. (2015). *QSR International Pty Ltd. Version 11*. Melbourne. https://lumivero.com/products/nvivo/

Reidy, J. (2021). Reviewing school uniform through a public health lens: Evidence about the impacts of school uniform on education and health. *Public Health Reviews*, *42*.

Rudel, T. K. (2019). *Shocks, states, and sustainability: The origins of radical environmental reforms*. Oxford University Press.

Sharplin, G., Smith, A., & Roth, F. (2013). The national survey of Australian primary schools' sun protection policy and practices: Evaluating the national SunSmart schools program. *Cancer Council SA: Adelaide*.

Sinatra, G. M., & Hofer, B. K. (2016). Public understanding of science: Policy and educational implications. *Policy Insights from the Behavioral and Brain Sciences*, *3*(2), 245–253.

Somboonwong, J., Sanguanrungsirikul, S., & Pitayanon, C. (2012). Heat illness surveillance in schoolboys participating in physical education class in tropical climate: An analytical prospective descriptive study. *BMJ Open*, *2*(4), e000741.

Townsend, L., & Wallace, C. (2017). The ethics of using social media data in research: A new framework. In *The ethics of online research* (Vol. 2, pp. 189–207). Emerald Publishing Limited.

Wattchow, B., Jeanes, R., Alfrey, L., Brown, T., Cutter-Mackenzie, A., & O'Connor, J. (2016). *Socioecological educator*. Dordrecht: Springer.

World Health Organization. (1986). Ottawa charter for health promotion, 1986 (No. WHO/EURO: 1986-4044-43803-61677). *World Health Organization and Regional Office for Europe*. Retrieved from https://apps.who.int/iris/handle/10665/349652

World Health Organisation. (2022). *Sun protection*. Retrieved from www.who.int/news-room/questions-and-answers/item/radiation-sun-protection?msclkid=e7576940cec811ecac36962b60805c64

Xu, P., Huang, Y. J., Miller, N., Schlegel, N., & Shen, P. (2012). Impacts of climate change on building heating and cooling energy patterns in California. *Energy*, *44*(1), 792–804.

Zander, K., Botzen, W. J. W., Kjellstrom, T., Oppermann, E., & Garnett, S. T. (2015). Heat stress has a substantial economic impact on the Australian workforce. *Nature Climate Change*, *5*, 647–651.

Zanocco, C., Boudet, H., Nilson, R., Satein, H., Whitley, H., & Flora, J. (2018). Place, proximity, and perceived harm: Extreme weather events and views about climate change. *Climatic Change*, *149*(3), 349–365.

Zivin, J. G., & Shrader, J. (2016). Temperature extremes, health, and human capital. *The Future of Children*, pp. 31–50.

6 Building and School-Playground Design to Protect From Weather Extremes

Jennifer Vanos and Sebastian Pfautsch

This chapter provides insight into key knowledge, applications, guidelines and progress surrounding school-environment design on mitigating the impacts of extreme weather, with a focus on weather extremes most related to climate change, including thermal exposures (extreme heat and cold), flooding (hurricanes/cyclones/typhoons, extreme rainfall), severe storms (thunderstorms) and wildfire impacts causing poor air quality. The chapter further emphasises the planning of landscapes according to local climatology using detailed assessment methods and design parameters to reduce extreme heat as well as energy use in school buildings. Such thinking aids in important decisions to protect schoolchildren from weather extremes today and into the future.

Weather Extremes and Schools

All extreme weather events are important and potentially harmful; they can, and do, affect schools and the users of school spaces. Given the connections between precipitation changes (including drought) and air-temperature increases with climate change, this chapter primarily focuses on how school design can help mitigate and adapt to these weather extremes that are predicted to become more rapid, intense and prolonged. Emphasis is placed on the planning of landscapes according to local climatology based on seasonal considerations of air temperature, precipitation, windspeed and direction, and latitude to encourage climate-sensitive design. We consider weather-protective techniques, materials, insulation strategies, "Smart" programs and technologies, shading and/or surfacing structures and natural greening for protecting staff and students from weather extremes. Decisions around building type, shading and orientation, outdoor ground and surfacing types and school-ground equipment and vegetation influence environmental exposures today and in the future.

Making decisions around extreme heat requires properly quantifying "heat" (i.e., combining temperature, humidity, wind and radiation). Extreme heat based on the area's climate may result in potentially cancelled play or impact learning. Moreover, the relative nature of heat affects how design,

DOI: 10.4324/9781003103165-6

adequate resources and education can support cooler, shadier environments, and thus outdoor activity, even on hot days (see Chapter 2). Similarly, the use of localised air-quality information can support decision-making at schools during extreme heat or wildfire events (see Chapter 3), with recent research in this space increasingly focusing on excessive air pollution levels caused by wildfires (Di Virgilio et al., 2021; Holm et al., 2021). These weather-related issues require design-driven solutions for minimising indoor and outdoor pollution exposure, yet little research exists on how to support decisions around traffic- or industry-related exposures, which can be more chronic in nature, depending on location and source. A recent study by Requia et al. (2021) found that of the 186,080 schools assessed across Brazil, 25% were located ≤ 250m of a major roadway. Similarly, nearly 8,000 U.S. public schools lie within 500 feet of highways, truck routes and other roads with significant traffic (Smith-Hopkins, 2017). These examples highlight the need for schools to use numerous bioclimatic-design strategies to establish methods to reduce damage from acute and chronic weather extremes, promote healthy physical activity and enhance the general ability of schools to withstand extremes.

Weather "Smart" School Programs

Globally, various "smart schools" programs exist related to weather extremes and are largely based on the types of protective designs of the school, including outdoor and building design. Moreover, many schools also integrate the notion of environmental extremes and mitigation into their environmental literacy and learning. Thus, "smart schools" can help cope with weather extremes and enhance learning.

"Storm Smart Schools"

The EPA (2017) has created a guide for "*Storm Smart Schools*," which integrates green stormwater infrastructure and designs into plans in a way that helps to meet regulatory compliance and promote environmental literacy through learning. Similarly, "*StormReady Schools*" certifies schools that have completed the necessary training and preparedness for storms in the U.S. Similarly, many countries have storm preparedness guides for schools outlining the steps to take in the face of severe weather, particularly fast-moving and unexpected weather.

According to the US National Weather Service (NWS, 2022), steps to be taken *before* the storm include 1) education for staff and students, 2) action planning (e.g., notifications, shelters, school buses), 3) practice and review and 4) using reputable source of weather information. During the storm, schools are guided to monitor weather conditions closely and act according to action plans. The Federal Emergency Management Agency (FEMA,

2009) states that storms with sufficient windspeeds can cause damage to weak schools; thus, all schools should be designed, constructed and maintained to avoid wind damage. FEMA also states that extra consideration is given to designing and constructing portions of schools within tornado-prone regions.

"Heat Smart Schools"

"*Heat Smart Schools*" support health and educational practices during physical activity outdoors, with proposed policies needed to protect students from extreme heat depending on location (see Hyndman, 2017). *Five key action areas* holistically work together to create heat-smart schools to protect and ensure child well-being. The five action areas were based upon the consolidation of policies, practices, research and guidelines for schools from a diverse range of organisations concerning heat protection:

1. School policy (flexible scheduling of activities, uniform/clothing during heat extremes)
2. Heat-supportive environments (shade, hydration, heat-protection guidelines)
3. Heat-protection community action (communication and preparation; feedback from the community on strategies)
4. Heat-protection community skills (resources; monitoring hydration; nutritional considerations)
5. Heat-illness prevention (monitoring; aligning with curricular content).

Other ideas for heat preparedness and "HeatReady" schools (Shortridge et al., 2022) that also encompass these five actions have also been introduced in the United States (see Chapter 2 and Chapter 7).

"Sun Smart Schools"

Sun Smart Schools were created by the Cancer Council in Australia, and are common in Australia, particularly for younger children at child centres and primary schools. Schools and centres can receive "SunSmart" status and recognition by reaching the following targets (Cancer Council Australia, 2022):

- A sun-protection policy that meets minimum standards relating to sun-protective behaviours, environmental design and curriculum
- A plan to reschedule/minimise outdoor activities in direct sun during peak UV periods of the year
- Ability to teach, model and reinforce positive sun-protection behaviour
- Agreeing to complete regular policy reviews with the relevant state or territory Cancer Council to ensure their policy meets current guidelines and recommendations.

The "SunSmart" School Program has been evaluated by Sharplin et al. (2013). Other countries may have similar initiatives, yet Australia has led the way in protecting children from excess sun exposure through behaviour and design. Cumberland City in New South Wales built a UV Smart playground (Cumberland City Council, 2022). Other techniques may also focus on ensuring adequate sun in the wintertime to support vitamin D synthesis and warmth, yet provide proper shade in the summertime for UV protection and cooling (e.g., see Kennedy et al., 2020 for example design ideas from Canada). Notably, an important future research area involves assessing how various surface types and colours may increase or decrease UV exposure (i.e., UVB and UVA). As noted previously, while a higher solar reflectivity may decrease surface temperature, the heightened radiation reflected toward users can increase overall heat load (Middel et al., 2020) and thus would increase heat stress to schoolchildren. The wavelengths reflected from a surface differ based on the surface properties, with certain coatings reflecting visibly and near infrared, yet not UVB or UVA (Middel et al., 2021; Schneider et al., 2023). Finding a balance between these considerations depending on location and time of year is an important future research contribution.

"Fire Smart Schools"

In Australia, the most flammable continent, federal and state government agencies provide policy frameworks for schools, kindergartens and early learning centres to become fire smart. The Australian Fire and Emergency Services Authorities Council has developed a special educational program for schools to teach students about the importance of bushfire preparedness (*Li'l Larikkins Bushfire Safety Program*). The state government of Victoria operates a risk register that identifies educational facilities at high risk to grassfires (www.education.vic.gov.au/about/programs/health/Pages/category4.aspx). Facilities listed in Category 4 of this register are required to close during days when fire danger is deemed "Catastrophic." The New South Wales Department of Education also introduced bushfire syllabi for all year-5 and -6 students.

In response to wildfires in 2018 and 2019, the Californian state government has prepared special programs and materials that explain how schools can prepare for these extreme events (www.cde.ca.gov/ls/ep/wildfires.asp). As fire risks increase in Australia, the western USA, Mediterranean countries and elsewhere, it is necessary to develop infrastructure solutions that increase fire resilience of schools and other educational facilities. While evidence-based practices, frameworks and immersive-learning tools have been developed to teach fire safety (e.g., Molan et al., 2022; Pooley et al., 2021), design guidelines for fire-smart school buildings and surrounding landscapes are largely missing. It is important to note that students and staff in schools are not only at risk from direct impacts of bush- or wildfires, but can also suffer from impacts after fire, such as contaminated drinking water. Truly fire-smart schools can focus on providing infrastructure solutions that can also deal with these post-event impacts.

Bioclimatic Design at Schools: A Global Lens

Bioclimatic design is an approach to designing buildings and landscapes based on local climate (Watson, 2013). Such thinking incorporates principles of local plant ecology and soil (e.g., tree and grass species) by climate zone, latitude and solar angle (including variations in short- and long-wave radiation), wind patterns across the seasons (thus using wind roses), precipitation (rain, snow) patterns, structure/object orientation and colour (e.g., building, slide, bench), sky view factor (SVF) and water source (Brown & Gillespie, 1995; Olsen et al., 2019; Pfautsch & Wujeska-Klause, 2021b). These factors are assessed by season and function of the space. For example, designing a school playground in Rome, Italy to be comfortable in the winter or summer will differ and require knowledge of predominant wind direction using wind roses or weather radials (see Figure 6.1) that will consistently influence the thermal comfort at a school. These are available for any city and country. In very cold cities, designers can try to block the wind (thus lowering the "windchill" factor) and allow sun exposure for warmth. Wind-flow patterns also help to understand locations of snow drifting. Conversely, designing for thermal safety and comfort in an equatorial region requires knowledge of the

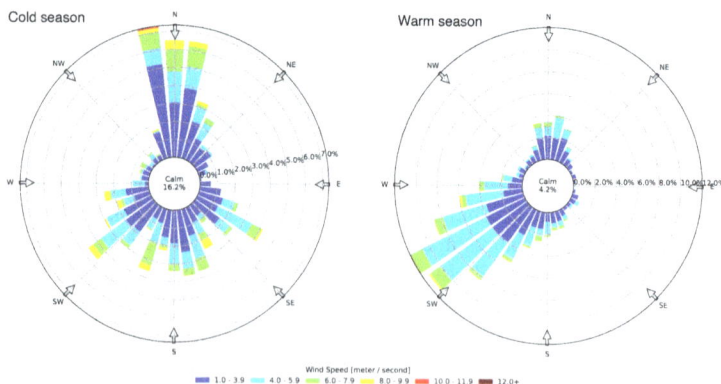

Figure 6.1 Example of wind roses for Rome, Italy in the cold season (left) and warm season (right)

Source: Data accessed via Iowa Environmental Mesonet (IEM, 2022)

Note: The predominant slow and faster winds form from the north in the cold season, while the warm season sees slower winds and prevailing flows of warm air from the southwest.

Building and School-Playground Design 99

patterns of high temperature, sun and humidity and ensuring open ventilation to support cooling evaporation from wind.

Green Infrastructure

School playgrounds and their outdoor areas for play are optimal locations to provide green infrastructure (GI) that can minimise urban flooding and provide ecosystem services, which are often lacking in dense urban areas. According to the EPA (2016), green infrastructure uses vegetation, soils, and other elements and practises to restore some of the natural processes required to manage water and create healthier urban environments. Green infrastructure is a patchwork of natural areas that provides habitat, flood protection, cleaner air, and cleaner water at the city or county scale. At the neighbourhood or site scale, stormwater management systems that mimic nature soak up and store water.

Thus, supporting water infiltration through permeable surfaces (dirt, grass, stones, etc.) minimises the amount of urban flooding (Zellner et al., 2016). An example of a new bioswale garden and play area used in a high-flood risk area in Phoenix, Arizona, USA is shown in Figure 6.2.

Additionally, GI provides nature exposure, which aids in mental health and reduces anxiety (Nutsford et al., 2013) and has been linked to cognitive development in schoolchildren (Dadvand et al., 2015), reduction in emotional stress (Flouri et al., 2014) and improved school performances (Wu et al., 2014). Areas experiencing amplified drought (i.e., lack of precipitation based on climate norms) will increasingly need to consider native GI to support the efficient use

Figure 6.2 Retention area and bioswale for floodwaters in South Phoenix at Paideia Academies School

Note: The bioswale captures runoff from the roof and plays a vital role in the monsoon season when flash flooding can occur. Retaining water within the play space also supports vegetation growth in an otherwise dry region

of available water for vegetation health, utilise native vegetation that is drought tolerant and find novel ways to harvest or retain stormwater runoff and/or air-conditioning condensate for plant uptake (Galindo, 2019). Tree selection should also consider native vegetation planted to withstand windstorms and receive proper maintenance to avoid dangers of falling branches during play.

Additional GI elements, such as vertical green walls, green facades adjacent to playgrounds, and green roofs help school playgrounds and buildings increase their capacity to cope with high temperatures through evapotranspiration and additional stored water onsite (e.g., within bioswales). Trellis structures to support fast-growing vines over playgrounds can have a similar cooling effect and reduce exposure to harmful UV radiation in summer. By reducing air and surface temperatures, radiant heat loads and waste heat from anthropogenic activities will also decline (e.g., air-conditioning; Salamanca et al., 2014). Trees can also help reduce building energy needs for summertime air-conditioning by shading buildings and lowering air temperatures with sufficient tree coverage (Soares et al., 2011). Finally, for cold-season considerations, the use of wind blocks (such as coniferous trees) as a barrier to predominant cold-season winds (see Figure 6.1) to reduce wind chill protects children from the cold and reduces building energy use (Brown & Gillespie, 1995; Vecellio et al., 2022).

Advancements are needed in bioclimatic design applications in areas of heat and sun mitigation, yet the physical and meteorological evidence base at the correct spatial scale (i.e., playground or schoolyard scale) for use by designers is limited (Graça et al., 2022; Kennedy et al., 2020). Research shows that extreme heat, sun and thermal comfort are often given minimal consideration in playground designs (Vecellio et al., 2022). Moreover, many new or updated school playgrounds increasingly lack vegetation and natural surfacing and have artificial surfaces to reduce maintenance costs, increase accessibility and/or provide cushioning for falls (CPSC, 2010). However, like rubber, artificial surfaces radiate substantial amounts of infrared heat toward children and cause tiny surface heat islands. Artificial surfacing does not support important natural exposure, flood control via permeability or vital urban ecosystem services that GI often provides.

Sun Exposure, Surfacing and Extreme Heat

Making school-based cooling-design strategies as effective as possible requires a sound understanding of the sources of direct and indirect heating within the environment. Excessive solar radiation is a significant predictor of sunburn, heat imbalance of the body, thermal discomfort and urban heat storage (Middel & Krayenhoff, 2019; Vanos et al., 2017a, 2017b). Thus, reducing sun exposure protects schoolchildren from both heat exposure and harmful UV radiation. While schools worldwide have implemented programs to protect children from harmful solar-UV exposure (Boldemann et al., 2011; Montague et al., 2001), similar programs that protect schoolchildren from heat are missing. An important priority for UV-protection programs would be to define UV thresholds by location that would change behaviour, similar to heat action thresholds. For example, heat action thresholds for human adaptation, including acclimatisation, can differ by location based on human and environmental factors as well as the relative definition of what constitutes extreme heat (e.g., McElroy et al., 2020; Xu et al., 2016).

While the perception of heat by individuals may differ, the immediate impact of high air temperatures on learning outcomes is well documented (Park et al., 2021; Wargocki et al., 2019), and has been confirmed in field studies (Laurent et al., 2018) and controlled conditions (Seppanen et al., 2006). Overexposure to extreme heat also impacts children's health (Morrison & Sims, 2014) (see Chapter 2). Schoolchildren are susceptible to heat stresses due to their limited capacity for self-assessment and adjustment (Teli et al., 2012), and thus ensuring appropriate outdoor designs are in place for an easy escape from sun and heat is vital.

Given the impacts of heat and UV radiation on children's health are well known, how can it be that design guidelines for heat-resilient, adaptive and thermally safe outdoor schoolyards are missing? The answer to this question may be found in the space between affordability, priorities in design approach, tradition and inexperience. However, exposure to heat extremes is increasing worldwide (Coffel et al., 2017), making it necessary to develop, adopt and implement new strategies that will support safe outdoor play in schools (Pfautsch et al., 2020a). Further concerns about heat in schoolyards and children's health, well-being and learning implications are discussed in Chapter 2.

We argue that strategic planning for high-quality shade and cooler spaces should become a primary focal point considered early in the design process for school playgrounds. If for some reason shade cannot be implemented (or existing shade via trees cannot be incorporated adequately), then design considerations to optimise the thermal performance of school playgrounds are necessary (Lanza al., 2021; Pfautsch & Wujeska-Klause, 2021b; Pfautsch et al., 2020b; Vanos, 2015). Importantly, if existing shade is to be incorporated into school-playground design, shade audits covering both relevant diurnal and seasonal changes in shade-casting patterns will be necessary (see Downs et al. (2022), for novel playground-shade modelling examples). There is currently no universal standardised metric for assessing shade protection and designs in school playgrounds or parks (Downs et al., 2022; Holman et al., 2018; Schneider et al., 2020).

Extreme Surface Temperatures and Thermal Burns

School playgrounds represent complex spaces (i.e., diversity in materials)n, surface), whether within urban or rural areas. Detailed mation on how to reduce risks from hot outdoor surfaces and l burns (or contact skin burns) is often overlooked during the

Figure 6.3 Examples of warning signs used in playgrounds

Sources: Left: WriterInSoul (n.d.), Top Right: Shutterstock (n.d.), Bottom Right: Macie (2019)

design phase (Vanos et al., 2016). In the example of thermal burns, there is a mismatch in the scale of impact (touch-scale) compared to the scale used for design (often much coarser) (Solís et al., 2017). Thermal burns on children from using playground equipment can be found in the media and online articles around the world (e.g., Ferri, 2020; Lefroy, 2022; Riga, 2018; Wilkins et al., 2008) and in peer-reviewed research (e.g., Strong et al., 2007). Evidence shows that unshaded playgrounds can become a health hazard for children in summer (Figure 6.3).

Depending on materials, colours and orientation, unshaded play equipment can reach dangerously high surface temperatures (Figure 6.4) that can burn schoolchildren's skin in just three seconds (Vanos et al., 2016) (see Table 6.1 and ISO13732, 2006). Exposed slides, rubber and artificial turf are the leading culprits of these burns (Ford et al., 2011). Important material characteristics include solar reflectivity, thermal mass, heat capacity and thermal conductance. The intensity of sunlight is also an important consideration based on the time of day and season, and duration of time a surface is exposed to sunlight. Together, these factors will determine surface temperatures (Campbell & Norman, 2012; Vanos et al., 2016) (see Figures 6.4–6.7).

For example, relative to the surface temperatures of the darker, more heat-absorbing mulch and concrete bricks, light-coloured concrete will have a lower surface temperature due to higher solar reflectivity (Figure 6.5, middle), whereas unshaded impact attenuating rubber surfaces (with low

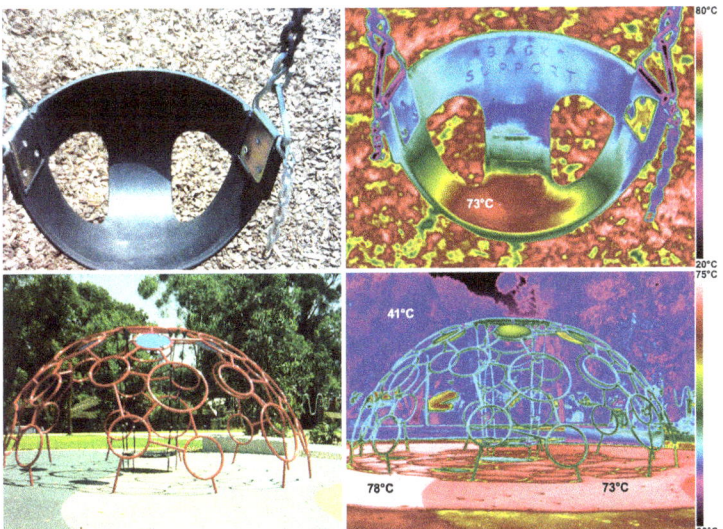

Figure 6.4 Infrared images of playground equipment captured during a heat wave in January 2019 in western Sydney, Australia

Source: Images © S. Pfautsch

Note: Surface temperatures of unshaded playground equipment varied due to thermal properties of materials used. (Top) Black rubber seat of a swing over dark bark mulch with maximum surface temperature of 73°C; the image was taken at 1:58 pm on 18 January 2021 when the air temperature was 40°C, no post-processing for stainless steel objects. (Bottom) Red-coated metal climbing frame over dark (left side) and light (right side) coloured wet-pour rubber; the lower section of the climbing frame is warmer (51°C) compared to the upper section (45°C); the image was taken at 2:53 pm on 18 January 2021 when ambient air temperature was 42°C. Emissivity of infrared images was set to 0.95. All images were taken in sunny conditions.

reflectivity and high heat capacity) can become very hot (Figure 6.5, bottom). Both natural and synthetic materials are used widely across school grounds (Figure 6.5, top). Large sections of unshaded synthetic turf add heat to the microclimate of a school and decrease thermal comfort, especially during midday in summer. The extreme-heat impact of unshaded synthetic turf on human health is well known from sporting fields (EPA, 2016a; Guyer et al., 2021; Hardin & Vanos, 2018), where surface temperatures can reach over 80C, yet are much less understood in school playgrounds. In contrast, natural turf has much lower surface temperatures, regularly around ambient air temperature (lower if watered). The resulting surface and air-cooling effect can be particularly beneficial during hotter summer months. The examples shown in Figure 6.5 of healthy versus dry natural turf (also Figure 6.6, top) illustrate the importance of irrigation to keep plant cover well hydrated in summer.

Figure 6.5 Infrared images of common surface materials used in and around playgrounds across Sydney, Australia

Source: Image © S. Pfautsch.

Note: Marked surface-temperature differences between unshaded natural and artificial materials are shown. (Top) Natural turf next to synthetic turf; the image was taken at 1:30 pm on 16 January 2021 when ambient air temperature was 27°C. (Middle) Pine bark mulch, dark concrete pavers and concrete; the image was taken at 1:36 pm on 16 January 2021 when ambient air temperature was 28°C. (Bottom) Wet-pour rubber in two different colours, white-painted concrete and natural turf that, due to lack of water, had yellowed; the image was taken at 2:53 pm on 4 January 2020 when ambient air temperature was 45°C. Emissivity of infrared images was set to 0.95. All images were taken in sunny conditions.

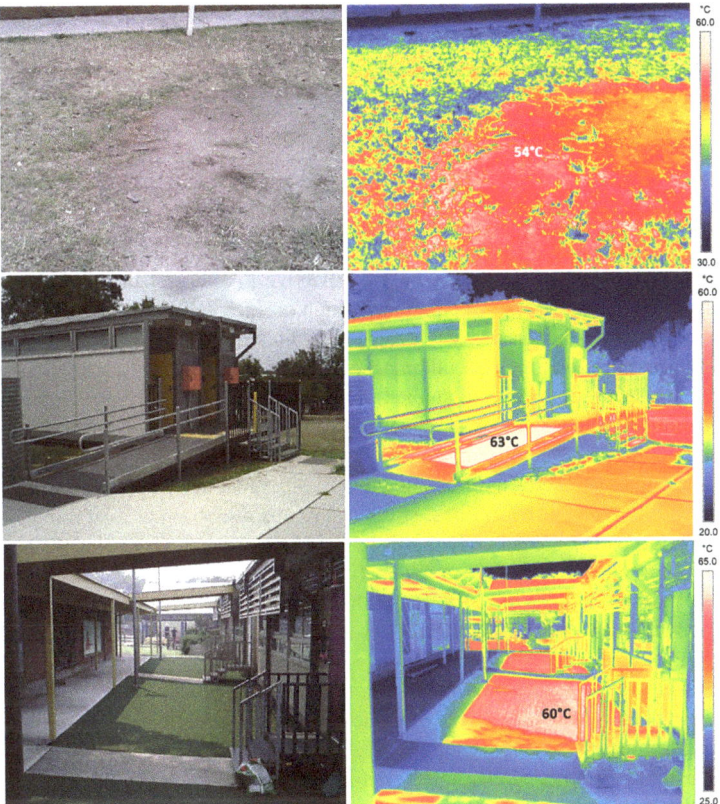

Figure 6.6 Infrared images showing high surface temperatures in school outdoor areas. High surface temperatures lead to high emission of infrared heat, which accelerates heat stress in children

Source: Image © S. Pfautsch

Note: (Top) Unshaded bare soil; a common problem when turf areas are not irrigated in summer as the dark surface has a very low reflectivity and thus absorbs high quantities of solar radiation; the image was taken at 12:40 pm on 14 January 2020 when ambient air temperature was 30°C. (Middle) Unshaded metal access ramp with dark anti-slip coating showing a very high surface temperature above 60°C; the adjacent unshaded light-coloured concrete pathway is 20°C cooler; the image was taken at 12:20 pm on 14 January 2020 when ambient air temperature was 29°C. (Bottom) Unshaded synthetic turf between school buildings; radiant heat from this surface warms the wall of the shaded classroom on the right side, which leads to greater need for air-conditioning inside the classroom; the image was taken at 12:03 pm on 19 December 2019 when ambient air temperature was 39°C. Emissivity of infrared images was set to 0.95. All images were taken in sunny conditions.

Where possible, larger play surfaces like climbing walls, slides and towers should be oriented away from direct summer sun (unlike, e.g., solar panels, which are great providers of shade) (Kennedy et al., 2020; Pfautsch & Wujeska-Klause, 2021b; Vanos et al., 2016). These design considerations will help reduce surface temperatures of the equipment and prevent burns.

Novel Considerations on Solar Reflectivity of School-Playground Surfaces

The observed differences in surface temperatures in Figure 6.5 are largely due to reflectivity of the surface (the percentage of incoming solar radiation reflected, 0–100%). Surfaces with low reflectively (dark asphalt, dark rubber) absorb more radiation, while those with high reflectivity (sand, light concrete) reflect more radiation and stay cooler. While taking advantage of the higher surface reflection to lower building-roof surface temperatures (where humans do not spend time) is well studied (e.g., Baniassadi et al., 2019), there are important trade-offs to consider with respect to heat stress on humans due to the additional reflected radiation.

Numerous studies have detailed that highly reflective surfaces often lead to increases in hyperlocal heat-stress conditions due to *extra* solar radiation imposed on the human body that is reflected from the surface, which is also bright to the eyes. This differential between reflective surfaces and decreased thermal comfort often results in a higher heat load for the users of such surfaces (Ferrari et al., 2019; Middel et al., 2020). According to Turner et al. (2022), increasing surface reflectivity without considering such unintended consequences of reflective impervious surfaces (along with the 3D urban environment and the central role of shade) will not necessarily provide thermal-comfort improvements. Stated simply: "cool surfaces cannot be considered a substitute for other cooling interventions" (Turner et al., 2022). Pfautsch and Wujeska-Klause (2021b) refer to the reduction of human thermal comfort on "cool" reflective surfaces as the *Trojan Effect* to describe the obvious blessings and hidden problems that come with high surface reflectivity that can occur within playgrounds. Classrooms next to reflective materials will also experience heightened solar reflection into the windows and glare.

Overall, careful strategic planning is required when introducing highly reflective surface materials in playgrounds, and we recommend that these types of materials and coatings are not used in unshaded, high-use locations in school grounds.

Sun-exposed surface materials and play equipment can also become heat traps (Choi et al., 2019). Pfautsch and Wujeska-Klause (2021a) found dangerous surface temperatures on unshaded dark-rubber equipment and surfaces (Figure 6.7, top and middle). However, synthetic turf repeatedly demonstrated the highest surface temperatures across a range of environmental conditions (Pfautsch & Wujeska-Klause, 2021a; Figure 6.7, bottom).

Building and School-Playground Design   107

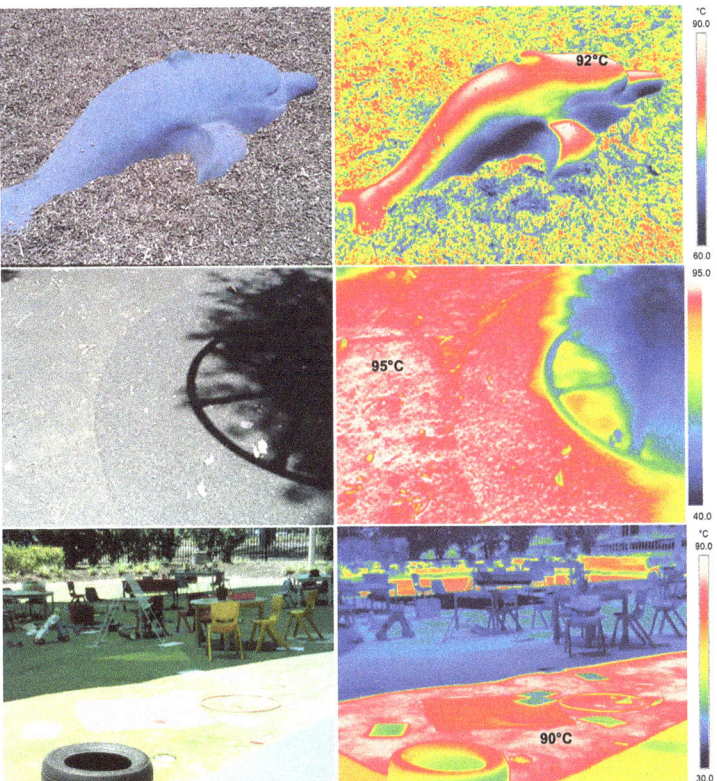

Figure 6.7 Infrared images of extreme surface temperatures observed during heat waves in playgrounds across Sydney, Australia

Source: Image © S. Pfautsch.

Note: (Top) An unshaded, dark blue dolphin made from high-density plastic reaching hazardous surface temperatures during a heat wave; the image was taken at 3:10 pm on 4 January 2020 when ambient air temperature was 45°C. (Middle) Dark unshaded wet-pour rubber surface; this surface was close to the boiling point of water during a hot summer day in the southwest of the Sydney Basin; shade provided by play equipment and a tree reduced surface temperature to 47°C, eliminating the potential contact-burn hazard; the image was taken at 12:45 pm on 24 January 2021 when ambient air temperature was 41°C. (Bottom) Synthetic turf in the outdoor play area of an early learning centre; the material was on average 90°C hot, making the area unplayable; surface temperatures close to 100°C were recorded on this unshaded surface during extreme heat, especially in high-use areas where the black webbing became increasingly visible; the image was taken on 18 January 2018 when ambient air temperature was 39°C. Emissivity of infrared images was set to 0.95. All images were taken in sunny conditions.

Table 6.1 Burn thresholds of skin according to ISO13732 (2006) for selected materials commonly found in outdoor play spaces

Material	Material characteristics	Burn threshold for human skin (°C) at given contact time		
		3 s	5 s	60 sec
Metal	uncoated	60°C	57°C	51°C
Coated metal	Powder: 90 µm	65°C	60°C	51°C
Stone material	Concrete, granite, asphalt	73°C	60°C	56°C
Plastic	Polyamide, acryl, duroplastic	77°C	74°C	60°C
Wood	Bare, low moisture	99°C	93°C	60°C

Source: Note the very short contact times for materials with high-contact thermal conductance like metal and the small change in temperature lowering the risk of thermal burns

The most important physical property to consider in relation to playground design for thermal burn protection is the capacity of a material to conduct heat to the skin. A guideline for the threshold contact time of different materials is provided in the ISO 13732 (2006) (Table 6.1). For example, although the surface temperature of unshaded dark bark mulch (wood) can reach 75–80°C, the low thermal conductance of the material makes contact burns unlikely (see Table 6.1). Play equipment that is made from wood usually displays a lower surface temperature in the sun, and has a lower thermal conductivity with human skin, thus a much lower risk for contact skin burns (ISO13732, 2006). Notably, thickness of the dermis and epidermis is much lower in children compared to adults (Manimegalai, 2015), leading to higher risk of contact skin burns for children and shorter threshold contact times. These injuries occur when the skin epidermis exceeds 44°C and their severeness increases logarithmically with the linear increase in surface temperature (Martin & Falder, 2017).

The United States Consumer Product Safety Commission (CPSC) has assembled a factsheet on Burn Safety Awareness on Playgrounds that warns about the risk of high surface temperatures in playgrounds and their potential to result in contact skin burns (CPSC, 2018). School personnel should be made aware of this fact and be educated about the potential for contact skin burns and how to treat such injuries.

Case Study: Novel Surfacing Considerations for Playgrounds to Reduce Heat Exposure

Systematic tests at Western Sydney University (Pfautsch & Wujeska-Klause, 2021a; Pfautsch et al., 2022) revealed that not only colour, but the type of plastic used to construct wet-pour rubber surfaces, dramatically influences surface temperatures (Figure 6.9). These tests used surface sample tiles made from styrene butadiene rubber (SBR), ethylene propylene diene polymer rubber (EPDM), thermoplastic olefin (TPO), four different types of synthetic turf

Building and School-Playground Design   109

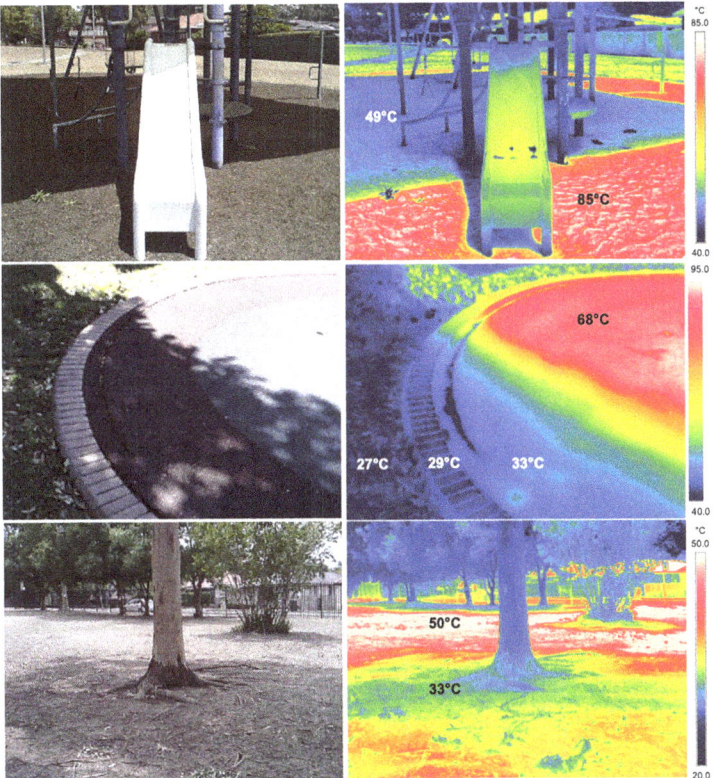

Figure 6.8 Infrared images documenting the surface-cooling effect of shade in playgrounds

Source: Image © S. Pfautsch

Note: (Top) Dark bark mulch commonly reaches very high surface temperatures when unshaded; maximum surface temperatures of unshaded bark mulch depicted here was 85°C; a shade sail cooled this surface material down to 49°C during a heat wave when ambient air temperature was 43°C; the image was taken at 12:00 pm on 4 January 2020. (Middle) Shade cooling on a range of surface materials commonly found in and around playgrounds: natural turf, brick pavers, wet-pour rubber; as depicted, shade reduced surface temperatures of natural turf from 41°C to 27°C, brick pavers from 48°C to 28°C and wet-pour rubber from 68°C to 33°C; the image was taken at 4:25 pm on 6 December 2020 when ambient air temperature was 31°C. (Bottom) Tree shade in schoolyards can reduce surface temperature of bare soil from 50°C to 33°C, thereby markedly reducing the exposure of students to radiant heat; tree shade in these locations also reduces exposure to direct UV and infrared radiation; the image was taken at 12:07 on 14 January 2020 when ambient air temperature was 29°C. Emissivity of infrared images was set to 0.95. All images were taken in sunny conditions.

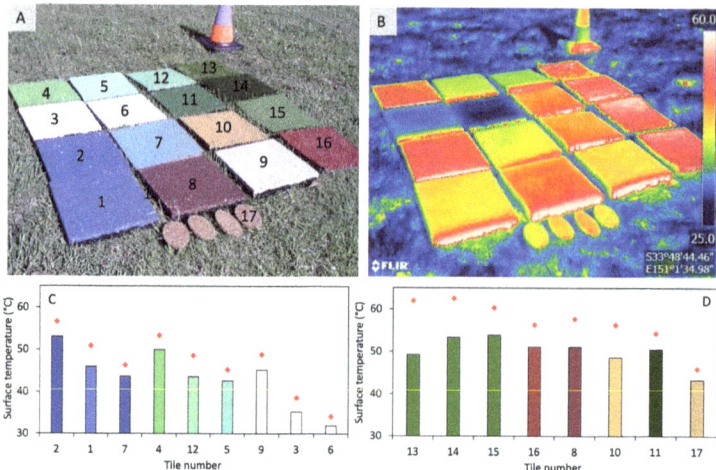

Figure 6.9 (A–D) Differences in surface temperature of common playground materials according to material type and colour

Note: Surfaces were exposed to full sunlight for 45 minutes (14:40–15:25) on 3 April 2019. Average air temperature during measurements was 29°C. Panel A: RBG image of test materials. Panel B: Thermographic image of Panel A with surface temperatures in °C represented by colours; scale is shown in panel; emissivity = 0.95. Panel C: Mean (bar) and maximum (diamond) temperature of rubber surfaces of similar colour (i.e., blue, light green, white). Panel D: Mean (bar) and maximum (diamond) surface temperature of additional materials and colours. Materials used: 1 = dark blue EPDM; 2 = dark blue SBR; 3 = white EPDM; 4 = light green SBR; 5 = aqua TPO; 6 = white TPO; 7 = dark blue TPO; 8 = brown EPDM; 9 = eggshell SBR; 10 = earth yellow SBR; 11 = dark green EPDM; 12 = light green EPDM; 13 = dark green synthetic turf (long pile); 14 = dark green synthetic turf (medium pile); 15 = dark green synthetic turf (short pile); 16 = maroon synthetic turf (short pile); 17 = light brown natural cork. EPDM: ethylene propylene diene polymer rubber. SBR: styrene butadiene rubber. TPO: thermoplastic polyolefin

and cork. Surface temperatures were calculated using more than 67,500 individual measurements across the surface of each sample tile (except for cork, where the number of measurements was lower) (Figure 6.9A, B).

The SBR is a recycling product made from car tires and the plastic granules are black throughout. Granules are coated in large tumblers with paint to achieve the desired surface colour. EPDM is a product made using virgin polymers in different colours. Like EPDM, TPO is made from virgin polymers.

Differences in material and surface characteristics were the origin in surface temperature variation among the three plastic types even when surface colours were relatively similar. The tests revealed that these differences were systematic when comparing dark blue, green and beige/white surface samples (Figure 6.9B, C). Surfaces made from SBR were always the warmest. Those made from EPDM and TPO were less hot, and absolute maximum surface temperatures were always the lowest on TPO surfaces.

The tests provide clear evidence that surface temperatures of wet-pour rubber surfaces can be influenced by strategic selection of colour and plastic granule type (Pfautsch & Wujeska-Klause, 2021a; Pfautsch et al., 2022). Further, samples where darker and lighter colours were mixed had lower surface temperatures compared to those that were made of a single darker colour. Lighter and earth-coloured surfaces also kept cooler compared to darker colours. Cork as an alternative surface material was also tested and found to have a very low surface temperature (Figure 6.9D).

After exposure to full sunlight during a clear summer day for 45 minutes, synthetic turf heated to > 60°C, twice as hot compared to white TPO. Clear differences in surface temperature existed among the four different synthetic-turf products (Figure 6.9). The systematic tests demonstrated that choices of materials and colours will determine temperatures of unshaded surfaces. Pfautsch and Wujeska-Klause (2021a) also reported surface temperatures of unshaded natural turf, bark mulch, concrete, brick pavers and a range of other materials. When constructing new or retrofitting existing school outdoor-play spaces where shade is absent or limited, strategic choices should be made to limit surface temperatures.

Beyond Design: Responsiveness to Climate Extremes by School Communities

Schools are increasingly seen as a vital community resource, one that provides functions beyond child education (FEMA, 2009). They represent hubs for the community that can provide safe spaces during extreme weather; however, this provision only exists if the school grounds, both indoor and out, are able to withstand extremes. Schools may act as storm shelters during severe storms for the community, cooling centres during extreme heat and general outreach and wellness centres for food, water and other resources during times of scarcity. With these roles in mind, general school code requires that schools are designed to provide more protection than other buildings (e.g., power generation during blackouts; withstand floodwaters and high windstorms) (FEMA, 2009); yet to our knowledge, no such requirements exist for heat. As compared to old designs from the early 20th century, new school-building designs are more focused on user thermal comfort, safety, education, lighting and protection against natural hazards (FEMA, 2009). There is still a need to incorporating such ideas into forward-thinking outdoor-design strategies for climate resilience in the face of intensifying and/or more frequent climate extremes.

Recommendations for building school resilience against climate extremes include:

Incorporate multi-hazard design: This process recognises various hazards and how they interact, thus ensuring that there is cross-hazard protection across all seasons that is integrated with outdoor- and building-design demands.

Budget to install and/or maintain vegetative shading: This recommendation ensures that shade is prioritised in funding throughout the building process, rather than being added after surfacing, and equipment only if sufficient funding exists. Maintaining shade trees that are already present can provide safe play and protection of schoolchildren from the health risks associated with extreme heat, and avoid overexposure to harmful UV radiation. Proper shading can also help reduce the costs of replacing equipment that becomes degraded due to UV light while also minimising sunburn, heat and thermal-burn injuries to the skin.

Use climate-sensitive designs: Designing outdoor spaces based on the local climatology will help ensure sustainable and impactful features for dealing with climate extremes. Considerations for such design involve knowledge of predication and temperature patterns across seasons, latitude, native plants species and windspeed and direction (e.g., see Figure 6.1).

Plan for maintenance time and costs: The costs of maintaining high-functioning outdoor spaces that aid in climate resiliency should be factored into planning. Schools can also incorporate maintenance of these spaces into outdoor classes and student tasks that can be connected to learning.

Incorporate outdoor spaces into curriculum: Schools can activate the use of outdoor spaces, particularly natural spaces, for learning rather than only at recess time. Such use provides more experiential learning that also supports holistic well-being of schoolchildren.

Conclusions

Current and increasing weather extremes result in emergent infrastructure and health risks and costs to society. School grounds, including outdoor play areas, can play critical roles in reducing such vulnerabilities while increasing safety and learning. Indeed, schools are important community hubs; thus, the environmental conditions and ability to adapt for climate resilience impact the full community. The current chapter detailed considerations linked to reducing the impacts of extreme weather on schools with emphasis on outdoor designs for well-known climate change impacts, such as flooding and extreme heat. Overall, ensuring that school spaces are appropriately designed for the given climate (and hence current and projected extremes) is vital to enhance preparedness for all climate extremes. The importance of advancing heat safety and climate-responsive approaches to school-playground design cannot be stressed enough. For example, school-playground designs targeting materials, colours, orientation of equipment, and assessing the outdoor areas for suitable locations where existing sources of shade (e.g., trees or buildings) can be incorporated in the design, are important considerations.

Research and applications into weather-protective designs, materials, insulation strategies, smart technologies, shading and/or surfacing structures and natural greening were presented, with critical new directions outlined for incorporating these ideas into the budgeting and design of schools and school playgrounds. Important knowledge exchange among schools, school districts and designers and operators of school infrastructure globally should actively exchange forward-thinking strategies. Collective knowledge is needed to increase the safe use of school grounds, amplifying adaption measures to future extremes while continuing to support health and well-being of children during learning and play. Finally, there is a critical need for designs, such as the use of nature, green infrastructure and permeability of surfaces that protect against multiple climate extremes and provide co-benefits to children's health and well-being.

References

Baniassadi, A., Sailor, D. J., & Ban-Weiss, G. A. (2019). Potential energy and climate benefits of super-cool materials as a rooftop strategy. *Urban Climate, 29*, 100495.

Boldemann, C., Dal, H., Mårtensson, F., Cosco, N., Moore, R., Bieber, B., Wester, U. (2011). Preschool outdoor play environment may combine promotion of children's physical activity and sun protection. Further evidence from Southern Sweden and North Carolina. *Science & Sports, 26*(2), 72–82.

Brown, R D, & Gillespie, T. J. (1995). *Microclimate landscape design*. John Wiley & Sons, Inc.

Campbell, G. S., & Norman, J. (2012). *An introduction to environmental biophysics*. Springer. Retrieved from https://books.google.com/books?id=QpsMBwAAQBAJ

Cancer Council Australia. (2022). *National SunSmart schools program*. Retrieved from www.cancer.org.au/cancer-information/causes-and-prevention/sun-safety/be-sunsmart/sunsmart-in-schools

Choi, Y. M., Chopra, T., Smith, D., & Moulton, S. (2019). Sun heated surfaces are an environmental hazard for young children. *Perspectives in Public Health, 139*(5), 264–270.

Coffel, E. D., Horton, R. M., & de Sherbinin, A. (2017). Temperature and humidity based projections of a rapid rise in global heat stress exposure during the 21st century. *Environmental Research Letters, 13*(1), 14001.

CPSC. (2010). *Handbook for public playground safety*. CPSC.

CPSC. (2018). Burn safety awareness on playgrounds. Retrieved from www.cpsc.gov/s3fs-public/3200.pdf

Cumberland City Council. (2022). *UV smart cool playground project*. Retrieved from www.cumberland.nsw.gov.au/uv-smart-cool-playground-project

Dadvand, P., Nieuwenhuijsen, M. J., Esnaola, M., Forns, J., Basagaña, X., Alvarez-Pedrerol, M., . . . Su, J. (2015). Green spaces and cognitive development in primary school children. *Proceedings of the National Academy of Sciences, 112*(26), 7937–7942.

Di Virgilio, G., Hart, M. A., Maharaj, A. M., & Jiang, N. (2021). Air quality impacts of the 2019–2020 black summer wildfires on Australian schools. *Atmospheric Environment*, 118450.

Downs, N. J., Vanos, J., Raj, N., Igoe, D., Butler, H., Beckman, M., . . . Parisi, A. (2022). The Playground Shade Index: A design metric for measuring shade and seasonal ultraviolet protection characteristics of parks and playgrounds. *Photochemistry & Photobiology*. https://doi.org/10.1111/php.13745

EPA. (2016). *Enhancing sustainable communities with green infrastructure*. Retrieved from https://www.epa.gov/sites/default/files/2016-08/documents/green-infrastructure.pdf

EPA. (2017). *Storm smart schools: A guide to integrate green stormwater infrastructure to meet regulatory compliance and promote environmental literacy (EPA 903-K-17-001)*. Retrieved from www.epa.gov/sites/default/files/2017-10/documents/storm_smart_schools_print_final_071317.pdf

FEMA. (2009). *Making schools safe against winds*. FEMA.

Ferrari, A., Kubilay, A., Derome, D., & Carmeliet, J. (2019). The impact of reflective and permeable pavements on the urban microclimate. *IBPSA Proceedings*. Retrieved from www.ibpsa.org/proceedings/BS2019/BS2019_210280.pdf

Ferri, L. (2020, January 27). Outraged parents claim a $10million playground is too dangerous for kids after a child burns his leg on a hot metal slide. *Daily Mail Australia*. Retrieved from www.dailymail.co.uk/news/article-7936217/Parents-claim-10million-playground-dangerous-child-burnt-leg-hot-metal-slide.html

Flouri, E., Midouhas, E., & Joshi, H. (2014). The role of urban neighbourhood green space in children's emotional and behavioural resilience. *Journal of Environmental Psychology, 40*, 179–186.

Ford, G., Moriarty, A., Riches, D., & Walker, S. (2011). Playground equipment: Classification & burn analysis. *Worcester*. Retrieved from https://web.wpi.edu/Pubs/E-project/Available/E-project-122111-202154/unrestricted/WPI_Final_Report_IQP-CPSC.pdf

Galindo, R. M. (2019). Air conditioning condensate: A potential water source and a creeping destroyer. In *Proceedings of international conference (ICTCBW 2019) at Cebu Technological University, Cebu, Philippines*. Retrieved from http://confe-jikei.org/ICTCBW/2019/proceedings/materials/proc_files/GS_ papers/camerareadymanuscript_GS_ICTCBW2019_A017. pdf

Graça, M., Cruz, S., Monteiro, A., & Neset, T.-S. (2022). Designing urban green spaces for climate adaptation: A critical review of research outputs. *Urban Climate, 42*, 101126. https://doi.org/https://doi.org/10.1016/j.uclim.2022.101126

Guyer, H., Georgescu, M., Hondula, D. M., Wardenaar, F., & Vanos, J. (2021). Identifying the need for locally-observed wet bulb globe temperature across outdoor athletic venues for current and future climates in a desert environment. *Environmental Research Letters, 16*(12), 124042. https://doi.org/10.1088/1748-9326/ac32fb

Hardin, A. W., & Vanos, J. K. (2018). The influence of surface type on the absorbed radiation by a human under hot, dry conditions. *International Journal of Biometeorology, 62*(1), 43–56. https://doi.org/10.1007/s00484-017-1357-6

Holm, S. M., Miller, M. D., & Balmes, J. R. (2021). Health effects of wildfire smoke in children and public health tools: A narrative review. *Journal of Exposure Science & Environmental Epidemiology, 31*(1), 1–20.

Holman, D. M., Kapelos, G. T., Shoemaker, M., & Watson, M. (2018). Shade as an environmental design tool for skin cancer prevention. *American Journal of Public Health*, e1–e6.

Hyndman, B. (2017). 'Heat-Smart'schools during physical education (PE) activities: Developing a policy to protect students from extreme heat. *Learning Communities Journal: International Journal of Learning in Social Contexts (Special Edition), 21*. Retrieved from www.cdu.edu.au/files/2021-06/learning-communities-journal-2017-21.pdf#page=60

IEM. (2022). *Iowa environmental mesonet.* Retrieved from https://mesonet.agron. iastate.edu/sites/dyn_windrose.phtml?station=LIRU&network=IT__ASOS&bin0=2&bin1=5&bin2=7&bin3=10&bin4=15&bin5=20&units=mps&nsector=36&fmt=png&dpi=100&year1=2020&month1=5&day1=1&hour1=0&minute1=0&year2=2020&month2=9&day2=22&hour2=0&min

ISO13732. (2005). *ISO 13732: Ergonomics of the thermal environment – methods for the assessment of human responses to contact with surfaces.* ISO.

Kennedy, E., Olsen, H., & Vanos, J. K. (2020). *Thermally comfortable playgrounds: A review of literature and survey of experts (Technical Report).* Retrieved from www.scc.ca/en/system/files/publications/SCC_Playgrounds_Report_EN_WEB.pdf

Lanza, K., Alcazar, M., Hoelscher, D. M., & Kohl, H. W. (2021). Effects of trees, gardens, and nature trails on heat index and child health: Design and methods of the Green Schoolyards Project. *BMC Public Health, 21*(1), 1–12.

Laurent, J. G. C., Williams, A., Oulhote, Y., Zanobetti, A., Allen, J. G., & Spengler, J. D. (2018). Reduced cognitive function during a heat wave among residents of non-air-conditioned buildings: An observational study of young adults in the summer of 2016. *PLoS Medicine, 15*(7), e1002605.

Lefroy, E. (2022). Mum's playground warning after toddler left with horrific burns. *Yahoo!News.* Retrieved from https://au.news.yahoo.com/mums-playground-warning-after-toddler-left-with-horrific-burns-215416482.html

Macie, D. (2019, June 27). *Playground equipment too hot for children, Tips to stay safe.* Retrieved from www.shutterstock.com/image-photo/caution-playground-surface-equipment-may-be-2047079510

Manimegalai, S. (2015). *Age changes in human skin from 3 years to 75 years of age.* PSG Institute of Medical Sciences and Research.

Martin, N. A., & Falder, S. (2017). A review of the evidence for threshold of burn injury. *Burns, 43*(8), 1624–1639.

McElroy, S., Schwarz, L., Green, H., Corcos, I., Guirguis, K., Gershunov, A., & Benmarhnia, T. (2020). Defining heat waves and extreme heat events using sub-regional meteorological data to maximize benefits of early warning systems to population health. *Science of the Total Environment, 721,* 137678.

Middel, A., & Krayenhoff, E. S. (2019). Micrometeorological determinants of pedestrian thermal exposure during record-breaking heat in Tempe, Arizona: Introducing the MaRTy observational platform. *Science of the Total Environment, 687,* 137–151.

Middel, A., Turner, V. K., Schneider, F. A., Zhang, Y., & Stiller, M. (2020). Solar reflective pavements – A policy panacea to heat mitigation? *Environmental Research Letters, 15*(6), 64016.

Middel, A., Vanos, J. K., Hondula, D. M., Kaloush, K., Sailor, D., Medina, J. R., . . . Campbell, B. (2021). *Cool pavement pilot program: Joint study between the city of Phoenix and Arizona State University.* Retrieved from https://keep.lib.asu.edu/items/160731

Molan, S., Weber, D., & Kor, M. (2022). Shaping children's knowledge and response to bushfire through use of an immersive virtual learning environment. *Journal of Educational Computing Research, 60*(6), 1399–1435.

Montague, M., Borland, R., & Sinclair, C. (2001). Slip! Slop! Slap! and SunSmart, 1980–2000: Skin cancer control and 20 years of population-based campaigning. *Health Education & Behavior, 28*(3), 290–305.

Morrison, S. A., & Sims, S. T. (2014). Thermoregulation in children: Exercise, heat stress, and fluid balance. *Annales Kinesiologiae, 5*(1).

Nutsford, D., Pearson, A. L., & Kingham, S. (2013). An ecological study investigating the association between access to urban green space and mental health. *Public Health, 127*(11), 1005–1011.

NWS. (2022). *Severe weather preparedness guide for schools*. Retrieved from www.weather.gov/grb/schools

Olsen, H., Kennedy, E., & Vanos, J. (2019). Shade provision in public playgrounds for thermal safety and sun protection: A case study across 100 play spaces in the United States. *Landscape and Urban Planning, 189*, 200–211.

Park, R. J., Behrer, A. P., & Goodman, J. (2021). Learning is inhibited by heat exposure, both internationally and within the United States. *Nature Human Behaviour, 5*(1), 19–27. https://doi.org/10.1038/s41562-020-00959-9

Pfautsch, S., Rouillard, S., Wujeska-Klause, A., Bae, A., Vu, L., Manea, A., . . . Leishman, M. (2020a). *School microclimates*. Retrieved from https://researchdirect.westernsydney.edu.au/islandora/object/uws:57392

Pfautsch, S., & Wujeska-Klause, A. (2021a). *Cool roads trial 2021*. Western Sydney University. Retrieved from https://doi.org/10.26183/hstd-bj72

Pfautsch, S., & Wujeska-Klause, A. (2021b). *Guide to climate-smart playgrounds: Research findings and application*. Western Sydney University. Retrieved from https://doi.org/10.26183/2bgz-d714

Pfautsch, S., Wujeska-Klause, A., & Rouillard, S. (2020b). *Benchmarking Tree Canopy in Sydney's Hot Schools*. Western Sydney University. Retrieved from https://doi.org/10.26183/kzr2-y559

Pfautsch, S., Wujeska-Klause, A., & Walters, J. (2022). Outdoor playgrounds and climate change: Importance of surface materials and shade to extend play time and prevent burn injuries. *Building and Environment, 223*. https://doi.org/10.1016/j.buildenv.2022.109500

Pooley, K., Nunez, S., & Whybro, M. (2021). Evidence-based practices of effective fire safety education programming for children. *Australian Journal of Emergency Management, 36*(2), 34–41.

Requia, W. J., Roig, H. L., & Schwartz, J. D. (2021). Schools exposure to air pollution sources in Brazil: A nationwide assessment of more than 180 thousand schools. *Science of the Total Environment, 763*, 143027.

Riga, R. (2018, November 8). Toddler suffers second-degree burns from metal plate in Ipswich park. *ABC News*. Retrieved from www.abc.net.au/news/2018-11-08/toddler-burns-feet-standing-on-metal-plate-ipswich-park/10477340

Salamanca, F., Georgescu, M., Mahalov, A., Moustaoui, M., & Wang, M. (2014). Anthropogenic heating of the urban environment due to air conditioning. *Journal of Geophysical Research: Atmospheres, 119*(10), 5949–5965.

Schneider, S., Bolbos, A., Kadel, P., & Holzwarth, B. (2020). Exposed children, protected parents; shade in playgrounds as a previously unstudied intervention field of cancer prevention. *International Journal of Environmental Health Research, 30*(1), 26–37.

Schneider, F. S.,* Cortez, J., Vanos, J. K., Sailor, D. S., Middel, A. (2023) Evidence-based guidance on reflective pavement for urban heat mitigation: A case study in Phoenix, Arizona. *Nature Communications. 14*, 1467. https://doi.org/10.1038/s41467-023-36972-5

Seppanen, O., Fisk, W. J., & Lei, Q. H. (2006). *Room temperature and productivity in office work*. US Department of Energy. Retrieved from https://www.osti.gov/biblio/903492

Sharplin, G., Smith, A., & Roth, F. (2013). The national survey of Australian primary schools' sun protection policy and practices: Evaluating the national SunSmart schools program. *Cancer Council SA: Adelaide.*

Shortridge, A., Walker VI, W., White, D. D., Guardaro, M. M., Hondula, D. M., & Vanos, J. K. (2022). HeatReady schools: A novel approach to enhance adaptive capacity to heat through school community experiences, risks, and perceptions. *Climate Risk Management, 36,* 100437. https://doi.org/https://doi.org/10.1016/j.crm.2022.100437

Shutterstock. (n.d.). *Playground sign.* KNRV.

Smith-Hopkins, J. (2017). *The invisible hazard afflicting thousands of schools.* Retrieved from https://publicintegrity.org/environment/the-invisible-hazard-afflicting-thousands-of-schools/

Soares, A. L., Rego, F. C., McPherson, E. G., Simpson, J. R., Peper, P. J., & Xiao, Q. (2011). Benefits and costs of street trees in Lisbon, Portugal. *Urban Forestry & Urban Greening, 10*(2), 69–78. https://doi.org/http://dx.doi.org/10.1016/j.ufug.2010.12.001

Solís, P., Vanos, J. K., & Forbis, R. E. (2017). The decision-making/accountability spatial incongruence problem for research linking environmental science and policy. *Geographical Review, 107*(4). https://doi.org/10.1111/gere.12240

Strong, D., Tahir, A., & Verma, S. (2007). Not fun in the sun: Playground safety in a heatwave. *Emergency Medicine Journal: EMJ, 24*(2), e9.

Teli, D., Jentsch, M. F., & James, P. A. B. (2012). Naturally ventilated classrooms: An assessment of existing comfort models for predicting the thermal sensation and preference of primary school children. *Energy and Buildings, 53,* 166–182.

Turner, V., Rogers, M. L., Zhang, Y., Middel, A., Schneider, F. A., Ocón, J. P., . . . Dialesandro, J. (2022). More than surface temperature: Mitigating thermal exposure in hyper-local land system. *Journal of Land Use Science, 17*(1), 79–99.

Vanos, J. (2015). Children's health and vulnerability in outdoor microclimates: A comprehensive review. *Environment International, 76,* 1–15.

Vanos, J. K., McKercher, G. R., Naughton, K., & Lochbaum, M. (2017a). Schoolyard shade and sun exposure: Assessment of personal monitoring during children's physical activity. *Photochemistry and Photobiology, 93*(4), 1123–1132. https://doi.org/10.1111/php.12721

Vanos, J., Herdt, A., & Lochbaum, M. (2017b). Effects of physical activity and shade on the heat balance and thermal perceptions of children in a playground microclimate. *Building and Environment, 126,* 119–131.

Vanos, J. K., Middel, A., McKercher, G. R., Kuras, E. R., & Ruddell, B. L. (2016). Hot playgrounds and children's health: A multiscale analysis of surface temperatures in Arizona, USA. *Landscape and Urban Planning, 146.* https://doi.org/10.1016/j.landurbplan.2015.10.007

Vecellio, D. J., Vanos, J. K., Kennedy, E., Olsen, H., & Richardson, G. R. A. (2022). An expert assessment on playspace designs and thermal environments in a Canadian context. *Urban Climate, 44,* 101235. https://doi.org/https://doi.org/10.1016/j.uclim.2022.101235

Wargocki, P., Porras-Salazar, J. A., & Contreras-Espinoza, S. (2019). The relationship between classroom temperature and children's performance in school. *Building and Environment, 157,* 197–204.

Watson, D. (2013). Bioclimatic design– Sustainable built environments. In V. Loftness & D. Haase (Eds.), *Sustainable built environments* (pp. 1–30). Springer. https://doi.org/10.1007/978-1-4614-5828-9_225

Wilkins, J., Hays, E., & Monahan, R. (2008, July 20). A sole priority. Angry parents make removal of dangerous overheated playground mats. *Daily News Writers*. Retrieved from https://www.nydailynews.com/new-york/angry-parents-remove-dangerously-overheated-playground-mats-article-1.351142

WriterInSoul. (n.d.). *Signs of problems*. Retrieved from https://writerinsoul.wordpress.com/2015/04/17/signs-of-problems/

Wu, C.-D., McNeely, E., Cedeño-Laurent, J. G., Pan, W.-C., Adamkiewicz, G., Dominici, F., . . . Spengler, J. D. (2014). Linking student performance in Massachusetts elementary schools with the "greenness" of school surroundings using remote sensing. *PLoS One*, *9*(10), e108548.

Xu, Z., FitzGerald, G., Guo, Y., Jalaludin, B., & Tong, S. (2016). Impact of heatwave on mortality under different heatwave definitions: A systematic review and meta-analysis. *Environment International*, *89–90*, 193–203. https://doi.org/https://doi.org/10.1016/j.envint.2016.02.007

Zellner, M., Massey, D., Minor, E., & Gonzalez-Meler, M. (2016). Exploring the effects of green infrastructure placement on neighborhood-level flooding via spatially explicit simulations. *Computers, Environment and Urban Systems*, *59*, 116–128.

7 Future Protection From Extreme Weather Influences in School Communities

Brendon Hyndman and Jennifer Vanos

Schools are the nucleus of our society, serving as an important hub for communications and events, and can also act as a shelter during significant extreme weather events (Augustino, 2017). The community hub that schools provide also builds upon the foundations wherein teachers and schoolchildren spend approximately one-third of their waking time – or around 30 hours per week – on school campuses (Glander, 2016). An absence of funding and prioritisation within the school sector – especially upon outdoor spaces for weather protection – are key factors in optimising the ability of school administrators to better protect schoolchildren and teachers (Augustino, 2017; Hyndman & Zundans-Fraser, 2021). Scholars report that school policies relating to extreme-weather protection could be enhanced if there was a greater understanding concerning the myriad of effects on children's development (Mermer et al., 2018; Gellman, 2020; Hyndman & Zundans-Fraser, 2021).

It is apparent based on all chapters within *The Impact of Extreme Weather on School Education: Protecting School Communities* that there are major, multilevel considerations for schools requiring focused attention on mitigating impacts from extreme weather. These needs are present both outside and within classrooms to optimise schoolchildren's development. Moreover, from this series of chapters, it is possible to suggest that school communities and educational leaders of all levels can be better informed on strategies that support schoolchildren's protection from extreme weather.

Over the past two decades, the world has become more aware of the importance of schoolchildren meeting physical-activity recommendations to prevent ill health. Higher-quality outdoor school environments are also seen as vital to ensure children can appropriately engage in and develop habitual physical activities. With most school-based physical activities undertaken outdoors, improving the protection of outdoor schoolyards has become a vital developmental consideration for educational communities, including the development of cognitive, social- and affective-well-being domains (Hyndman et al., 2016; Hyndman, 2017a). The risks of not considering how to better protect outdoor school environments for developmental activities becomes

DOI: 10.4324/9781003103165-7

even more pertinent when considering that certain extreme weather events are set to become more intense, frequent and longer lasting in coming years and decades (IPCC, 2021). This book addresses various types of extremes, from heat to heavy precipitation. Related to schoolchildren's bioclimates, this book assesses how schoolchildren's learning and development can be adversely impacted if measures are not put in place to ensure appropriate levels of thermal comfort concerning the temperature, surface temperatures (e.g., choice of colours and materials), shade provision, airflow, leniency with uniform provisions, density within classrooms and air quality.

Overall, the chapters provide crucial insight into the various influences of extreme weather and potential variables that need to be monitored, planned and developed via "micro-climate" assessments and modifications. Similarly, there is high importance when weather extremes force school closures or for migration/relocation of children to other locations or regions due to the impacts of the extreme weather events (e.g., wildfires, hurricanes). Throughout this book, key insights are provided into both thresholds and strategies that must be considered both during and after a school community is exposed to an extreme weather event of a significant scale. Rather than governments forcing policies on education communities, important public perceptual insights are also articulated into what can be considered for any future school-policy implementation.

In the United States, the Federal Emergency Management Agency (FEMA) details that most American schools now have outdated building standards and "older school facilities are particularly vulnerable to natural disasters and in most cases school administrators do not have the financial resources to address these vulnerabilities" (FEMA, 2017). Similarly, many school leaders across Australian schools have acknowledged that many fixed school-playground contexts are over 50 years old, even though such playground designs may not be optimal for schoolchildren's development (Chancellor, 2013; Hyndman, 2017a). Facility experts recommend that school buildings require improved vulnerability assessment of the facilities, utilisation of insights from best practices and the formulation of preparatory school and community operations plans.

The book details the impacts of extreme heat on schoolchildren (and other school-based attendees) in Chapter 2. The chapter underlines the direct and strong reliance of the education sector on sports/athletic heat guidelines. Yet developing more tailored, school-specific and holistic protection from extreme heat has been limited due to a lack of research and confusing messages from a diverse range of disciplines and organisations. The majority of heat-related research insights into school-based heat policies or guidelines have emerged from either public health and scientific disciplines, and only recently have researchers endeavoured to consolidate the various messages received by schools into a more educationally focused package (Hyndman, 2017b;

Shortridge et al., 2022) or more school-specific design guidelines for heat mitigation (Madden et al., 2018).

Despite the lack of educationally focused literature relating to heat influences on schoolchildren, the scientific literature provides strong rationale to provide further support and resources within schools to protect schoolchildren and teachers from the impacts of heat. For instance, schoolchildren can be at higher risk to heat-related illness (Bergeron et al., 2011), have longer delays in being able to acclimatise compared to adults (Pryor et al., 2015), can fail to recognise heat-stress symptoms (Vanos et al., 2017), have higher body-mass-to-area ratios compared to adults (Falk & Dotan, 2008) and produce less sweat overall (Morrison & Sims, 2014) that aids body cooling (Gomes et al., 2013). Despite adults being the gatekeepers to many of the design decisions within schools relating to the outdoor environments, schoolchildren express a need to be more involved in decisions relating to weather extremes (Haisma et al., 2018). Hyndman, Vanos and Shortridge express in Chapter 2 that within educational contexts there are also more subtle influences on a child's development – from a lack of thermal comfort that can negatively impact learning endeavours within timetabled classes, to low hydration awareness leading to concentration/behavioural impacts and overexposure to unsuitable schoolyard surface temperatures. The authors believe that now is the time to better connect with schoolchildren's viewpoints concerning school design affecting comfort and microclimate conditions.

Paths forward to ensure improved heat protection in schools should consider recent education-focused projects from Australia (Hyndman, 2017b), the United States (Shortridge et al., 2022) and Sweden (Bäcklin et al., 2021). After multiple years in northern, tropical Australia where wet-bulb globe temperatures were almost always exceeding the maximum sporting temperature guidelines for safe physical-activity participation (Hyndman, 2015), Hyndman (2017b) identified and sought to use robust health-promotion frameworks to capture and package the many sporadic, inconsistent heat-protection guidelines for schools. The guidelines emerged from government departments, health, environmental and sporting organisations, as well as peer-reviewed research and nonacademic reports that were all directed towards schools with sporadic utilisation of the guidelines. Hyndman (2017b) reviewed various investigations, implementations, reports and/or guidelines for schools, initially captured using the multidimensional social–ecological-model framework for health behaviour (and, increasingly, education behaviours). The review then consolidated each of the findings into five key action areas based upon the World Health Organisation's Ottawa Charter for Health Promotion (1986) of what a holistic, national school heat-protection policy could resemble, which was later supported by the general public (Hyndman & Zundans-Fraser, 2021).

The areas included:

1. A heat protection program to build healthy school policy (flexible scheduling of activities, uniform adaption); 2. Heat supportive environments to be created in schools (shade provisions, hydration strategies, development of heat protective guidelines and charts); 3. Heat protective community action to be strengthened (development of communicative methods to parents such as social media, provision of preparatory information to parents, feedback from the community on strategies); 4. Heat protective community skills to be developed (skill development on accessing heat protective resources; monitoring hydration skills; nutritional considerations;); and 5. A focus on the prevention of heat illness (monitoring of staff and students; aligning with curricular content).

(Hyndman & Zundans-Fraser, 2021, p. 77)

Similarly, Shortridge and colleagues (2022) utilised the same Ottawa Charter action areas to later build upon this initial research to create a resource, specific to the climate and culture of Phoenix, Arizona, that schools could then check if they were sufficiently "Heat Ready" for extreme heat waves within their schools. Similar to Hyndman, gaining insights and endorsement from broader stakeholders (e.g., the public), Shortridge and colleagues (2022) consulted with a range of school-community and public health stakeholders to initially find that heat-safety resources are not fully utilised within schools, and there should also be consideration of site-specific needs. From the multiple stages of interviews and the Delphi process used, the Ottawa Charter framework was used to develop a 30-item resource that could be adapted or applied to a specific school context.

In addition to the holistic heat-protective approaches outlined, there has also been evidence of school-athlete programs in the United States focusing specifically on the wet-bulb globe-temperature index, guiding thresholds for the frequency and duration of recovery periods, maximum practice duration times and types of protective equipment that should be removed (Cooper et al., 2020). Hyndman (2015) has previously criticised the guidelines and accuracy of wet-bulb globe-temperature-index guidelines due to the extremes of humidity of tropical jurisdictions, yet the widespread use for sporting/athletics endeavours continues to be well supported.

These studies answer the international call for the improved development and operationalisation of schools to audit the level of preparation and resources required to counter the extremes of heat. Shortridge and colleagues (2022, p10) state that "Efforts to make schools Heat Ready are an essential step towards ensuring that future generations have access to comfortable and safe learning environments without risks associated with heat exposure, even as temperatures rise in cities across the globe." A comprehensive Western Sydney University report from researchers in Australia (Madden et al., 2018) outlined that air temperatures had been regularly reaching greater than 40 degrees Celsius and that several indices that guide the population on indoor thermal comfort or heat stress may be largely unsuitable within schools. Conclusions called for more accounting of thermal "microvariations" in classrooms for teachers to restore thermal comfort for schoolchildren. The authors of the report encourage all schools to ensure there are more natural features to offer fresher air, shade, recreation and learning opportunities for schoolchildren during occurrences of extreme weather. Like Hyndman's (2017b) earlier published research, the Western Sydney University report also called for more connectivity between other disciplines and organisations to improve school spaces to buffer extreme weather. The holistic development of a multidimensional, multi-item auditing system could perhaps be moulded and adapted for wider, yet school-specific adoption for other weather extremes outlined in this book.

Another growing policy issue affecting schoolchildren involves hazardous exposures to air pollution (Wolfe et al., 2021). Similar to the detrimental impacts of extreme heat on schoolchildren, air-pollution exposure is associated with impaired cognitive development (Rivas et al., 2018) and increased susceptibility to asthmatic illness from being exposed to various air pollutants (Carrion-Matta et al., 2019). Schoolchildren are often exposed to high levels of traffic-based pollution en route to school campuses with peak school times resulting in nitrogen oxide (which irritates and damages the respiratory system) being higher than at other times of the day (Varaden et al., 2021). In Chapter 3, Di Virgilio and colleagues detail the complex nature of air pollution and potential impacts to school communities based on onset, duration and severity of air-pollution episodes. The authors indicate a need for improved understanding of the impacts of poor air quality on schoolchildren during: 1) journeying to and from school; 2) class-based activities; and 3) classwork at home (via homework or if a child is home-schooled). The authors also detail the advances in technology that are now available to enable more widespread monitoring of air-pollution levels at reasonable cost; such technology could be useful for school communities to improve spatial congruence of air pollution across time as well as localised pollutant concentrations.

Further, the World Health Organization (WHO) guidelines have recently been revised with updated air pollution exposure-limit details, thus affecting actions that should be taken by schools at certain levels. The authors of Chapter 3 emphasise that the WHO guidelines are the most suitable guiding principles for school communities to adhere to or aim towards through air pollution exposure-reduction actions. Lastly and similar to Hyndman's (2017b) drive towards consolidating messages around extreme heat for school communities, Di Virgilio and colleagues call for more consistent messages within geographic areas to at-risk groups, such as schoolchildren, regarding pollution concentrations and actions. These actions will be especially pertinent as bushfires, wildfires and sand or dust storms increase in many regions globally (Di Virgilio et al., 2019).

Chapter 4 unearthed the colder end of the temperature extremes, along with the unpredictable and major intensities of various storms, such as cyclonic events and tornadoes. For lesser weather extremes, the chapter highlights how simply providing more comfortable conditions within outdoor schoolyards during wet weather periods could prolong activity participation by almost six weeks across a school year (Li, 2019). The transition from indoor neutral temperatures to outdoor cold temperatures was deemed to be more favourable for schoolchildren when intermittent exposures were provided to slowly adapt to outside temperatures, rather than going from a fully heated classroom into the extremely cold air (Figueiro, 2013). Figueiro (2013) also indicates that artificially bolstered indoor temperatures should be avoided as much as possible, and suggests the use of naturally sourced sunlight to improve indoor comfort levels, mood, behaviour and overall health in cold climates. Providing opportunities to engage with naturally cool conditions and snow was encouraged in Chapter 4, as features such as snow can facilitate unique physical activities such as skiing, sledding, sliding and skating (Button et al., 2020; Rasi et al., 2017). Literature reflects greater amounts of science and health research related to extreme heat, yet further research is required into the developmental impacts of cold-weather extremes on school activities in places like Europe and North America (Rasi et al., 2017).

Adult stakeholders across Minnesota schools in the United States identified the need for improved outdoor-play policies depending on weather influences (Hughes et al., 2017). Many schools that are in extreme-cold climatic zones have various temperature-specific thresholds (including ones based on the wind-chill factor) which trigger school or school bus cancellations, and such decision-making is sporadic based on different backgrounds, beliefs, people involved, spaces available and school expectations (Hughes et al., 2017). Heavy precipitation in the form of snow, sleet, freezing rain or rain all can elicit school closures and bus cancellations, which are more straightforward decisions to make based on direct road and sidewalk safety compared to temperature-based decisions (heat or cold).

At the classroom level, more holistic, formalised training for schoolteachers may be helpful for informed decision making during cold weather that may impact schoolchildren's ability to engage in play (Chancellor & Hyndman, 2017). In Chapter 4, the authors provide a range of forward-thinking suggestions based on the diverse international research. First, further investigation into the perceptions of risk of school decision-makers is needed concerning extreme cold and inclement weather. Second, greater attention from schools is needed to provide more thermal comfort and encouragement for physical-activity engagements through improved resources during extremely cold weather (that do not meet the specific thresholds for school cancellation). Third, professional development that encourages a variety of cold-weather activities applied (safely) within the curriculum can support schoolchildren's activity levels; these can be tailored across the school communities. Fourth, the alignment of broader extreme weather school-policy strategies, based on greater pools of research from other extreme weather events, can support school policies related to extremely cold weather events. For example, schools can draw upon frameworks and considerations from other weather impacts (e.g., Hyndman, 2017b) to limit overall impacts of severe weather in general. Lastly, new online technologies may support schoolchildren's participation and effective engagement in learning when temperatures reach school-closure thresholds.

In relation to the more severe risks of extreme weather patterns that cause flooding and other damage, Chapter 4 underlines the importance of schools regularly assessing their resource capabilities, such as the standards of buildings and the appropriateness of the locations of school structures and terrains. For instance, there could be space available within school playgrounds to implement a new play feature, yet if it is at a low point of a hilly playground, this could result in hazardous play conditions (e.g., flood risk, snowdrift risk), or, depending on the materials, the new features could get ruined by weather extremes. Moreover, Chapter 4 demonstrates how school closures occur in many jurisdictions and the impacts of rain, snow, windstorms, flooding, cyclones, bushfires and tornadoes have become almost as common for school closures as an illness pandemic. Chapter 4 also points to the need for rapid educational recovery from any school displacement from extreme weather occurring to try and to prevent schoolchildren's anxieties from the disruptions on their learning routines. It is suggested that any disruption to school attendance or participation is challenging for schoolchildren's development, yet the more prolonged the disruption to learning routines, the greater the potential for negative consequences on academic progress. Therefore, effective planning to fast-track learning routines or to be able to continue with scheduled activities as much as possible through improved resourcing (for safety and comfort) are important considerations in the future.

All chapters clearly underline the importance of more consistent, consolidated policy to better inform educational stakeholders and to ensure educational communities have established foundations to adequately protect school attendees from extreme weather influences – a message that is reinforced in Chapter 5. For example, the argument against more restrictive uniforms within schools is growing (Reidy, 2021), with evidence for more suitable clothing to better facilitate physical activities. Given that most extreme weather events are becoming more intense and frequent, unhelpful uniform protocols will need to be better addressed by schools internationally.

Chapter 5 documents that school communities are lagging behind other workplaces (that are more adult based) when it comes to protection from weather extremes. Research links less involvement from schoolchildren in weather-protection planning provisions, which in turn may cause differential exposures to unconducive indoor environments between school leadership (e.g., air-conditioned offices) versus classrooms, which may lack air-conditioning, thus affecting learning. Acclimatisation protocols have had some success in hot/cold protection and should be further considered for such weather extremes in the future. Hyndman's (2017b) proposed heat policy suggested that teachers could make some subjective judgements on schoolchildren's acclimatisation based on time of season, yet there is value in considering how students might adapt on short or long timescales to extreme cold. Physiological acclimatisation to extreme heat and cold are very different processes, especially for safe exercise in said conditions, and thus require different policies if put in place. For heat acclimatisation, Kerr and colleagues (2019) outlined key acclimatisation guidelines for high school football preseason training, which include limiting the number of sessions during the first five days of training, capping the duration of training sessions (e.g., three hours for a single session, five hours for a double session), having three-hour recovery periods between practice and walk-through sessions, and not allowing full protective equipment to be worn until day six of training. Similar to the recommendations from Chapter 3, the use of previously developed health models, frameworks and benchmarks are effective lenses to package the key preventive considerations for school communities across weather extremes. Further, negative health impacts on schoolchildren from extreme weather tends to capture public concern over health and educational attainment. Midford and colleagues (2020) demonstrate that health and learning cannot be separated; both elements are delicately intertwined when considering a human's development from early childhood into adulthood. The scholars emphasise the importance of "synergistic investment in the health and education of children to maximise potential for productive and meaningful lives" (Midford et al., 2020, p. 8). Dodd (2008, p. 95) previously stated,

> A person as a unitary being, where mind and body are integrated, has been the most difficult conception to elaborate in Western thought. The implications and consequences for being based on this conceptualisation are only just beginning to be explored.

Similarly, Santrock outlined that "biological processes can influence cognitive processes and vice versa . . . we are talking about the development of an integrated individual with a mind and body that are interdependent" (Santrock, 2011, p. 16). Thus, in connection with providing conducive environments in the face of chronic or acute extreme weather events, supporting safe schooling environments are critical. It is more recognised than ever that with a brain processing around 20% of the body's metabolism through cognitive engagement, the physical impacts upon oxygen, hormones and glucose use affects the brain's capacities to optimally perform and support learning (e.g., attention, memory, perception, concentration and beyond) (Ogoh & Ainslie,

2009). Rather than the brain operating entirely on its own, it is the very link with the physical functioning of the body that can dictate the performance of a schoolchild's brain (Hyndman et al., 2020).

In Chapter 6, complexities of schoolground designs are underlined in relation to extreme weather influences. There are many aspects of design for play that may be overlooked yet may affect schoolchildren's optimal development. For instance, in the extreme cold of northern Canada, school play designs must carefully consider the most predominant wind directions during the most intense extreme-cold periods (and to understand locations of snow drifting), while also ensuring that there is sufficient sunlight exposure to provide natural warmth in the cold season. Yet in the warm seasons and tropical regions, designs must support thermal comfort through ventilation (wind flow) for cooling via evaporation of sweat. These examples show that there are various dimensions of "bioclimatic design" that can be overlooked in the design process for school plans, yet involve various complexities based on location and time of year.

A common concern that need to be considered for children's play include the surfacing of equipment in relation to sun and heat exposures (Pfautsch et al., 2022). As noted in Shortridge et al.'s (2022) recommendations, natural features and vegetation in school play areas help generate protective cooling where schoolchildren play. It has also been identified that natural features such as trees and vegetation can effectively reduce wind chill in the winter (Coder, 2011; Vecellio et al., 2022), while school greening supports broader restorative spaces for students and development (Paddle & Gilliland, 2016; Hyndman, 2017a). Yet many school-design choices rely on artificial surfaces to reduce potential maintenance, costs, cushion falls and promote accessibility (USCPSC, 2010). Thus, when it comes to artificial surfacing and structures, there are a number of considerations to address, as specified in Chapter 6, connected to extreme temperatures. These considerations include added shade, the level of reflectivity, thermal mass, thermal conductance and how much direct sunlight the surface or structures will receive across a school day. Several recommendations are provided to reduce the risks of injury from extreme temperatures: (1) shade all artificial surfaces; (2) avoiding dark-coloured/coated metals and plastics in favour of lighter colours; (3) prioritise play equipment that is constructed from treated wood, which has lower surface temperatures and thermal conductivity to the skin; and (4) orient larger play structures, like slides, away from the direct sunlight. In Chapter 6, Vanos and Pfautsch also detail how the school play design process/order of decisions can be rethought. For example, the provision of shade should not be an afterthought, yet should be included/prioritised throughout. Then, designers can consider the play themes, accessibility, developmental aspects and other characteristics of the play area in and around these shaded, comfortable spaces. Often due to the costly burdens of school-playground structures, shade is traditionally only considered if there is funding remaining. Thus, it's easy to see unshaded playgrounds, even despite the growing knowledge that prioritising schoolchildren's protection from various weather extremes, like heat, will support sufficient levels of physical activity and participation (Remmers et al., 2017; Button et al., 2020).

The insights provided from across the chapters raise awareness and build foundations towards the impact of extreme weather on school and educational communities. These topics are of growing importance with the wide projections that many extremes are increasing in frequency and intensity across most global regions (Hoegh-Guldberg et al., 2018). The data and examples provided point to global areas that have not been as vulnerable to extreme weather events (Hoegh-Guldberg et al., 2018), yet may become more susceptible in the future. As a society, we now require more evidence-based research than ever to develop and apply practices and interventions that leverage the efficacy of weather-protection policies, especially in schools, to protect the next generation. Seddighi and colleagues (2020) reviewed the international literature to unearth suggestions for some broader, more generic yet modern strategies that school communities can consider for enhanced education and preparedness of schoolchildren to extreme weather events. These methods included:

- The use of virtual reality as a platform to improve academic knowledge and preparation of schoolchildren; this tool also supports case study scenarios that are useful for schoolchildren with disabilities.
- Simulation games related to extreme weather events and protective actions that can be conveniently accessed via portable devices; these are often already available and have been, or can be, purchased by schoolchildren.
- Arts-based approaches that consider interactive modes (games, music, stories, dramatic plays and artistic expression) related to extreme weather that also include parents in the activities.
- More consideration of virtual platforms, interactive digital resources (with multiple languages) and forums for education towards weather extremes, with context-specific content.
- Involvement of schoolchildren as agents of change with the goals of also having family/community influence on protective behaviours that can impact new generations.
- Educational training for all adult stakeholders whom schoolchildren will rely on during an extreme weather event.
- Improved local and community-focused policy for schools, as well as community education for parents, that can strengthen and empower parents and the full school community regarding extreme weather events.

To protect against the evolving range of sustainable challenges our world now confronts, the 2015 UN Sustainable Development Goals detail key priority areas for international action towards reaching a better world. These are focused on

Future Protection From Extreme Weather Influences on Schools 129

ensuring that well-being and healthy lives are promoted across all ages (SGD 3) and providing quality, accessible educational opportunities (SDG 4). The book aligns with both of these prioritised areas and brings together a compilation and holistic showcase of present insights into the impacts and strategies that can be undertaken related to these goals as well as inform schoolchildren's educational opportunities. The evidence presented across the chapters makes it clear that schoolchildren's educational attainment and opportunities do not exist in isolation from weather and its extremes. There is high value in enhancing efforts for preparedness and protection of schoolchildren and their communities.

Finally, the comprehensive evidence compiled across the book showcases the substantial benefits that could be realised with increased prioritisation to address the impacts of extreme weather on schools. Clear messages delivered throughout the chapters include:

(1) Sustainable futures for schoolchildren and their well-being requires improved prioritisation of policies surrounding extreme weather preparedness, protection and response plans that effectively address both health and educational outcomes.
(2) A wide range of educationally protective strategies exist that should be made available to students and teachers from the commencement of schooling; these can protect schoolchildren's learning, health and future developmental outcomes.
(3) There is high impact-potential from embedding the compiled practical implications and perspectives from the book within teacher-preparation programs (in-service and pre-service) and within related training for school-community decision-makers and stakeholders. Related, teachers' or supervisors' preparation/training for school-recess supervision is a necessity to facilitate children's safe outdoor development.
(4) Improved investment in schools (infrastructural, technological and educational) can help reduce the adverse impacts of extreme weather and the potential educational harm within the learning process.
(5) Investment into achieving the necessary weather-protective educational outcomes for school communities needs to be cross-sector (e.g, child protection, health, education, family services, environmental organisations), including multiple levels of government; these activities can be enhanced through schoolchildren's and family's inputs.

School communities are continuing to face the challenges and consequences of extreme weather events (Chawla, 2020), yet impacts are increasing as adaptation resources may be comparatively decreasing. Schools have the responsibility to ensure that their communities are equipped to prepare and cope with the changing extremes. Unfortunately, across the globe, schoolchildren and young people of all ages have elevated sadness, fears, and worries about environmental changes they are experiencing (Chawla, 2020). Strife (2012) previously captured the fears of fifth graders in the United States, revealing that they worried that there would be less nature in the future, and felt betrayed and dismayed by a lack of action to protect the population from extreme weather impacts. Additionally, there is increasing concern that school activities across learning and physical activity may be adversely affected. Overall, there are two major focuses regarding extreme weather protection in schools that underline the impacts of poor decision-making that can be counterproductive for the holistic well-being of schoolchildren, staff and other education stakeholders.

> 1. The loss of time (developmentally) . . . due to cancellation of activities during moderate to high-risk conditions when the activities could safely occur with appropriate modifications and provisions; and 2. Placing the health and safety of students, staff and other stakeholders at risk by continuing to run an activity, as previously scheduled, during extreme risk conditions.
>
> (Shannon et al., 2009, p. 272)

We hope this book, in its entirety, provides guidance through evidence-based information to elicit positive and impactful actions that protect schoolchildren from extreme weather and thus support the critical role of schools.

References

Augustino, J. (2017). Invest in resilient public school infrastructure. *Federal Emergency Management Agency (FEMA)*. Retrieved from www.21csf.org/best-home/docuploads/pub/342_BASIC_Resilient_Public_School_Infrastructure-Update.pdf

Bäcklin, O., Lindberg, F., Thorsson, S., Rayner, D., & Wallenberg, N. (2021). Outdoor heat stress at preschools during an extreme summer in Gothenburg, Sweden-Preschool teachers' experiences contextualized by radiation modelling. *Sustainable Cities and Society*, *75*, 103324.

Bergeron, M. F., DiLaura Devore, C., & Rice, S. G. (2011). Climatic heat stress and exercising children and adolescents. *Pediatrics*, *128*(3), e741–e747.

Button, B. L., Tillmann, S., & Gilliland, J. (2020). Exploring children's perceptions of barriers and facilitators to physical activity in rural Northwestern Ontario, Canada. *Rural and Remote Health*, *20*(3), 5791–5791.

Carrion-Matta, A., Kang, C. M., Gaffin, J. M., Hauptman, M., Phipatanakul, W., Koutrakis, P., & Gold, D. R. (2019). Classroom indoor $PM_{2.5}$ sources and exposures in inner-city schools. *Environment International*, *131*, 104968.

Chancellor, B. (2013). Primary school playgrounds: Features and management in Victoria, Australia. *International Journal of Play*, *2*(2), 63–75.

Chancellor, B., & Hyndman, B. (2017). Adult decisions on students' play within primary school playgrounds. In *Contemporary School Playground Strategies for Healthy Students* (pp. 37–55). Springer.

Chawla, L. (2020). Childhood nature connection and constructive hope: A review of research on connecting with nature and coping with environmental loss. *People and Nature, 2*(3), 619–642.

Coder, K. (2011). *Identified benefits of community trees & forests. Community forests series.* Retrieved from https://esploro.libs.uga.edu/view/pdfCoverPage?instCode=01GALI_UGA&filePid=13662225040002959&downloa d=true

Cooper, E. R., Grundstein, A. J., Miles, J. D., Ferrara, M. S., Curry, P., Casa, D. J., & Hosokawa, Y. (2020). Heat policy revision for Georgia high school football practices based on data-driven research. *Journal of Athletic Training, 55*(7), 673–681.

Di Virgilio, G., Evans, J. P., Blake, S. A., Armstrong, M., Dowdy, A. J., Sharples, J., & McRae, R. (2019). Climate change increases the potential for extreme wildfires. *Geophysical Research Letters, 46*(14), 8517–8526.

Dodd, G. D. (2008). *Toward a broader appreciation of human motion in education: The value of human motion.* VDM Publishing.

Falk, B., & Dotan, R. (2008). Children's thermoregulation during exercise in the heat – A revisit. *Applied Physiology, Nutrition, and Metabolism, 33*(2), 420–427.

Federal Emergency Management Agency (FEMA). (2017). *Safer, stronger, smarter: A guide to improving school natural hazard safety.* www.fema.gov/sites/default/files/2020-07/fema_earthquakes_p-1000-safer-stronger-smarter-a-guide-to-improving-school-natural-hazard-safety_aug2017.pdf

Figueiro, M. G. (2013). An overview of the effects of light on human circadian rhythms: implications for new light sources and lighting systems design. *Journal of Light & Visual Environment, 37*(2–3), 51–61.

Gellman, M. D. (2020). Behavioral medicine. In *Encyclopedia of behavioral medicine* (pp. 223–226). Springer International Publishing.

Glander, M. (2016). Selected statistics from the public elementary and secondary education universe: School year 2014–2015. US Department of Education. *National Center for Education Statistics.* Retrieved from https://eric.ed.gov/?id=ED569170

Gomes, L. H. L., Carneiro-Júnior, M. A., & Marins, J. C. B. (2013). Thermoregulatory responses of children exercising in a hot environment. *Revista Paulista de Pediatria, 31*, 104–110.

Haisma, H., Yousefzadeh, S., & Boele Van Hensbroek, P. (2018). Towards a capability approach to child growth: A theoretical framework. *Maternal & Child Nutrition, 14*(2), e12534.

Hoegh-Guldberg, O., Jacob, D., Bindi, M., Brown, S., Camilloni, I., Diedhiou, A., . . . & Zougmoré, R. B. (2018). Impacts of 1.5 C global warming on natural and human systems. *Global Warming of 1.5 C. An IPCC Special Report.* Retrieved from https://helda.helsinki.fi/handle/10138/311749

Hughes, A. C., Zak, K., Ernst, J., & Meyer, R. (2017). Exploring the intersection of beliefs toward outdoor play and cold weather among Northeast Minnesota's formal education and non-formal EE communities. *International Journal of Early Childhood Environmental Education, 5*(1), 20–38.

Hyndman, B. (2015). *What is the impact of sweating out HPE in top-end Northern Territory schools.* ACHPER Australia. Retrieved from www.achper.org.au/blog/blog-what-is-the-impact-of-sweating-out-hpe-in-top-end-nt-schools

Hyndman, B. (Ed.). (2017a). *Contemporary school playground strategies for healthy students.* Springer.

Hyndman, B. (2017b). 'Heat-Smart' schools during physical education (PE) activities: Developing a policy to protect students from extreme heat. *Learning Communities Journal: International Journal of Learning in Social Contexts (Special Edition)*, 56–72.

Hyndman, B., Benson, A., & Telford, A. (2016). Active play: Exploring the influences on children's school playground activities. *American Journal of Play, 8*(3), 325–344.

Hyndman, B., Winslade, M., & Wright, B. (2020). Physical activity and learning. In *Health and education interdependence* (pp. 179–204). Springer.

Hyndman, B., & Zundans-Fraser, L. (2021). Determining public perceptions of a proposed national heat protection policy for Australian schools. *Health Promotion Journal of Australia, 32*(1), 75–83.

IPCC. (2021). Climate change 2021: The physical science basis. In V. Masson-Delmotte, P. Zhai, A. Pirani, S. L. Connors, C. Péan, S. Berger, N. Caud, Y. Chen, L. Goldfarb, M. I. Gomis, M. Huang, K. Leitzell, E. Lonnoy, J. B. R. Matthews, T. K. Maycock, T. Waterfield, O. Yelekçi, R. Yu, & B. Zhou (Eds.), *Contribution of working group I to the sixth assessment report of the intergovernmental panel on climate change* (pp. 2061–2086). Cambridge University Press. https://doi.org/10.1017/9781009157896.015

Kerr, Z. Y., Scarneo-Miller, S. E., Yeargin, S. W., Grundstein, A. J., Casa, D. J., Pryor, R. R., & Register-Mihalik, J. K. (2019). Exertional heat-stroke preparedness in high school football by region and state mandate presence. *Journal of Athletic Training, 54*(9), 921–928.

Li, Y., Song, Y., Cho, D., & Han, Z. (2019). Zonal classification of microclimates and their relationship with landscape design parameters in an urban park. *Landscape and Ecological Engineering, 15*(3), 265–276.

Madden, A. L., Arora, V., Holmes, K., & Pfautsch, S. (2018). *Cool schools*. Western Sydney University. Retrieved from https://doi.org/10.26183/5b91d72db0cb7

Mermer, G., Donmez, R. O., & Daghan, S. (2018). The evaluation of the education for earthquake preparation addressed to middle school students. *JPMA. The Journal of the Pakistan Medical Association, 68*(12), 1809–1815.

Midford, R., Hyndman, B., Nutton, G., & Silburn, S. (2020). A preview of how health and education interact to influence the course of a child's development. In *Health and Education Interdependence* (pp. 3–11). Springer.

Midford, R., Nutton, G., Hyndman, B., & Silburn, S. (Eds.). (2020). *Health and education interdependence: Thriving from birth to adulthood*. Springer.

Morrison, S. A., & Sims, S. T. (2014). Thermoregulation in children: Exercise, heat stress & fluid balance. *Annales Kinesiologiae, 5*(1).

Ogoh, S., & Ainslie, P. N. (2009). Cerebral blood flow during exercise: mechanisms of regulation. *Journal of Applied Physiology, 107*(5), 1370–1380.

Paddle, E., & Gilliland, J. (2016). Orange is the new green: Exploring the restorative capacity of seasonal foliage in schoolyard trees. *International Journal of Environmental Research and Public Health, 13*(5), 497.

Pfautsch, S., Wujeska-Klause, A., & Walters, J. (2022). Outdoor playgrounds and climate change: Importance of surface materials and shade to extend play time and prevent burn injuries. *Building and Environment*. https://doi.org/10.1016/j.buildenv.2022.109500

Pryor, R. R., Bennett, B. L., O'Connor, F. G., Young, J. M., & Asplund, C. A. (2015). Medical evaluation for exposure extremes: Heat. *Wilderness & Environmental Medicine, 26*(4), 69–75.

Rasi, H., Kuivila, H., Pölkki, T., Bloigu, R., Rintamäki, H., & Tourula, M. (2017). A descriptive quantitative study of 7-and 8-year-old children's outdoor recreation, cold exposure and symptoms in winter in Northern Finland. *International Journal of Circumpolar Health, 76*(1), 1298883.

Reidy, J. (2021). Reviewing school uniform through a public health lens: Evidence about the impacts of school uniform on education and health. *Public Health Reviews, 42*.

Remmers, T., Thijs, C., Timperio, A., Salmon, J. O., Veitch, J., Kremers, S. P., & Ridgers, N. D. (2017). Daily weather and children's physical activity patterns. *Medicine and Science in Sports and Exercise, 49*(5), 922–929.

Rivas, I., Querol, X., Wright, J., & Sunyer, J. (2018). How to protect school children from the neurodevelopmental harms of air pollution by interventions in the school environment in the urban context. *Environment International, 121*, 199–206.

Santrock, J. W. (2011). *Life-span development* (13th ed.). McGraw-Hill.

Seddighi, H., Yousefzadeh, S., López, M. L., & Sajjadi, H. (2020). Preparing children for climate-related disasters. *BMJ Paediatrics Open, 4*(1).

Shannon, H., Stewart, I., & Stewart, K. (2009). Preventing physical activity induced heat illness in school settings. In *Creating active futures: Edited proceedings of the 26th ACHPER international conference* (pp. 271–281). School of Human Movement Studies and Queensland University of Technology.

Shortridge, A., VI, W. W., White, D. D., Guardaro, M. M., Hondula, D. M., & Vanos, J. K. (2022). HeatReady Schools: A novel approach to enhance adaptive capacity to heat through school community experiences, risks, and perceptions. *Climate Risk Management*, 100437.

Strife, S. J. (2012). Children's environmental concerns: Expressing ecophobia. *The Journal of Environmental Education, 43*(1), 37–54.

US Consumer Product Safety Commission (USCPSC). (2010). *Public playground safety handbook*. Government Printing Office.

Vanos, J. K., Herdt, A. J., & Lochbaum, M. R. (2017). Effects of physical activity and shade on the heat balance and thermal perceptions of children in a playground microclimate. *Building and Environment, 126*, 119–131.

Varaden, D., Leidland, E., Lim, S., & Barratt, B. (2021). "I am an air quality scientist"– Using citizen science to characterise school children's exposure to air pollution. *Environmental Research, 201*, 111536.

Vecellio, D. J., Vanos, J. K., Kennedy, E., Olsen, H., & Richardson, G. R. (2022). An expert assessment on play space designs and thermal environments in a Canadian context. *Urban Climate, 44*, 101235.

Wolfe, M. K., McDonald, N. C., Arunachalam, S., Baldauf, R., & Valencia, A. (2021). Impact of school location on children's air pollution exposure. *Journal of Urban Affairs, 43*(8), 1118–1134.

World Health Organization. (1986). Ottawa charter for health promotion, 1986 (No. WHO/EURO: 1986-4044-43803-61677). *World Health Organization and Regional Office for Europe*. https://apps.who.int/iris/handle/10665/349652

Index

Note: Page numbers in *italics* indicate a figure and page numbers in **bold** indicate a table on the corresponding page.

absences 8; *see also* school closures
acclimatisation 22, 23, 24, 88, 126; *see also* adaption
action areas: for air quality improvement 41–42, 123–124; for extreme heat protection 27, 96, 121–123; for storm smart schools 95–96; for weather-protection strategies 80–81; *see also* mitigation; recommendations
adaption: to cold weather 62, 70, 124, 126; to extreme heat 19, 83, 126; to extreme weather, generally 9–10; thermal comfort and 26; weather-protection strategies addressing 10, 83, 87, 91
air conditioning: air quality and 40, 42, 50; extreme heat and use of 19, 27, 84, 85; weather-protection strategies addressing 84, 85, 89–90
air quality and air pollution 38–52; in Black Summer (case study) 46–50, *48–49*; building and playground design addressing 95, 99; bushfire/wildfire effects on 5, 11, 39–40, 42–43, 46–50, 95, 124; challenges and opportunities for 51–52; citizen-science projects tracking 43, *44–45*, 44–46, 50; climate change and 39–40; data networks on meteorology and 42–43; deaths caused by poor 5, 38; extreme heat and 8, 47, 95; health effects of 8, 38–41, 47, 123; indoor 11, 38, 40–41, 42, 50–51; indoor monitoring (case study) 50–51; mitigation actions for 41–42; monitoring networks on 43–46, *44–45*, 47–51; outdoor pollution 38–40 (*see also* bushfires/wildfires *subentry*); overview of effects of 11, 38, 123–124; policies and standards on 41–42, 51–52, 123–124; public communication and education on 52, 123; scientific understanding of 51
artificial surfaces 21, 100, 103–108, *104–105*, *107*, 110, *110*, 127

bioclimatic design 98–108, 127
bioswales 99, *99*
Black Summer 46–50, *48–49*
building and playground design 94–113; air quality and 95, 99 (*see also* indoor air quality); bioclimatic 98–108, 127; for bushfires/wildfires issues 97–98; case study of novel playground surfacing in 108–111, *109–110*; for cold weather 98, *98*, 100, 127; for extreme heat 26, 85–86, 94–95, 96, *98*, 98–112, 127; green infrastructure in *99*, 99–100; outdated 120;

overview of 12, 94, 112–113, 127–128; recommendations for climate extreme responsiveness in 111–112, 127–128; reflective surfaces in 97, 106–108, *107*; shade in 97, 100–101, *109*, 112, 127–128; Smart Schools programs in 80, 95–98; for storms 95–96, 125; for sun protection 96–97, 100–101; for surface temperature control 21, 97, 100–111, *102–105*, *107*, **108**, *109–110*, 127; thermal comfort considerations in 26, 85–86 (*see also* cold weather and extreme heat *subentries*); weather-protection strategies addressing 85–86, 89–90
burns *see* thermal burns
bushfires/wildfires: air quality effects of 5, 11, 39–40, 42–43, 46–50, 95, 124; Black Summer of 46–50; building and playground design addressing 97–98; climate change and 40, 42; deaths from 5; health effects of 39–40; increase in 40, 42, 124; school closures due to 39, 66
Button, Brenton 12, 60

climate change: air quality and 39–40; bushfires/wildfires and 40, 42; extreme heat and 3, 18, 19, *20*; extreme weather and 3–4 (*see also* extreme weather)
climate extremes 2; *see also* extreme weather
closures *see* school closures
clothing 26–27, 61, 72, 86, 90, 125
cold weather 60–72; adaption to 62, 70, 124, 126; building and playground design addressing 98, *98*, 100, 127; climate change and 3; health effects of 61; increase in 6; mitigating impacts of 61, 71–72, 124; outdoor physical activity and 12, 60–62, 67–72, 79–80, 124–125; overview of effects of 12, 60–62, 124–125; policies on 70–72, 80, 86, 124–125, 126; teacher training on 61, 70–71, 72, 124–125;

weather-protection strategies addressing 83–90, 126
communication: on air quality issues 52, 123; on cold weather and storms 72; of extreme weather warnings 7; of tornado warnings 65–66
COVID-19 pandemic 50, 63, 67, 71
curricula: cold weather coverage in 61, 72; extreme heat coverage in 25; extreme weather coverage in 9; outdoor space incorporation into 112; storm preparedness and mitigation in 64, 72
cyclones 3, 7, 62, 63–64; *see also* hurricanes

deaths: air quality causing 5, 38; extreme heat causing 5, 18, 19, 24; extreme weather leading to 5; from lightning strikes 65; from suicide 6
decision making: on building and playground design 127; on cold weather play 70–71, 72, 124; on school closures 7, 120; *see also* policies
dehydration 24, 87–88
developmental risks: of air quality/air pollution 38, 123; of extreme heat 22–25, 121; future protection strategies to minimise 119–120, 126–127; health intersection with 126–127; of physical activity lack 88; of school closures 62, 66–67
displacement *see* school displacement
Di Virgilio, Giovanni 38
droughts 3, 6, 7, 18, 99–100

earthquakes 5
Education for Sustainable Development 9
El Niño 7
ethylene propylene diene polymer rubber (EPDM) 108, 110, *110*
exercise *see* physical activity
extreme cold *see* cold weather
extreme heat 18–32; acclimatisation to 22, 23, 24, 88, 126; air quality and 8, 47, 95; building and playground design for 26, 85–86, 94–95, 96, *98*, 98–112, 127; bushfires associated

136 *Index*

with (*see* bushfires/wildfires); climate change and 3, 18, 19, *20*; deaths from 5, 18, 19, 24; developmental risks of 22–25, 121; health effects of 8, 18–24, *20*, 47, 80, 83, 87–88, 101, 121; increase in 6, 18; across international school contexts 26–31, **28–30**, 88, 90; mitigation of impacts of *20*, 26; negative effects of, generally 8; outdoor physical activity and 8, 11, 19, *20*, 21–24, 80, 122; overview of effects of 11, 18–19, 31–32, 120–121; policies and guidelines addressing 19, 22, 24–25, 27, 31, 80, 121–123, 126; recommendations for response to **28–30**, 120–123; surface temperatures and (*see* surface temperatures); thermal comfort and *20*, 23, 25–26; weather-protection strategies for 83–90, 126

extreme weather: adaption to (*see* adaption); building and playground design for protection from (*see* building and playground design); climate change and 3–4 (*see also* climate change); cold and (*see* cold weather); communication on 7, 52, 65–66, 72, 123; curricula on 9, 25, 61, 64, 72, 112; definition of 3; future protection from 12, 119–130; heat and (*see* extreme heat); mitigation of impacts of 6–10 (*see also* mitigation); school community impacts of, generally 1–13; storms and (*see* storms); strategies for protection from (*see* weather-protection strategies); *see also* climate extremes

fires *see* bushfires/wildfires
Fire Smart Schools 97–98
flooding 6, 7, 64–65, *70–71*, *99*, 99–100, 125
future protection strategies 12, 119–130

Green, Donna 38
green infrastructure *99*, 99–100

Hart, Melissa 38
health effects: of air quality/air pollution 8, 38–41, 47, 123; of bushfires/wildfires 39–40; of climate extremes *2*; of cold weather 61; development intersection with 126–127; of extreme heat 8, 18–24, *20*, 47, 80, 83, 87–88, 101, 121; of extreme weather, generally 8, 11; learning process intersection with 84, 126; mental 6, 99; overprotection from 87–88; of physical activity 22, 60–61, 119–120; strategies for protection from (*see* weather-protection strategies); of sun exposure 80; of thermal burns 22, 101–106, 108, **108**; *see also* COVID-19 pandemic; deaths; illnesses
heat extremes *see* extreme heat
Heat Ready Schools 27, *31*, 96, 122
Heat Smart Schools 96
hurricanes 5, 7, 62, 64–65
Hyndman, Brendon 1, 11, 12, 18, 60, 78, 119

illnesses: heat 18, 19, 22, 23–24, 121; physical activity and 22; school closures for contagious 62–63, 67; *see also* COVID-19 pandemic; health effects
individual levels of influence 83–84, 87–88
indoor air quality 11, 38, 40–41, 42, 50–51
indoor cooling *see* air conditioning
interpersonal (social) levels of influence 84, 89

La Niña 7
learning process: air quality effects on 41; climate extremes effects on *2*; extreme heat effects on 8, *20*, 24, 80, 84, 87–88; health intersection with 84, 126; overprotection of 87–88; school closure effects on 62, 66–67, 125; storms disrupting 64–65, 125; thermal comfort effects on 25 (*see also* extreme heat *subentry*); weather-protection strategies to protect 83–84, 87, 126
lightning 4, 7, 65

Maharaj, Angela 38
microclimates 12, 21, 120
mitigation: of air quality issues 41–42; of cold weather impacts 61, 71–72, 124; of extreme heat impacts 20, 26; of extreme weather impacts, generally 6–10; of storm impacts 64, 71–72, 124–125
mudslides 5

Ottawa Charter 80–81, 121–122
outdoor play: cold weather and 12, 60–62, 67–72, 79–80, 124–125; extreme heat effects on 8, 11, 19, 20, 21–24, 80, 122; playground design effects on 12, 119–120 (see also building and playground design); storm effects on 65, 67–72, 68–71, 124; surface temperatures and (see surface temperatures); see also physical activity; playgrounds

parental support 6
Pfautsch, Sebastian 12, 94
physical activity: cold weather and 12, 60–62, 67–72, 79–80, 124–125; extreme heat effects on 8, 11, 19, 20, 21–24, 80, 122; health effects of 22, 60–61, 119–120; outdoor (see outdoor play; playgrounds); storm effects on 65, 67–72, 68–71, 124
physical education 24, 68, 72, 86
physical-environmental levels of influence 84–86, 89–90
play see physical activity
playgrounds: design of (see building and playground design); outdoor play on (see outdoor play); shade on (see shade); surface temperatures of (see surface temperatures)
policies: adaption through 10; on air quality/air pollution 41–42, 51–52, 123–124; on cold weather 70–72, 80, 86, 124–125, 126; on extreme heat 19, 22, 24–25, 27, 31, 80, 121–123, 126; schoolchildren's exclusion from 5, 121; on storm mitigation and response 64, 71–72, 124–125; on sun protection 80, 96–97; on weather-protection strategies 78–91, 125–126
policy-organisational levels of influence 86, 90
precipitation see rain; snow
professional development see teacher training

rain 3, 62, 67–71, 69–71, 124
recess 22, 67–68, 79–80, 88–89; see also outdoor play; playgrounds
recommendations: on air quality opportunities 51–52, 123–124; for building and playground design resilience to climate extremes 111–112, 127–128; on cold weather response 62, 70–72, 124–125; for enhanced preparedness for weather events 128; on extreme heat response 28–30, 120–123; on future weather-protection strategies 12, 119–130; on storm impact mitigation 71–72, 124–125; for weather-protection strategies 125–126; see also policies
reflective surfaces 97, 106–108, 107

SBR (styrene butadiene rubber) 108, 110, 110
school closures: bushfires/wildfires causing 39, 66; decision making on 7, 120; developmental risks of 62, 66–67; extreme weather causing 1–2, 120; online learning and 67, 71, 125; storms causing unplanned 7, 62–67, 84, 124–125; weather-protection strategies addressing 84
school displacement 5, 6, 65–66, 67, 125
school recess 22, 67–68, 79–80, 88–89; see also outdoor play; playgrounds
school uniforms 26–27, 86, 90, 125
shade: building and playground design including 97, 100–101, 109, 112, 127–128; extreme heat and 21, 21–22; sun protection with

97; weather-protection strategies including 86
Shortridge, Adora 11, 18
Smart Schools programs 80, 95–98
snow 3, 60, 62–63, *68*, 124
social-ecological model 82–83, 87
social (interpersonal) levels of influence 84, 89
solar electricity 90
storms 62–72; building and playground design for 95–96, 125; climate change and 3; mitigating impacts of 64, 71–72, 124–125; outdoor physical activity and 65, 67–72, *68–71*, 124; overview of effects of 12, 124–125; policies on 64, 71–72, 124–125; school closures due to 7, 62–67, 84, 124–125; storm cells *4*; weather-protection strategies addressing 84; *see also specific types of storms*
Storm Smart Schools 95–96
styrene butadiene rubber (SBR) 108, 110, *110*
suggestions *see* recommendations
sun protection: building and playground design for 96–97, 100–101; policies for 80, 96–97; reflective surfaces and 97, 106–108; shade for (*see* shade); *see also* solar electricity; ultraviolet (UV) radiation
Sun Smart Schools 80, 96–97
surface temperatures: artificial surfaces and 21, 100, 103–108, *104–105*, *107*, 110, *110*, 127; building and playground design and 21, 97, 100–111, *102–105*, *107*, **108**, *109–110*, 127; global average rise in 18; reflective surfaces and 97, 106–108, *107*; thermal burns from 22, 101–106, 108, **108**
synthetic turf *see* artificial surfaces

teacher training: on cold weather safety and decision making 61, 70–71, 72, 124–125; on extreme heat safety 25, 32; for Storm Smart School program 95–96
thermal burns 22, 101–106, 108, **108**

thermal comfort: building and playground design for 26, 85–86 (*see also under* building and playground design); cold weather and 62 (*see also* cold weather); definition of 25; extreme heat effects on *20*, 23, 25–26 (*see also* extreme heat)
thermoplastic olefin (TPO) 108, *110*, 110–111
thermoregulation 22, 23, 26
tornadoes 3, *4*, 7, 62, 65–66, 96
transportation: air quality and 38–42, 51, 95, 123; physical activity and 42, 68; storms and 68, *68*
trees 26, 100–101, *107*, 112, 127
Trojan Effect 106
typhoons 7; *see also* hurricanes

ultraviolet (UV) radiation 3, 21–22, 80, 97, 100–101, 106; *see also* sun protection
uniforms, school 26–27, 86, 90, 125
UN Sustainable Development Goals 128–129
urban areas: air quality in 43; building and playground design in *99*, 99–100; extreme heat in 18, 19–21, *20*; growth of 18, 43
urban growth 18, 43
urban heat islands 18, 19

Vanos, Jennifer 1, 11, 12, 18, 94, 119

weather, defined 3; *see also* extreme weather
weather-protection strategies 78–91; action areas and elements of 80–81; adaption with 10, 83, 87, 91; building and playground design in 85–86, 89–90; context for findings on 87–91; data collection and analysis for 81–82; funding for 85–86, 89, 119; future 12, 119–130; importance of 4–5; individual influence on 83–84, 87–88; interpersonal (social) influence on 84, 89; overview of 12, 78–79, 90–91, 125–126; physical-environmental influence on 84–86, 89–90; policy-organisational influence

on 86, 90; public perceptions of 78–91; research considering 79–80; schoolchildren's input on 89; social-ecological model for 82–83, 87

wet weather 3, 62, 67–71, *69–71*, 124

wildfires *see* bushfires/wildfires

winds: building and playground design addressing 96, 98, *98*, 100, 127; bushfire/wildfire effects of 47–49, *49*; storms including 7, 62, 64–65

For Product Safety Concerns and Information please contact our EU representative GPSR@taylorandfrancis.com
Taylor & Francis Verlag GmbH, Kaufingerstraße 24, 80331 München, Germany

www.ingramcontent.com/pod-product-compliance
Lightning Source LLC
Chambersburg PA
CBHW070550170426
43201CB00012B/1797